C000132577

Overcoming Historical Injustices
Land Reconciliation in South Africa

Overcoming Historical Injustices is the last entry in James L. Gibson's "overcoming" trilogy on South Africa's transformation from apartheid to democracy. Focusing on the issue of historical land dispossessions – the taking of African land under colonialism and apartheid – this book investigates the judgments South Africans make about the fairness of their country's past. For instance, should land seized under apartheid be returned today to its rightful owner? Gibson's research zeroes in on group identities and attachments as the thread that connects people to the past. Even when individuals have experienced no direct harm in the past, they care about the fairness of the treatment of their group to the extent that they identify with that group. Gibson's analysis shows that land issues in contemporary South Africa are salient, volatile, and enshrouded in symbols and, most important, that interracial differences in understandings of the past and preferences for the future are profound.

James L. Gibson is currently the Sidney W. Souers Professor of Government at Washington University in St. Louis. He has published more than 100 refereed articles and chapters in a wide range of national and international social-scientific journals, including all of the leading political science journals. He has also published five books, including the award-winning *Overcoming Apartheid: Can Truth Reconcile a Divided Nation?* and *Citizens, Courts, and Confirmations: Positivity Theory and the Judgments of the American People* (co-authored with Gregory A. Caldeira, forthcoming). Gibson has served as the President of the Midwest Political Science Association and as an officer of the American Political Science Association. His research has been recognized with numerous awards. Gibson's overall research agenda on democratization was recognized with the 2005 Decade of Behavior Research Award.

CAMBRIDGE STUDIES IN PUBLIC OPINION AND POLITICAL PSYCHOLOGY

Series Editors

DENNIS CHONG, *Northwestern University*

JAMES H. KUKLINSKI, *University of Illinois, Urbana-Champaign*

Cambridge Studies in Public Opinion and Political Psychology publishes innovative research from a variety of theoretical and methodological perspectives on the mass public foundations of politics and society. Research in the series focuses on the origins and influence of mass opinion; the dynamics of information and deliberation; and the emotional, normative, and instrumental bases of political choice. In addition to examining psychological processes, the series explores the organization of groups, the association between individual and collective preferences, and the impact of institutions on beliefs and behavior.

Cambridge Studies in Public Opinion and Political Psychology is dedicated to furthering theoretical and empirical research on the relationship between the political system and the attitudes and actions of citizens.

Books in the series are listed on the page following the Index.

Overcoming Historical Injustices

Land Reconciliation in South Africa

JAMES L. GIBSON

Washington University in St. Louis

CAMBRIDGE
UNIVERSITY PRESS

CAMBRIDGE UNIVERSITY PRESS

Cambridge, New York, Melbourne, Madrid, Cape Town, Singapore, São Paulo, Delhi

Cambridge University Press
32 Avenue of the Americas, New York, NY 10013-2473, USA

www.cambridge.org
Information on this title: www.cambridge.org/9780521517881

© James L. Gibson 2009

This publication is in copyright. Subject to statutory exception
and to the provisions of relevant collective licensing agreements,
no reproduction of any part may take place without the written
permission of Cambridge University Press.

First published 2009

Printed in the United States of America

A catalog record for this publication is available from the British Library.

Library of Congress Cataloging in Publication Data

Gibson, James L., 1951–
Overcoming historical injustices : land reconciliation in South Africa / James L. Gibson.
p. cm. – (Cambridge studies in public opinion and political psychology)
Includes bibliographical references and index.
ISBN 978-0-521-51788-1 (hardback)
1. Land reform – Law and legislation – South Africa. 2. Land tenure – Law and legislation –
South Africa. 3. Reparations for historical injustices – South Africa. I. Title.
KTL3056.G53 2009
346.6804'32–dc22   2008038080

ISBN 978-0-521-51788-1 hardback
ISBN 978-0-521-14440-7 African edition paperback

Cambridge University Press has no responsibility for the persistence or accuracy of URLS
for external or third-party Internet Web sites referred to in this publication and does not
guarantee that any content on such Web sites is, or will remain, accurate or appropriate.
Information on prices, travel timetables, and other factual information given in this work
are correct at the time of first printing, but Cambridge University Press does not
guarantee the accuracy of such information thereafter.

This book is dedicated to Monica E. Kinsella,
without whom there would be no
worthwhile past, present, or future.

Contents

List of Figures

List of Tables

Preface and Acknowledgments

Anyone who lives in South Africa for extended periods of time, as I have, cannot help but be impressed with how pervasive issues of land are. Virtually every day, the newspapers report a land story, be it one about the evictions of squatters from public property, the efforts of dispossessed peoples to regain their land and their treasure, or the plight of farmer workers and their efforts to establish tenure on their living places. Land issues are everywhere, nearly all the time.

And there is no shortage of policy attention to the problems of land. Conferences are held regularly involving scholars, activists, and NGOs, and some amount of published material is emerging on the land problem in South Africa. Everyone seems to recognize the importance of "the land problem" for the future of South Africa's nascent democracy.

What is missing from much of the discussion is any systematic attention to the expectations, experiences, and preferences of ordinary South Africans. Most students of land politics know practically nothing about the beliefs, attitudes, and behaviors of the average person-in-the-street. Part of this omission is a function of the lack of survey research skills among South African scholars and students – and certainly the costs of conducting surveys are well beyond the means of most scholars and many funding agencies – but perhaps a larger part goes to the disdain that many hold for ordinary people. A slice of this attitude is infected by serious racism, through which Africans in particular are judged to be not smart enough to be able to grasp complex political issues. But much more pervasive is elitism, the belief that political controversies are best handled through inter-elite competition. We know little about what ordinary people think, in part, because most do not care what ordinary people think.

The obvious premise of this book is that the views of ordinary people matter on issues such as land. I guess, in truth, this is both a scientific hypothesis and something of a normative commitment on my part. Anyone who studies public opinion harbors in the back of his or her mind the view that public opinion in a democratic system *should* matter. Even if disagreement on the normative issue is appropriate, before the views of the public are dismissed entirely, it is fruitful to know what they are. My hope in writing this book is that both political scientists and pundits will pay more attention to the beliefs, values, attitudes, and behaviors of ordinary South Africans when it comes to issues of land.

I have often said that this is the third (and last) entry in what I term the "overcoming" trilogy. The first book published in the series was *Overcoming Intolerance in South Africa: Experiments in Democratic Persuasion* (with Amanda Gouws, published by Cambridge University Press). That book was conceived during the tense days of the intergroup political conflict in 1990–1994 in South Africa and focused on ways in which political intolerance in the country might be nourished and enhanced. The second book in the series, *Overcoming Apartheid: Can Truth Reconcile a Divided Nation?* (published in 2004 by the Russell Sage Foundation in the United States and the HSRC in South Africa, with an American paperback edition released in 2006), dealt with how South Africa might overcome its terrible apartheid past. In that book, tolerance was reconsidered, but primarily by conceptualizing tolerance as one of the pillars of the meta-concept "reconciliation." *Overcoming Apartheid* was written because, at the time, getting through the initial transitional period in South Africa, when no one knew whether the tentative peace would give reconciliation a chance, was the most important issue in South African politics.

"Truth and reconciliation" were undoubtedly crucial during the early days of South Africa's transition. Now, however, "justice and reconciliation" represent the primary problem when it comes to dealing with the country's past, and the various land issues represent one of the most important aspects of reconciling historical injustices. Thus is the origin of the need for a third book about the problems that South Africa must overcome.

That there will be no fourth entry in this series should not, of course, be taken to indicate that I see no further obstacles to the consolidation of democratic reform in South Africa.

Finishing this book has been more challenging than is typically the case, but that it is finished is in part due to the extraordinary efforts of Cindy White of the Washington University Research Office and Joseph Sklansky, one of Washington University's lawyers. Whenever one must acknowledge the assistance of one's university attorneys, one knows that the research path has been rocky. And without the support of Edward Macias, Executive Vice Chancellor and Dean of Arts and Sciences, it is entirely unclear that this project could have been brought to a successful conclusion. Not all university administrators are steadfastly committed to truth and justice. I am privileged to work at a university in which they are.

The (U.S.) National Science Foundation provided essential support for this project via the Law and Social Sciences Program (SES-0214451). Any opinions, findings, and conclusions or recommendations expressed in this material are those of the author and do not necessarily reflect the views of the National Science Foundation. I continue to be amazed and deeply impressed by NSF's commitment to social science and to using rigorous and reproducible methods to address important issues of theory and public policy.

Additional support for this research was provided by Steven S. Smith and the Weidenbaum Center on the Economy, Government, and Public Policy at Washington University in St. Louis. I also greatly appreciate the efforts of Gloria Lucy of the Weidenbaum staff on all aspects of this project.

A portion of this research was conducted in conjunction with the Institute for Justice and Reconciliation. I am indebted to Charles Villa-Vicencio, Karin Lombard, and the staff of IJR for valuable assistance on this project.

I am also indebted to the Department of Political Science at Stellenbosch University (where I hold the position of Professor Extraordinary) and to the Centre for Comparative and International Politics at Stellenbosch University (South Africa), where I am a Fellow.

For valuable assistance on framing the questions about knowledge of South African history, I am indebted to Chris Willemse and Christopher Saunders (University of Cape Town, Department of History).

Bertus de Villiers provided most useful help on the formulation of the land policy questions. From Lungisile Ntsebeza I learned a great deal about the politics of land in South Africa.

Portions of this book have appeared elsewhere in earlier versions. Chapter 4 is derived from a paper delivered at the 2005 Annual Meeting of the American Political Science Association, September 1–4, 2005, and at the spring meeting of the Working Group on African Political Economy, University of California at Los Angeles, May 13–14, 2005, Los Angeles, California; delivered as the Keynote Address at the "Justice Preconference" at the Society for Personality and Social Psychology annual meeting, January 20–22, 2005, New Orleans, Louisiana; and presented at the 63rd Annual National Conference of the Midwest Political Science Association, April 7–10, 2005, Chicago, Illinois. The paper was also published as "Group Identities and Theories of Justice: An Experimental Investigation into the Justice and Injustice of Land Squatting in South Africa," *Journal of Politics* 70, no. 3 (July 2008) 700–716. I am indebted to John Darley, Linda Skitka, Tom Tyler, David A. M. Peterson, and Raymond Duch for comments on an earlier version of that paper. I also acknowledge the valuable research assistance of Marc Hendershot, Jessica Flanigan, and Briana Morgan.

For the 2005 version of Chapter 4, I was the recipient of the 2005 Lucius Barker Award, "for the best paper investigating race or ethnicity and politics honoring the spirit and work of Professor Barker," awarded by the Midwest Political Science Association, and the paper received an Honorable Mention for the Sage Paper Award for the Best Paper in the Field of Comparative Politics presented at the 2005 Annual Meeting of the American Political Science Association, awarded by the Comparative Politics Organized Section, American Political Science Association.

Many people have commented on various aspects of this work. I am particularly indebted to my friend and colleague Amanda Gouws. It was Amanda who first introduced me to South Africa; I will be forever grateful for that.

This book was written during a most difficult period of time for Monica and me. Without the support of our beloved friends in Camps Bay – Chris Willemse, Linda Holmes, Cheryl Gibbon, and Judy Kruger – it would have been difficult to go forward. I deeply appreciate the friendship of these folks.

One of the joys of my life has been the opportunity to learn about and come to love South Africa. An unexpected bonus of this journey has been my friendship with Chris Willemse. Chris is a friend of unending insight, quick wit, and quicker intelligence, and from him I have learned immensely about the politics of South Africa. I deeply appreciate his unwavering friendship, in times that have been both good and bad.

Finally, this book is dedicated to Monica E. Kinsella. Monica will surely claim one day an honorary degree in political science – she has certainly put up with enough of it to deserve such recognition. But our experiences associated with this book have been unique, and, for what she has endured, she deeply deserves this dedication.

Cape Town
August 2007

Land Reconciliation and Theories of Justice, Past and Present

One of the most compelling issues for worldwide socio-legal studies has to do with how to reconcile competing historical claims to land. Countries as diverse as the United States, Argentina, and the Philippines are confronted with extremely complex and divisive issues of rectifying land injustices from the past. These conflicts are intractable in part because they implicate exceedingly difficult issues of law, justice, and history.

Nowhere is the issue of *land reconciliation*[1] more salient than in South Africa. Because the apartheid system and its predecessors were so obsessed with efforts (largely successful) to expropriate the vast majority of the land in the country for the use of the tiny white minority, South Africa's past is now colliding with its present, as demands for land reconciliation are growing in both number and intensity. And with the ever-present specter of Zimbabwe-style land invasions,[2] the issue is seen by many as threatening to the very political and economic stability of the country. How South Africa deals with the injustice of historical land practices will have much to do with the success of the country's attempt at consolidating its nascent democracy.

---

[1] I use the term "land reconciliation" to refer to a panoply of issues related to competing claims to land. As will become clear below, a number of specific issues are involved here.

[2] Zimbabwe's land problems figure heavily in the salience of the land issue in South Africa, with most South African elites perceiving the controversy as having had a ruinous effect on that country.

But land reconciliation is more than "just" an important policy issue. In addition, matters of land injustice are central to the growing inter-disciplinary attention to issues of *transitional justice* (see Hayner 2001, who claims that a new field of research on "transitional justice" has recently emerged). Scholars in this field are analyzing a variety of special problems of historical injustices[3] that confront regimes attempting to create a more democratic polity out of an authoritarian past. At the micro-level, the complementary development in political psychology is the emerging specialty of "justice research" (see Miller 2001, who describes how this subfield was created). Fueled partly by dissatisfaction with the dominance of the rational choice paradigm, these researchers are exploring ways in which feelings of justice and injustice shape socio-legal preferences and behavior, and ultimately political institutions and transitions. This body of research contends that satisfaction with political and legal outcomes is not solely a function of instrumental considerations but is instead conditional upon perceptions of fairness. Whether people believe that the institutions and processes of a new regime are more *fair* – not just more effective – than the old ones may be crucial to the success of political and legal transitions.

But fairness is a complicated concept, and unfortunately, competing claims to land are typically grounded in competing theories of justice. For instance, deeply cherished values such as rule of law, due process, and property rights are pitted against the injustice of apartheid, the unfairness of "legal" means of forcing Africans off their land and into so-called Bantustans, and the simple need for a place to live for millions of people.[4] In many respects, the problem of land reconciliation is a problem of the conflict between legality and justice, and thus the land issue is classically what Sniderman and his colleagues refer to as a "clash of rights," as their book is titled (Sniderman et al. 1996). How

---

[3] du Bois (2008, 116) defines the concept as follows: "I use the term 'historical injustice' to refer to injustices committed in a setting that has become historical by virtue of some fundamental and lasting change in the socio-political structure such as the end of slavery, colonial rule, or nonrepresentative government. Because of the break in continuity all these situations raise the question of how political institutions should deal with injustices that are not of their own making."

[4] The law on land in South Africa is based on the "implicit recognition that some of these rights [to land] had been acquired through a morally reprehensible if not strictly speaking illegal process of apartheid-inspired dispossessions" (Visser and Roux 1996, 92).

(and whether) such controversies get negotiated and managed is a matter of considerable importance to the future of South Africa's democratic transition.

Thus, the specific objective of this book is to develop and test a theory of justice values and apply it to South African preferences and judgments on issues of land reconciliation. I then test hypotheses derived from this theory using data from a nationally representative survey of ordinary people. In the broadest terms, my objectives include answering the following questions:

1. How are the issues of land reconciliation understood by South Africans? How much does history – including historical injustices – shape contemporary understandings of land politics? Which aspects of justice (distributive, procedural, retributive, or restorative) are most salient? How do the various issues and justice concerns get dimensionalized in the minds of people?

2. How much support exists for various aspects of land reconciliation in South Africa? Is support based solely on material self-interests, or do larger symbolic concerns predominate? What is the relative influence of contemporary and historical factors?

3. How can competing views of land be reconciled? Are land positions so deeply rooted in conflicting value systems that reconciliation is impossible, or can people be persuaded to alter and moderate their views?

4. Is land reconciliation an example of the more general phenomenon of people caring about the justice of socio-legal disputes, even when their immediate self-interests are not directly implicated?

5. How does support for land reconciliation vary across the various subcultures in South Africa? Are subcultural differences connected to such basic values as the sanctity of private property and preferences for European-style individualism or African-style communalism?

6. To what degree do land issues engage group identities, rendering the issue more volatile and intransigent?

Consequently, three overriding themes structure this research: To what degree are the politics of the present shaped by feelings of injustice from the past? To what degree are feelings of justice and injustice bound up within group identities and attachments? And to what degree are land issues further complicated by a clash of cultures within South Africa's multicultural context? South Africa thus offers an extremely fecund laboratory for testing psychological theories of transitional justice, since land reconciliation is at the forefront of the list of injustices wrought by apartheid.[5]

Thus, this is a book about how ordinary people apply principles of justice to complex policy issues within the domain of land reconciliation. It may not be immediately obvious that a study of the beliefs, attitudes, and preferences of ordinary people are of much relevance to issues of land reconciliation. More relevant might be a study of land litigants (plaintiffs and defendants), land activists, land policy makers, or even land claimants. What can a study of the justice thinking of a representative sample of South Africans tells us about the land issue and/or theories of justice?

COMMONSENSE JUSTICE

Justice research is a field of inquiry in the making (Miller 2001), and applications of justice theory to actual issues of law and politics are becoming increasingly common (e.g., Hamilton and Sanders 1992; Gibson and Gouws 1999; Gibson 2002). Indeed, the publication of an encyclopedic review of justice research – the *Handbook of Justice Research in Law*, by Sanders and Hamilton – will most likely contribute enormously to the institutionalization of the field. It is now well established that the justice judgments of ordinary citizens ("commonsense justice" – see, for examples, Finkel 1995, 2001) are of considerable importance to both psychologists and political scientists.[6]

The basic insight of this research is that, when it comes to law and politics, *justice matters*. Generally speaking, justice research examines

---

[5] For many, land is a central element of transitional justice politics and reconciliation in South Africa. For instance, Roux (2006) treats land restitution as a form of reconciliation. On reconciliation more generally, see Gibson 2004a.

[6] Investigations of justice theories can be found in far-flung places, including normative treatises on social justice (e.g., Barry 2005), experimental treatments inspired by distributive justice theories (e.g., Michelbach et al. 2003), both experimental and survey studies of procedural justice (e.g., Tyler et al. 1997; see also Tyler and Lind 2001), qualitative studies of how ordinary citizens think about fairness (e.g., Hochschild 1981), and large cross-national quantitative research on cultural differences in understandings of fairness (e.g., Kluegel, Mason, and Wegener 1995).

people's conceptions of the justness of law and politics under the presumption that people care about whether legal and political outcomes are fair. "What qualifies such research as justice research is the assumption that outcome satisfaction is mediated by perceptions of outcome fairness" (Miller 2001, 528). Thus, justice research moves beyond a concern with narrow calculations of individual self-interest (costs and benefits), arguing that in addition to interests, people judge legal and political outcomes by whether they comport with their standards of fairness. Indeed, a long line of research has demonstrated that "what's fair" is a terribly important criterion – perhaps even the most important criterion – in the calculus of opinion formation (e.g., Hochschild 1981). In addition, institutions that rely on principles of justice not widely shared by the citizenry are likely to have a rocky existence, since unjust institutions are unlikely to be accorded legitimacy, and without legitimacy, compliance becomes problematical (i.e., it becomes more closely related to calculations of costs and benefits).[7] Of course, some social scientists have long argued that material instrumentalism rarely provides a full account of legal and political issues (e.g., the "symbolic politics" literature – e.g., Tarman and Sears 2005; see also Funk 2000), but there now seems to be an acknowledgment across many areas of the social sciences that fairness – even fairness for *others* rather than for oneself – is one of the most sought after "commodities" in law and politics. Citizens are often lay philosophers, applying principles of justice to complex issues of public policy (e.g., Chong and Marshall 1999). And justice matters in part because one does not have to be a party to a dispute to care about the fairness of its outcome – people care about injustices done to others.[8]

Justice considerations, however, are rarely unidimensional; rather, people typically apply multiple aspects of justice when evaluating political conflicts. Scholars have addressed several different types of justice, such as distributive, procedural, retributive, and restorative

[7] The large body of research conducted under the general rubric of "political culture" is grounded in the hypothesis that democratic institutions require certain cultural and value commitments on the part of citizens to be effective. See, e.g., Gibson, Duch, and Tedin 1992. For a study of the degree of congruence between justice principles in law and in lay intuitions of justice, see Robinson and Darley 1998. See also Caldeira and Gibson 1995 on democratic values and support for judicial institutions, and Duch and Palmer 2004 on the cultural requisites of a market economy.

[8] This notion of "disinterested justice" has emerged from the literature on retribution and revenge (for an excellent review, see Vidmar 2001).

justice. Within each domain, various criteria of justice exist.[9] For instance, the major criteria on which distributive justice judgments are made include desert, need, and equality (e.g., Miller 1999).[10] Procedural justice judgments often rely on criteria such as neutrality in decision making and status recognition by the decision maker (e.g., Tyler and Lind 1992). Justice values, like justice itself, are pluralistic.

Justice assessments are especially complicated when criteria within domains conflict with one another, since there is no clear metric on which citizens can trade units of need for units of desert, for example. The problem of justice conflict is exacerbated when tension across justice domains also exists. How does one, for instance, exchange a quantity of procedural justice voice for a portion of distributive justice desert or retributive justice proportionality? Social justice theories recognize that views of justice are pluralistic (Miller 1999, 63), and that "very often people decide what a fair distribution consists in by balancing claims of one kind against claims of another" (Miller 1999, 63; see also Scott et al. 2001, 751).[11] But little progress has been made either theoretically or empirically on identifying a stable hierarchy of justice principles or criteria that enables predictions of how ordinary people adjudicate justice conflict in real political controversies.[12]

For example, granting amnesty to gross human rights violators may be judged in terms of distributive, procedural, retributive, and restorative justice considerations (Gibson 2002). The analysis in that work shows that these different dimensions of justice can be fungible. Although awarding amnesty to gross human rights violators does indeed create a retributive justice shortfall, other forms of justice (distributive, procedural, and restorative) can compensate for the inability to extract retribution. In judging political and social controversies and policies,

---

[9] I use the term "domains" to refer to the major types of justice, and "criteria" to refer to the principles by which justice is allocated within a domain. So, for instance, within the domain of distributive justice, desert is regarded as an important criterion, or principle of allocation. In the justice literature, no standard terminology has yet been produced and accepted.

[10] For a useful review of the distributive justice literature, see Hegtvedt and Cook 2001.

[11] Or as Scott et al. (2001, 751) note: "individuals use several allocation principles in distributive justice judgments."

[12] An analogous literature exists on the role of value conflict in opinion formation. For recent examples of research on this problem, see Alvarez and Brehm (2002), Grant and Rudolph (2003), and Jacoby (2005).

citizens typically do not apply unidimensional justice thinking; instead, pluralism prevails. Unfortunately, however, although the relative influence of different justice considerations can be estimated empirically, little theory exists to help understand how (and under what conditions) one justice value trumps another.[13]

Moreover, to complicate the issue further, context matters. As Miller (1999, 63) asserts, "the social context in which the distribution has to be made – or more precisely how that context is perceived by those making the judgment – will determine which principle stands out as the relevant principle to follow." What's fair depends on a variety of factors idiosyncratic to contexts – for example, whether those seeking justice are part of an ingroup or are representatives of an outgroup, as in relational models of procedural justice (Tyler and Lind 1992).

We have also established that justice judgments may be formed in reference to individual or group interests, or in egocentric or sociotropic terms. Undoubtedly some people draw conclusions about justice in terms of what they think is fair to them, but many base their views on what is fair to their group, or even what is fair to groups of which they are not even members.[14] Mutz and Mondak (1997) introduce the concept of "sociotropic justice" to refer to how people judge not fairness to themselves, but rather fairness to the group of which they are members. Since it is well established that people typically assess political disputes by far more than simply what they think is beneficial to their immediate self-interests (see, e.g., Funk 2000), any attempt to understand justice judgments must pay attention to justice for groups, even groups of which the judgment maker is not a member.

---

[13] Another nice example of justice pluralism can be found in the work of Chong and Marshall (1999), who illustrate the crucial role that multidimensional judgments of justice played in the decision of the residents of Williamson County in Texas not to grant tax relief to Apple computer company owing to its policy on benefits for homosexual and unmarried heterosexual couples. Chong and Marshall describe the conflict that arose in the minds of people between moral and economic values; how individuals derived their positions on the Apple controversy depended on the way in which moral and economic senses of justice were prioritized. Again, however, we have little theory regarding these processes of prioritization of justice values.

[14] The concern many expressed about the treatment of Afghan women is a primary example of this phenomenon. At least some white men in the United States care deeply about whether Afghan girls are treated fairly when it comes to political equality, access to education, etc.

Thus, justice matters in part because one does not necessarily have to be a party to a dispute to care about the fairness of its outcome – people care about injustices done to others. Being forcefully removed from one's living quarters by the apartheid regime is obviously an example of both group and individual victimization. Consequently, the desire for retributive justice is stimulated. The important insight of this literature, however, is that people respond strongly to harms done to people and groups with whom no personal or immediate relationship exists. The important unanswered question is, why?

Strong feelings of injustice may be aroused by sympathy with the person or group who is victimized, based on sharing an identity with the victim. But they may also be a more general reaction to the socio-legal system, with some viewing victimization as a violation of the "social contract" between the individual and the state (and hence Tyler et al. 1997 refer to this as the "relational model"). Central to this contract is a set of normative assumptions about how citizens ought to be treated, which is of course the basic building block of a polity based on the rule of law (Vidmar 2001, 42). The offense against an individual is sometimes generalized to an offense against a group or a community, a violation of the contract. To the extent that this occurs, the systemic relevance of individual injustices is vastly multiplied.

Thinking about justice for groups raises obvious connections with social identity theory (e.g., Tajfel 1981; for a useful review, see Huddy 2001). Although most approaches to understanding justice judgments adopt an individualistic perspective, relying on attributes of the individual to predict conclusions about justice, of late, scholars have become concerned with the role of group identities in shaping thoughts about justice and injustice (e.g., Tyler et al. 1997).[15] As Vidmar (2001, 43) notes, " 'disinterested' retributive justice is not disinterested at all: The response of the individual is based on identification with her or his group and the threat to values held by the group." People seem to feel the need to vindicate their value in society by ensuring that some form of retributive or restorative justice takes place. This is particularly important for those who draw much of their identity from their group

---

[15] Some cross-national differences in justice thinking may have to do with how people conceptualize relations among groups, as in, for example, individualistic or collectivist terms (e.g., Hamilton and Sanders 1992).

affiliation, and especially if the group has been subject to systematic victimization in the past.

Consequently, an obvious hypothesis drawn from social identity theory (e.g., Tajfel 1981; Gibson and Gouws 2000) is that to the extent that an individual identifies with a victimized group, reactions to the victimization of an individual group member will be stronger, more salient, and of greater socio-political relevance. Land reconciliation is certainly an important issue for those directly victimized by apartheid. But through mechanisms of group identification, group comparison, and disinterested justice, the victimization takes on larger proportion and meaning for the political system. Because such feelings of injustice aroused by failure to punish wrong-doers typically generate anger and the desire to strike out at the offender, behavioral consequences of these attitudes often materialize (as perhaps in criminal behavior against the privileged minority, or in Zimbabwe-style "land grabs"). Failure to sanction offenders can lead to a more general sense of the illegitimacy of the socio-political system.[16] Apparently, people feel the need to vindicate their value in society by ensuring that some form of retribution and restitution take place. This is especially important for those who draw much of their identity from their group affiliation, especially if the group has been subject to systematic victimization and lack of respect for the rule of law.[17]

Land repression in South Africa was obviously directed against both individuals and groups.[18] Where individuals could live was determined by their group membership (race), as ascertained by law. There was no ambiguity about the value of group comparisons – whites assigned themselves the superior position and blacks the decidedly inferior position. Thus, the harm of forced removal was experienced both directly by those who were required to move their residences and by those who, while not directly affected, were subject to the law requiring forced

---

[16] See Vidmar (2001, 56), who concludes that the question is as important as existing empirical research is sparse.

[17] Huo and Tyler (2000) report the interesting finding that identification with a group does not undermine legal authority, even if failure to identify with the United States does.

[18] On the importance of this issue, Leung and Morris (2001, 371) note: "very little research has examined [the dispossession of native peoples] from a justice perspective. We believe that this is a major area that should be tackled in future research."

removals. Consequently, land reconciliation is likely to be of great concern to all black South Africans because until such reconciliation takes place, blacks cannot have their status as equal citizens of the country affirmed.[19]

Identity theory may therefore provide some basis for establishing a hierarchy of justice values. Skitka (2003), for instance, has argued that although *justice principles* may not be hierarchically organized themselves, different types of *identities* are arrayed in a hierarchy – and become salient under different, contextually defined circumstances – and different types of identities give rise to different types of justice concerns. For instance, following group values and relational models of justice (Lind and Tyler 1988; Tyler and Lind 1992), she hypothesizes that "people are influenced more by socio-emotional outcomes like standing, status, and respect as the relative salience of their social identity concerns increases" (Skitka 2003, 290). In addition, "when people's material interests are threatened, they will first look for violations of the equity norm, and when their social status or standing is threatened, they will first look for evidence of procedural impropriety (e.g., a biased judge) or violations of group norms" (Skitka 2003, 292). Thus, people define themselves socially; sociotropic concerns are at least as important as egocentric goals and are associated with assigning priority to procedural justice; and group identities, norms, and values are therefore important when people assess the fairness of outcomes.

In sum, extant research has shown that citizens typically evaluate justice claims using multidimensional frameworks. To understand the politics of such claims, one must be able to assess which justice domains are dominant, whether group identity concerns are activated, and how conflicts among justice domains are adjudicated. Since the land issue implicates a variety of justice values, it provides a useful context for an inquiry into commonsense justice.

---

[19] This suggests the hypothesis that whether one was victimized by apartheid is unlikely to be a strong predictor of positions on land reconciliation (just as the risk of victimization has been found to have little impact on attitudes toward California's "three strikes" sentencing laws – see Tyler et al. 1997). In fact, based on the limited data available from our 2001 survey (see Gibson 2001), this hypothesis receives little empirical support. Experiences of this sort seem to have only a very small influence on the attitudes South Africans hold toward land reconciliation.

LAND ISSUES IN SOUTH AFRICA

One of the central aims of both the English and Afrikaans governments in the twentieth century was to secure for white South Africans the exclusive use of the most valuable land in the country (see Turner and Ibsen 2000 for a valuable review of land reform in South Africa; see also and Walker 2005a, 2005b, 2007, Hall 2007, Hall and Ntsebeza 2007). Beginning with the 1913 Natives' Land Act[20] – which restricted the areas where Africans could live and stripped African cash tenants and sharecroppers of their land, replacing land ownership with labor tenancy, and which restricted black[21] land ownership to the 7% of the country designated as "homelands" or native reserves – the South African parliament adopted a variety of pieces of legislation dispossessing blacks of their land. The 1936 Development Trust and Land Act No. 18 expanded the reserves to a total of 13.6% of the land in South Africa (for 80% of the total South African population) and authorized the Department of Bantu Administration and Development to eliminate "black spots" (black-occupied land surrounded by white-owned land).[22] Roughly 470,000 black South Africans were relocated due to "black spot" cleansing (de Villiers 2003, 46). It was these relocation areas that were later to become the so-called Bantustans that would constitute the "homelands" for blacks in South Africa. The Surplus People Project (1983) estimates that, between 1960 and 1983, 1.29 million people were evicted from farms, and 614,000 were resettled during the abolition of "black spots" and homeland consolidation processes (see Turner and Ibsen 2000 for details). Moreover, Villa-Vicencio

---

[20] I begin this history of land dispossessions in South Africa with the Natives' Land Act No. 27 of 1913, not because no land was expropriated before 1913, but rather because the Restitution of Land Rights Act 22 of 1994 limited its jurisdiction to racially motivated land dispossessions taking place after the passage of the Natives' Land Act of 1913.

[21] Race in South Africa is a complicated construct so I have prepared a detailed discussion of South Africa's racial/ethnic/linguistic groups in Appendix A.

[22] A least a few whites were also affected by this policy of ethnic cleansing. For instance, the Opperman family has filed a claim before the Land Claims Court alleging that their family was compelled to sell their farm land north of Pretoria as part of the government's scheme to create the Lebowa homeland. The family claims that they were forced to accept compensation at less than the fair value of the land. The family further contends that it was targeted by the government due to its efforts to promote nonracialism in sports in South Africa. See Hofstätter 2004.

and Ngesi (2003, 283; see also Platzky and Walker 1985) claim: "Between 1963 and 1985, approximately 3.5 million blacks were removed from areas designated for whites and sent to the homelands." Even if the methods by which these various estimates are derived are rarely transparent, in the end, the "ethnic cleansing" of vast proportions of both urban and rural land was extremely successful. By the twilight of the apartheid regime, little of South Africa was owned by blacks.

Indeed, the extent to which various South African administrations have been preoccupied with the land issue is documented to some degree by Table 1.1, which lists some of the major land legislation between 1913 and the fall of the apartheid regime in 1994. This table makes plain that land repression did not begin with the installation of the apartheid regime in 1948, even if the apartheid government made considerable progress in its scheme to separate South Africa's racial groups. It is also obvious that the South African government has devoted some considerable energy over time to legislating on various land issues.

Land Reform Under the Post-Apartheid Government

Although land reform began under the final apartheid government (e.g., the Abolition of Racially Based Land Measures Act 108 of 1991), the major pillars of contemporary public policy are found in the new constitution and several pieces of legislation enacted by the post-apartheid government. With majority rule in 1994, the new government passed several laws designed to deal with historical dispossessions, the most important of which is the Restitution of Land Rights Act of 1994 (for a superb historical and legal analysis, see Miller with Pope 2000; see also Murphy 1996). The principal elements of the policy were: (1) *land restitution* – the right to restoration or compensation for dispossessions as a result of past racially discriminatory laws or practices, (2) *land redistribution* – an assistance program through which the government aids individuals seeking to purchase land (primarily for agricultural purposes),[23] and (3) *land tenure*

---

[23] Particularly important in establishing the broad contours of land policy is the government's White Paper on South African Land Policy promulgated in April 1997. Redistribution relies on a system of grants to individual citizens to allow them to purchase land on the open market, based on the principle of the "willing buyer/ willing seller." This policy is currently being reconsidered and revised (e.g., Benjamin 2006).

TABLE 1.1. *Adoption and Implementation of South African Land Legislation*

1874: *Native Location Act* authorized one-man-one-plot in Cape Colony, occupation without ownership.[a]

1887: *Squatter Laws (Transvaal)* allowed five African families for every white household.[a]

1894: *Glen Grey Act* converted land tenure in the Transkei and Ciskei to permanent quitrent, reduced the size of land holdings, and imposed a labor tax, effectively preventing African commercial farming in these areas.[b]

1908: *Native Occupation of Land Act (Transvaal)* reduced the number of Africans allowed on white farms.[a]

1913: *Natives' Land Act (No. 27)* restricted the area of land for lawful African occupation and stripped African cash tenants and sharecroppers of their land and consequently replaced sharecropping and rent-tenant contracts with labor tenancy. The *Natives' Land Act* resulted in only 7% of the land being reserved for blacks.[b]

1921: The first large-scale forced eviction from land by the police took place at Bulhoek near Queenstown in the Eastern Cape.[c]

1923: *Native (Urban Areas) Act (No. 21)* established separate residential areas for Africans in urban locations.[b]

1927: *Black (Native) Administration Act (No. 38):* Section 5(1)(b) provided that "whenever he deemed it expedient in the public interest, the minister might, without prior notice to any person concerned, order any tribe, portion thereof, or individual black person, to move from one place to another within the Republic of South Africa."[d]

1934: *Slums Clearance Act* laid down minimum standards for housing and allowed for evictions and the expropriation of properties deemed to be slums.[a]

1936: *Native Trust and Land Act (No. 18)* expanded the reserves to a total of 13.6% of the land in South Africa and authorized the Department of Bantu Administration and Development to eliminate "black spots" (black-owned land surrounded by white-owned land).[d]

1937: *Natives Laws Amendment Act (No. 46)* was enacted to control rural-urban migration by prohibiting Africans from buying land in urban areas.[b]

1945: *Natives (Urban Areas) Consolidation Act (No. 25)* introduced influx control to black males only. People who were deemed to be leading idle or dissolute lives or who had committed certain specified offenses could be removed from an urban area.[e]

1950: *Group Areas Act (No. 41)* racially segregated areas with respect to residence and business and controlled interracial property actions.[a]

(continued)

TABLE I.I *(continued)*

1951: *Prevention of Illegal Squatting Act (No. 52)* empowered the government to evict squatters from public or private land at its discretion and required local authorities to set up emergency camps for evicted people.[b]

1952: *Native Laws Amendment Act (No. 54)* narrowed the definition of the category of blacks who had the right of permanent residence in towns to those who had been born there and had lived there continuously for not less than 15 years or who had been employed continuously there for at least 15 years or who had worked continuously for the same employer for at least 10 years.[b]

1954: *Native Resettlement Act (No. 19)* gave the state the authority to remove Africans from any area in the magisterial district of Johannesburg, enacted so as to remove the African residents of Sophiatown, in the west of the city.[a]

1956: *Natives (Prohibition of Interdicts) Act (No. 64)* denied Africans the right of appealing to the courts against forced removals.[f]

1957: *Group Areas Act (No. 77)* consolidated the law relating to the establishment of group areas and the control of the acquisition of immovable property in those areas.[g]

1978: *Black (Urban) Areas Amendment Act (No. 97)* introduced a 99-year leasehold system. Full ownership was not attainable until 1986.[b]

1984: *Black Communities Development Act (No. 4)* enabled Africans to acquire land in urban areas and stated that only a "competent person" could lease or rent property.[a]

1986: *Abolition of Influx Control Act (No. 68)* repealed those sections of the Native (Urban Areas) Consolidation Act not abolished by the Black Communities Development Act of 1984. A degree of freedom of movement was granted to South African "citizens," but "non-citizens," including workers from the "independent" homelands, lost rights.[a]

1994: *Restitution of Land Rights Act (No. 22)* set up the land restitution process whereby individuals and communities who were dispossessed of their land have the right to claim restitution against the state. All claims must first be submitted to the Commission on the Restitution of Land Rights, whose role is to investigate the merits of claims and attempt to settle them through mediation. Where a claim cannot be settled through mediation, the Commission refers the claim to the Land Claims Court for final determination.[g]

1996: *Land Reform (Labour Tenants) Act (No. 3)* grants secure tenure to labor tenants on privately owned farms. A process to acquire full ownership of land occupied by labor tenants was created.[i]

(continued)

TABLE I.I *(continued)*

1997: *Extension of Security of Tenure Act (No. 62)* provides for measures, with state assistance, to facilitate long-term security of land tenure, regulates the conditions of residence on certain land (the conditions on and under which the rights of persons to reside on land may be terminated), and regulates the conditions and circumstances under which persons whose right of residence has been terminated may be evicted from land.[j]

1998: *Prevention of Illegal Evictions from and Unlawful Occupation of Land Act (No. 19)* provides that an unlawful occupier of land may not be evicted without a court order and establishes procedures for the eviction of unlawful occupiers, except for those who are subject to the Extension of Security of Tenure Act.[i]

2003: *The Restitution of Land Rights Amendment Act (No. 48)* allows the minister of land affairs and agriculture to expropriate land for the purposes of restitution without a court order.[i]

2004: *Communal Land Rights Act (No. 11)* recognizes and formalizes the African communal land tenure system, provides security of tenure to those within this tenure system, and provides for the administration of communal land. It also provides for compensating people who hold old, insecure land rights in communal land areas, which the state is unable to legally secure.[i]

[a] Fair Share, School of Government, University of the Western Cape, "How the South African Economy Works," March 2001. http://www.uwc.ac.za/fairshare/Pubs/ SA%20Economy/Feb%20-%20Land.pdf (August 2, 2007).

[b] Rodney Davenport and Christopher Saunders, *South Africa: A Modern History*, 5th ed. (New York: St. Martin's, 2000), 190–1.

[c] Anthony Minnaar and Phineas Ngoveni, "The Eviction of Squatters in South Africa: Post-1994 Victims and the Role of the Police," paper presented to the 10th International Symposium on Victimology, Montreal, August 6–11, 2000.

[d] Muriel Horrell, *Laws Affecting Race Relations in South Africa 1948–1976* (Johannesburg: South African Institute of Race Relations, 1978), 204.

[e] Truth and Reconciliation Commission of South Africa, *Final Report*, Vol. 1 (1998), 452.

[f] John Dugard, *Human Rights and the South African Legal Order* (Princeton: Princeton University Press, 1978), 78.

[g] South African History Online. "South African History Timelines: Apartheid Legislation." http://www.sahistory.org.za/pages/chronology/special-chrono/ governance/apartheid-legislation.html (August 2, 2007).

[h] Land Claims Court of South Africa, "Information About the Land Claims Court." http://wwwserver.law.wits.ac.za/lcc/about.html (August 2, 2007).

[i] The Centre for Development and Enterprise, *Land Reform in South Africa: A 21st Century Perspective.* CDE Research Report No. 14 (Johannesburg: CDE, 2005), 24.

[j] Extension of Security of Tenure Act No. 62, *Government Gazette of the Republic of South Africa* 389, no. 18467 (November 28, 1977).

reform – changes in the legal basis of land ownership to provide legal standing and security in land ownership (e.g., the formalization of informal land rights, especially in rural areas and the former "homelands").[24] Particularly important was the establishment of the Commission on Restitution of Land Rights and the Land Claims Court, before which 63,455 claims have been filed (Hall 2007, 93).[25] As of June 30, 2005, some 62,127 of these claims had been settled (Hall 2007, 93), and the government has spent millions of rands for land restitution and land compensation.

Thus, although I speak of "land reconciliation" in South Africa, in fact, the land issue is actually a bundle of different and relatively distinct problems, including:

Land "grabs" by the urban landless: In the past several years, South Africa has experienced enormous emigration, with large numbers of the rural population relocating to the cities. This has swollen the size of the urban squatter communities and has led to a demand for land for the simple purpose of being able to live where jobs are. For instance, in July 2001, in one of the most poignant examples of squatting, a major "land grab" took place in Bredell (an area between Pretoria and Johannesburg). After squatters put up their shacks on vacant land, they were evicted by the government, which destroyed all the shacks and cleared the land.[26] Land grabs by urban

[24] Tenure security is based on two pieces of legislation, the Land Reform (Labour Tenants) Act of 1996 and the Extension of Security of Tenure Act (ESTA) of 1997. The primary focus of this legislation is on the security of tenure of labor tenants and farm workers. Walker (2002, 43) refers to tenure security as "the most politically difficult aspect of land reform to manage, as it brought the DLA [Department of Land Affairs] into conflict with two very different but equally hostile and defensive constituencies — commercial farmers, with respect to the tenure security of farm works and labour tenants living on the land they own, and traditional leaders and tribal authorities, with respect to tenure security for the residents of communal areas."

[25] The number of claims is ever-changing as group claims get split into subgroup and individual claims. Hall (2007, 93) estimates that there are about 80,000 claims as of about 2007. For analysis of the decisions of the Land Claims Court, see Roux 2004.

[26] On July 2, 2001, thousands of people converged on Bredell, Kempton Park, near Johannesburg International Airport, in the hope of securing some land for shelter after word spread that the Pan Africanist Congress (PAC) was "selling" plots for R25 each. On July 10, the court ruled in favor of the government and gave the squatters until 12 July to leave the land. Thereafter, 30 armored vehicles forced the squatters off the land, in a scene that was reminiscent for many of apartheid era dispossessions. See Norm Dixon, "South Africa: ANC Denounces 'Land Grab.'" Reprinted at www.greenleft.org.au/back/2001/456/456p18.htm (accessed August 6, 2003).

dwellers have become increasingly common throughout South Africa, clearly linking for many the South African land issue with the expropriation of farming land in Zimbabwe (see Mitchell 2001).

Rural land claims by farm workers: Legislation under the new government gave fairly specific land rights to farm workers who had long occupied (ten years) land. However, many new rural land issues have emerged (e.g., the right to bury deceased people on the land; how workers who are retrenched are to be resettled), and rights consciousness seems so low among farm workers that it is difficult to get them to pursue their legal rights.[27]

Claims by those subject to forced removals: By far the most difficult issue from a justice perspective is the problem of forced removals (see, e.g., O'Regan 1989). The apartheid government moved a massive number of black South Africans from their residences, often with the goal of providing land for whites. Some of these forced removals are notorious (e.g., District 6 in Cape Town), with so much controversy created by the removals that the land remained vacant for long periods of time. Dealing with the claims of the dispossessed has been a slow and arduous process.

Land Redistribution: Since whites own such a vastly disproportionate share of land in South Africa, the post-apartheid government has developed a program of land redistribution. Through these efforts, land is purchased from current owners and redistributed through a variety of grants, loans, subsidies, and so on. Many complain that black commercial farmers have been the primary if not exclusive beneficiaries of such programs.

Legal Land Transfers: Many black South Africans were dispossessed of their land through legal contracts between tribal leaders and land purchasers.[28] These controversies raise even more complicated justice issues since the conflicts often pit individuals against extremely powerful traditional leaders, and they also raise intractable questions of incompatibility between customary and civil law.

---

[27] Hall (2007, 95) asserts: "government and civil society organisations have acknowledged that implementation of both laws has been weak and ineffective."

[28] Banner (2000) notes that most land in New Zealand was actually transferred through legal means.

Gender: All aspects of these various land issues are deeply interwoven with questions of gender, especially in areas where traditional leaders are dominant.

Thus, the "land issue" in South Africa is actually an amalgamation of a variety of quite distinct political issues. Moreover, these various aspects of the land issue intersect with different theories of justice.

Land Politics

Politics in South Africa is strongly driven by competition among elites, and the land issue is no exception. Powerful interest groups (e.g., AgriSA, the interest group for big agriculture in South Africa) have recognized the importance of the land problem. It is therefore reasonable to ask what a study of the views of a representative sample of ordinary South Africans can tell us about the politics of the issue.

Zimbabwe's land problems differ in many important ways from the land problems of South Africa. But for many South Africans, Zimbabwe stands as a terrifying exemplar of how ruthless and unprincipled elites can mobilize the mass public in pursuit of a "solution" to the land problem. In South Africa, no effort to mobilize ordinary people has yet been successful, even though political parties have attempted to galvanize the people on land (e.g., the Pan Africanist Congress, and, more recently, the South African Communist Party).[29] The mass public can become a form of political capital as elite groups and organizations seek political advantage. Especially as the African National Congress (ANC) is increasingly divided over the questions of who will lead the party and the country, it seems quite likely that radical land reform might become a vehicle for challenging the current structure of power in the country. As Cousins (2007, 238) put it, "events in Zimbabwe have catapulted land reform into the headlines. Across the region, a variety of interest groups (including political parties, NGOs, farmers' unions, trade unions and donors) have responded to the implicit question: does the slow pace of land reform in their own country presage large-scale land invasions supported by powerful political interests?"

---

[29] The Landless People's Movement sought to mobilize ordinary South Africans on the land issue. However, by late 2006, the movement seemed to be in complete disarray (see Ntsebeza 2007, 128).

What are the views of ordinary South Africans on the various land issues?[30] Given the history of colonialism and apartheid, how legitimate are the vast land holdings of whites in the country? To what degree are proposals for radical land reform (e.g., expropriation) supported by ordinary South Africans? And perhaps most important, how "racialized" is the land problem? Is land simply one more subdimension of the vast interracial conflict characterizing South African politics? Do the positions people adopt on land reflect alternative sets of cultural values, as in a mini-version of the clash of cultures? Have class divisions arisen and how do they intersect with race? To date, little is known about what ordinary South Africans believe about land, and why they hold these beliefs. One purpose of this book is to attempt to fill that important lacuna in our understanding of the politics of land in South Africa.

JUSTICE CONSIDERATIONS IMPLICATED

In order to consider how conflicting views of justice affect these various issues of land reconciliation it is necessary to identify the key principles underpinning the land reform process in South Africa. These include (ranging loosely from the most explicit to the most implicit) the following.

Colonial dispossessions will not be reviewed: Only "modern" dispossessions will be considered, with land claims prior to June 19, 1913 (the date of passage of the Natives Land Act) not eligible for consideration and adjudication. Land lost through colonial conquest will not be restored and no compensation will be provided.

Rule of law: All transfers of property will be done within the context of the rule of law, including due process in all legal hearings. This principle forbids the lawless land seizures common in Zimbabwe and of growing frequency in South Africa (and more recently in Namibia).

---

[30] Only a handful of earlier studies have focused on either mass or elite opinions on land issues. See, e.g., Aliber, Reitzes, and Roefs (2005, 2006), Gran (2005), and du Toit (2006). Roberts (2006, 120) reports the results from a single land question within the context of attitudes toward the responsibilities of government. He finds vast racial differences on whether government should "redistribute land to black South Africans." Generally, though, no prior study examines land attitudes as comprehensively as this study does.

Formality is preferred to informality, with informal and customary land claims being converted to formal legal ownership wherever possible.

The sanctity of property rights: The rights of property owners shall be extended legal protections and given relatively high priority. When legality and fairness conflict, legality should generally dominate, through the principle of protecting property rights.

Voluntariness: Land will not be forcibly taken from its owners, and, if land is claimed in the name of the state, compensation will be given. Generally, compulsory acquisitions have not been common in South Africa as of yet.

Fair compensation: Compensation for land is to be based on the market price of the land *at the time it is acquired*, with little or no concern for any unjust enrichment that may have occurred as a result of apartheid.

Individualism: Individual rights are generally privileged over communal rights, although some elements of communal ownership are recognized and protected (especially in the former Bantustans). Individual citizens have rights in disputes with their traditional leaders.

Equality: Land arrangements cannot abrogate the right of all South Africans to equal treatment, including women. To the extent that customary law conflicts with civil law, the latter should prevail. Racial discrimination in land rights will not be tolerated, and the historical practice of maintaining a second-class system of land tenure for blacks must cease.

Land reconciliation is undoubtedly an issue of retributive justice, as the post-apartheid government seeks to rectify the sins of the country's apartheid past. But land reconciliation also implicates dimensions of justice other than retributive concerns. It is therefore useful to consider how the issue maps onto the other major building blocks of justice research: distributive, procedural, and restorative justice.

The Distributive Justice of Land Reconciliation

As noted, land reconciliation actually involves multiple distinct issues, including the question of whether the government ought to adopt more redistributive policies. Obvious aspects of such policies involve the distribution of government-owned land, purchasing and redistributing privately owned land, the exercise of eminent domain, and the means by which revenue can be raised to fund land reconciliation. Thus, land reconciliation may be thought of largely in terms of distributive justice dimensions.

The Procedural Justice of Land Reconciliation

Procedure is no doubt important in how people judge claims to land, since procedure lies at the heart of due process and the rule of law. But of course formal procedures are not all that matter for judgments of fairness. One of the most interesting findings from my research on the unfairness of amnesty is that granting people procedural justice ("voice") can compensate for failing to achieve any sort of retributive justice (Gibson 2002). To date, the procedural fairness of land reform has been widely criticized as being too slow, too bureaucratized, and giving virtually no process control to the participants. Some seem to envisage a zero-sum relationship between procedural fairness for those making land claims and those subject to land claims. One important question is whether there are procedural justice factors that can contribute to making land transfers more acceptable to ordinary South Africans.

The Restorative Justice of Land Reconciliation

Though the most obvious hypotheses of this research concern distributive and retributive justice, I also hypothesize that expectations of *restorative* justice are important for land reconciliation attitudes. Some argue that restorative justice is especially significant in the African context:[31]

In traditional African thought, the emphasis is on restoring evildoers to the community rather than on punishing them. The term *ubuntu*, which derives from the Xhosa expression *Umuntu ngumuntu ngabanye bantu* (People are people through other people), conveys the view that an environment of right

---

[31] The basis of law in much of rural South Africa remains "customary law," and restorative justice is a central element in that system. The new constitution did not abolish customary law, even if it did subordinate it to civil law. See Bennett (1995) and Chambers (2000).

relationships is one in which people are able to recognize that their humanity is inextricably bound up in others' humanity. *Ubuntu* emphasizes the priority of "restorative" as opposed to "retributive" justice. (Graybill 1998, 47)

When South Africans talk about restorative justice, they often refer to processes such as restoring the "dignity" of the victims (e.g., Villa-Vicencio 2000, 202).

One important form of restoration involves an apology. A considerable literature in political psychology investigates the effectiveness of apologies in mitigating blame (e.g., Darby and Schlenker 1989; Ohbuchi, Kameda, and Agarie 1989; Weiner et al. 1991; see also Vidmar 2001, 52–54). Generally, that literature concludes that apologies can contribute to forgiveness and reconciliation under some circumstances (e.g., Scher and Darley 1997).

In sum, extant research has shown that citizens typically evaluate justice claims using multidimensional frameworks. To understand the politics of such claims, one must be able to assess which justice domains are dominant, whether group identity concerns are activated, and how conflicts among justice considerations are adjudicated.

This research focuses specifically on the judgments of ordinary South Africans of the process of land reconciliation, and therefore it fits squarely within the socio-legal tradition of empirical research on legal cultures (e.g., Gibson and Caldeira 1996). However, it is probably a mistake to think of South Africa as constituting only a single legal or political culture. Instead, the country is an amalgam of cultures – from European to African to Asian – and that may well be a source of conflict over issues of land reconciliation.

MULTICULTURALISM AND THE JUSTICE OF LAND RECONCILIATION

Some extant research considers whether cultural values are in agreement with the value premises of law (e.g., Hamilton and Sanders 1992; Bierbrauer 1994; Blankenburg 1994). In the South African case, our earlier research investigated the degree to which ordinary people attribute blame for atrocities committed under apartheid in the same fashion (according to the same criteria) as the law granting amnesty to gross human rights violators (Gibson and Gouws 1999). A long tradition of socio-legal research addresses the degree of agreement between law and cultural values (e.g., Robinson and Darley 1995).

In the case of land reconciliation in South Africa, the law does indeed adopt certain normative positions on various aspects of land reconciliation. For instance, restitution is clearly limited to *land* rights, excluding other proprietary interests (e.g., business goodwill and lost profit). Correcting past dispossessions is also explicitly contingent on a judgment of whether the transfer of land is "feasible" (a decision the Minister of Land Affairs must make). "Feasibility" inevitably involves a comparison of the costs and benefits of land transfers that is inherently subjective – what is the "feasibility," for instance, of restoring land occupied by a white-owned golf and country club to its original owners? Compensation involves similar issues – is land to be valued by its current market value or its value at the time of the dispossession (Eisenberg 1993)? And what about unjust enrichment? Whether land reconciliation succeeds depends in significant degree on the congruence between how the law thinks about land reconciliation and how ordinary South Africans think about it.

Some scholars believe that land is an irreconcilable issue due to a clash between cultural values that ultimately rest on the values of individualism and communalism (on communalism, see Lahiff 2000). Western conceptions of land rights are grounded in liberal individualism and universalistic values, while African views are said to give priority to community interests over individual interests, and to particularism. As Cousins (2000, 19) notes: The fundamental "difficulty derives from the lack of fit between the exclusive nature of the Western concept of property ownership, and the inclusive, flexible and nested character of many African systems of property rights."[32] Bennett (1995, 130) goes so far as to argue that in South Africa " 'ownership' . . . is historically and culturally specific; it does not have an *a priori* meaning and it may well not exist in customary law." If those of

---

[32] Asabere (1994) prefers to call this a "corporate" form of land holding, and emphasizes that the local chief is often a trustee with no absolute control over community lands. Bennett (1995, 131) disagrees. Still, individuals have little ability in communal systems to use land as they please and virtually no ability to dispose of land. As Bennett notes (1995, 132), "communal" land rights are often treated dismissively, or at least regarded as less worthy of protection than individual land rights. For a useful study of land and traditional leaders, see Ntsebeza 2005.

European origin understand well "ownership" and if Africans do not, then obviously land reconciliation is unlikely to be very successful. Effective law may require a consensus on at least some basic principles of fairness. But in a multicultural, divided society like South Africa, such shared cultural orientations may not be common (see Gibson 2000). These differences in cultural values, if they exist, have very strong and clear implications for land reconciliation, since individualist and communalist solutions to South Africa's land problems may be quite at odds with each other.

Perhaps of even greater interest is the empirical question of how widespread is the commitment to communal land ownership. One can well imagine that various traditional leaders ("chiefs") support a system from which they profit so greatly, but that does not necessarily imply that ordinary people share such views. An important empirical contribution of this research will be to document the degree to which different cultures subscribe to different theories of land ownership. It is quite possible that communal attitudes describe a relatively small proportion of the black population (and may well be confined to rural areas), and that charges of communalism are largely a ploy by which whites maintain dominance over the legal system of land in South Africa. Thus, a portion of this research will assess whether cultural values (and which cultural values) are consistent with the principles undergirding the law of land reconciliation.

Are preferences on land reconciliation influenced by justice considerations that are independent of economic self-interests? From the point of view of *Homo economicus,* the land issue is pretty simple: Whites control most of the land, blacks control very little land, and land redistribution thus pits the economic interests of one group against another. Reactions to land reconciliation can therefore be expected to be largely if not entirely instrumental.[33] But our 2001 survey indicates that the proportion of the South African population with a direct stake

---

[33] I recognize that in some instances strictly instrumental behavior can dictate that land owners surrender a portion of their land in order to preserve their property. Some farmers in South Africa have voluntarily ceded land to their farm workers in order to coopt those workers into accepting the existing distribution of land. Farmers have also given farm workers land on the perimeter of their property in order to create a buffer against land invasions. Such strategic actions seem to be motivated by economic instrumentalism.

in land reconciliation is probably less than half. Without direct involvement in the issue, how can land reconciliation be of any real consequence for South Africa's transition?

Important research has recently questioned whether instrumental behavior is culturally specific. Experimental economists have encountered (and have been perplexed by) findings that culture matters when it comes to the basic values that undergird attitudes toward economic issues. For instance, Roth et al. (1991, 1091) find considerable out-of-equilibrium behavior in bargaining games, leading them to conclude that "bargainers' conceptions of fairness might be an important explanatory variable." Moreover, they observe important cross-cultural differences in bargaining behavior that may well reflect different cultural presumptions about what constitutes fairness.[34] If noninstrumental factors play such a large role in largely amoral activity such as economic bargaining, then one might well predict that in a highly normative activity such as politics – and especially land reconciliation – noninstrumental concerns may in fact dominate.

Part of the explanation for the importance of noninstrumental considerations requires that we return to the concept "disinterested justice" to which I have already referred – the strong emotions we feel "about an injustice because we sympathize with the person who was harmed or with his reactions to the harm" (Vidmar 2001, 36). Mutz and Mondak (1997) label this phenomenon as "sociotropic fairness." They recognize that people are concerned about how economic conditions affect their group, but they also argue that this influence is separate from self-interest, or even a group-based interest. They believe that people are concerned with how their group is treated within the political system – whether it is treated fairly. Consequently, they argue in favor of focusing on perceptions of fairness – and especially whether one's group is treated better or worse than other groups – in order to understand the political preferences and behaviors of people. This theory is similar to the relational theory developed by Tyler and Lind (e.g., Tyler et al. 1997). Concern with "sociotropic justice" transforms land reconciliation from an issue of direct self-interest (perhaps affecting few) to one with much broader consequences for the political and legal systems.

---

[34] This conclusion is very strongly reinforced in the profoundly important work of Henrich et al. 2001 (but see Duch and Palmer 2001).

The final link in the theory undergirding the analysis in the book is social identity theory (SIT). Loosely speaking, my central hypothesis here is that group identities provide a bridge from the present to the past. Because those who identify with a group also identify with the injustices done to the group in the past, identities provide a key connection to feelings of sociotropic injustice. Throughout the analysis in this book, group identities are carefully documented and explored, and the hypothesis that these identities connect the present with the past is thoroughly investigated.

SPECIFIC EMPIRICAL ISSUES ADDRESSED IN THIS RESEARCH

This research reports the results from a 2004 survey of the South African mass public on a variety of issues surrounding land reconciliation. With the data from the survey, I address the following questions:

1. What sorts of relationships do South Africans have with land, how common are such relationships, and how are they distributed across various groups? For instance, what proportion of black South Africans have no contemporary or historical claim of any sort to land? If land were reclaimed by South Africans, to what use would they put it?
2. How is the land issue seen in South Africa? Which of the various aspects of justice (distributive, procedural, retributive, and restorative) are most implicated by land reconciliation? Do different groups in South Africa perceive the issues along the same justice dimensions? What consequences flow from understanding land reconciliation as one form of justice versus another? For instance, if the issues are framed in distributive/redistributive justice terms (e.g., whether the state should allocate more money to purchase land for the landless), then the dynamics of political conflict are probably quite different from the case in which the issues are framed along retributive justice lines (e.g., whether whites should be punished for colonialism). Some forms of justice lead more readily to political compromise than other forms.
3. How much support is there for the various aspects of land reconciliation in South Africa? Issues of land restitution, redistribution, and land tenure will be addressed, and differences in

the meaning of these concepts in urban and rural areas will be considered as well.

4. Who supports land reconciliation? What accounts for variability in attitudes toward land? To what degree is support for land reconciliation a function of one's racial/linguistic/ethnic group? To what degree are positions on land reconciliation a function of the basic cultural and ideological values individuals hold? For instance, are positions on land issues related to the degree to which private property rights are judged to be sacrosanct? Do values associated with power and authority have any influence over land positions? Can racial differences be explained primarily by differences on these fundamental value dimensions?

5. For what proportion of the population does the resolution of the land issue have material consequences? To what degree do positions on land reconciliation reflect one's experiences and one's interests? Does whether one is "interested" or "disinterested" in land reconciliation have implications for the research questions addressed in this project?

6. How useful is social identity theory for accounting for land reconciliation attitudes? Do those who identify with a group attach more salience to the issue? Are their positions on land reconciliation distinctive? Do different aspects of justice become more or less relevant among those with strong group identities?

7. What role do contextual factors play in judgments of land claims? For instance, how relevant is the means by which the current owner acquired the land to judgments of the legitimacy of the owner's claim? What other contextual factors are significant? Do contextual costs and benefits influence land judgments? How influential are competing justice claims (balanced) in comparison to unrebutted or one-sided justice claims (unbalanced)?

8. Do South Africans approve of so-called land grabs? What conditions make such land invasions acceptable or unacceptable? To what degree are South Africans likely to engage in land grabs? To what extent is behavior motivated by instrumental versus expressive motives (e.g., Gibson 1997)?

9. Do the relative weights people attach to contemporary and historical injustices vary according to the nature of group identities?

AN OVERVIEW OF THE LAND RECONCILIATION SURVEY

In 2004, interviews were completed with 4,108 South Africans, including 1,549 Africans, 1,362 whites, 738 Coloured respondents, and 459 South Africans of Asian origin. Two different sampling strategies were used in this survey, one for the large African majority, the other for the three small racial minorities. Because the methodological issues involved are complicated, I defer a full discussion of them to Appendix B. In summary, conclusions from the black subsample warrant a great deal of confidence, since the sample was selected via probability methods with a very high response rate. The Coloured and Asian subsamples blend probability and quota methods and have a reasonable response rate, and therefore deserve a moderate degree of confidence. And the white subsample warrants relatively low confidence owing to the sampling methods, low response rates, and the need to correct nonrepresentativeness via fairly substantial poststratification.

A CHAPTER-BY-CHAPTER OVERVIEW OF THIS BOOK

My analysis of the politics of land in contemporary South Africa is structured as follows.

The purpose of Chapter 2 is to introduce the problem of land injustice in South Africa from an empirical viewpoint. On the basis of the survey data, considerable territory is covered in the chapter, ranging from the extent of land victimization and grieving to behavioral activism on land issues. In this chapter, I document the extent to which South Africans view themselves as victims of historical land injustices, and I also report that this sense of victimization is becoming more, not less, widespread over time. The chapter also examines the preferences of South Africans regarding various land policies, as well as evidence on whom South Africans blame for the vast land inequalities that exist today.

Chapter 3 introduces the central theory that guides most of the analysis of the book: social identity theory. Because the Land Reconciliation Survey devoted considerable effort to measuring various aspects of group attachments, this chapter treats social identities as multidimensional and examines how ordinary South Africans feel about various aspects of the groups to which they claim allegiance.

In the last half of the chapter, the analysis turns to the connection between group identities and land policy preferences, under the overarching hypothesis that group identities provide the bridge by which the present is linked with the past. I also examine the simple hypothesis that land policy preferences reflect individual self-interests. I find that hypothesis quite wanting; instead, policy preferences strongly reflect more abstract and symbolic attitudes about the past and present in South Africa. Because land is more than an economic issue, it is more politically volatile, and potentially more difficult to negotiate.

Based on formal experiments embedded within the survey, Chapters 4 and 5 report investigations into how South Africans apply principles of justice to highly contextualized land disputes. Utilizing hypothetical vignettes, Chapter 4 focuses on a woman named Patience, who is said to be engaged in an illegal land grab. My analysis shows how ordinary people judge the fairness of such disputes, and, in particular, how group identities structure these judgments. South Africans of all races oppose squatting, but many also view the eviction of squatters with suspicion and strong reservations. When squatters are given procedural justice, via the rule of law, the outcome is perceived to be much more fair. Squatting is a difficult and complex issue, and considerable interracial differences in viewpoints exist, but most South Africans are united on the need to acknowledge the legitimacy of squatters' claim to a place to live. It is this juxtaposition of the claim of contemporary versus historical injustices that makes land grabs so difficult (and so interesting to study from the point of view of commonsense justice).

Chapter 5 presents another vignette that is much more sharply focused on the race of the claimants to a piece of land. The vignette poses a conflict between claimants with contemporary claims to land and those with historical claims, based on dispossessions, and thus even more clearly juxtaposes the past with the present. Again, I find that group identities have much to do with how South Africans judge conflicts such as these. Those with more parochial group attachments are much more likely to incorporate past injustices into their decision making on contemporary issues. The analyses reported in these chapters are important because they demonstrate how the symbolic aspects of the land issue implicate and activate group identities. A central contention of this book is that identity-based political issues are more difficult to manage than issues that can be resolved via simple economics.

The concluding chapter begins by reviewing the principal empirical findings of the earlier chapters. After doing so, however, the chapter moves away from the data in order to speculate a bit about the importance of the land issue for the consolidation of democracy in South Africa. Because one cannot talk about land politics without thinking a bit about the experience of Zimbabwe, I present some evidence in this chapter about how South Africans view the experiences of their neighbor to the north. I conclude the book with some speculation about how land issues may become mobilized in the context of the upcoming struggle over the leadership of the African National Congress and the elections of 2009.

2

Naming, Blaming, and Claiming on Historical Land Injustices

The Views of the South African People

Apartheid and colonialism left a profound legacy of unrequited demands for land justice. Through its system of forced removals, restrictions on occupancy, the creation of Bantustans, and so on, apartheid dispossessed millions of South Africans of their land and land rights. Layered on top of apartheid's other sins is a system of communal land control that seems to have benefited few rural South Africans. And even apartheid's demise has exacerbated the land problem as countless rural poor people flock to the cities in hopes of some degree of economic subsistence. Apartheid, and its own ancestor, colonialism, created a tremendous need for land restitution, land redistribution, and a secure system of individual ownership of land and land resources.

How do South Africans view these issues of land reconciliation? Unfortunately, little is known beyond a handful of questions about the issue asked in our 2001 survey (see Gibson 2001). The data indicate that land reconciliation is broadly important to South Africans – concern over the problem is not limited to a landless few (or even the landless many). Enormous and profound racial differences exist, with virtually all blacks and no whites believing that whites hold land illegitimately. For instance, the respondents in our 2001 sample were asked whether they agree or disagree with the following statement: "Most land in South Africa was taken unfairly by white settlers, and they therefore have no right to the land today." An astonishing 85% of the black respondents agreed with that statement; only 8% of the whites held the same view. Most seriously, perhaps, a large majority of Africans is willing to risk the stability of the country to achieve their land goals: Two-thirds of blacks (68%) agree that "land must be returned to blacks in South Africa, no matter what the consequences are for the current owners and for political stability in the country." This Zimbabwe-style proposition elicits virtually unanimous disagreement from whites (91% disagree). Land seems to be an issue that will not easily be resolved in South Africa, since, ultimately, it combines black demands for justice through economic redistribution with the expectation of symbolic reparations for the crimes and sins of colonialism and apartheid. In light of the profound importance of the issue to the African majority, the controversy over land is unlikely to dissipate anytime soon.

These 2001 results provide only the most limited insights into popular views on various land issues. Consequently, the 2004 Land Reconciliation Survey addressed numerous aspects of contemporary land conflict and policy. The purpose of this chapter is to consider how ordinary South Africans judge the various components of land injustice. Based on interviews with more than 4,000 South Africans representing all parts of the country, all ages, all races, and so on, this chapter addresses several specific issues:

- Do South Africans perceive the land issue as salient and threatening to the country?
- To what degree do the various racial groups in South Africa differ in terms of their basic attitudes toward land, including its symbolic meaning, as well as general and abstract commitments to private property?
- Whom do South Africans blame for contemporary land inequality?
- How widespread are understandings of the history of land dispossessions in South Africa? Are the basic facts known of how whites came to own and control most of the valuable land in the country?
- Do South Africans perceive themselves as personally aggrieved by land injustices from the past?
- Do South Africans perceive their own land today as vulnerable to land grabs by other citizens or by the state?
- To what degree is a sense of historical land injustice pervasive in South Africa and what political consequences are likely to materialize?

- A variety of policy proposals are currently being considered; to what degree do South Africans support various different means of dealing with land problems? Are ordinary people willing to sacrifice the rule of law in order to rectify the injustices of the past?
- To what degree has land been an issue that mobilizes South Africans to protest or to take political action?
- To what degree are there racial differences in various attitudes toward land?
- Are other cleavages relevant to the land issue? For instance, are there any significant class divisions among blacks on attitudes and preferences about land?

These various questions are addressed here using data collected in a 2004 national survey (see Appendix A for details). Since black South Africans were the primary (but far from exclusive) victims of historical land injustices, I focus mainly on the views and experiences of blacks. However, comparisons across racial groups are typically presented (on race in South Africa, see Appendix A), since a comparison across groups often provides useful perspective. Finally, in some limited instances, this analysis is able to compare contemporary attitudes with the results from earlier surveys.

As noted, this is a study of the views of ordinary South Africans. The premise underlying this research is that, while public policy is rarely directly dictated by the preferences of ordinary people, those preferences can set the broad parameters of the range of acceptable policy options. Moreover, public opinion is a political resource for entrepreneurs seeking to gain political advantage. Thus, on important and salient issues of public policy, it is crucial to know what people prefer, or least what they will accept.

Throughout this portion of the analysis, I consider four primary variables that may divide South Africans: race, gender, age, and social class. Obviously, these four factors are not inclusive of all possible determinants of land attitudes, but it is entirely reasonable to hypothesize that land attitudes differ by race owing to differing experiences under apartheid; by gender, since much of the apartheid land legislation affected men and women differently; by age, inasmuch as for many South Africans, apartheid is a system of the increasingly distant past; and by class, since class divisions, especially among blacks, are becoming increasingly important.[1] To the extent that these factors influence the attitudes I consider, mention will be made of each.

The most important finding of this chapter is that land is an explosive and racially divisive issue.[2] South Africans of different races view land issues so differently that it is difficult to imagine how any sort of common ground can be forged. In the concluding section to this chapter, I address some of the policy implications of these empirical findings.

THE SALIENCE OF THE LAND ISSUE

Cousins (2007, 238) refers to South Africa's land issues as "a political time bomb." But do South Africans perceive the land issue as important to them and their country? Figure 2.1 reports the percentage of the sample rating each of the social problems about which we asked as "very important" (the most extreme point on the scale).

It should surprise no one that the most important problem in South Africa is unemployment, with 85% of all respondents rating it as very important. Racial differences on the importance of unemployment are statistically significant, although not especially large: 86% of Africans rate joblessness as very important, compared with 73% of whites, 89% of Coloured people, and 81% of those of Asian origin (data not shown). Other problems widely seen as vexing include HIV/AIDS, crime, and drugs.

---

[1] Social class is measured by three indicators: (1) the range of consumer goods the respondent owns, (2) interviewer assessments of the respondent's living standard, and (3) interviewer assessments of the respondent's social class. An index was created via factor analysis. Note that in the analysis that follows, class often has a significant bivariate relationship with variables of interest, but once considered within a multivariate equation including race, class has no independent impact. I attribute influence to social class only when it has an independent impact on the variable of interest.

[2] Numerous studies of South African public opinion have documented large if not vast interracial differences in political opinions, attitudes, values, and behaviors. For a sampling of the literature, see: Gibson and Gouws 2003 on political tolerance; Gibson 2004a on truth acceptance and reconciliation; Ferree 2006 and the various chapters reported in Piombo and Nijzink 2006 on party support and voting behavior; Seekings and Nattrass 2005 on economic matters, including inequality; Roberts 2006 on poverty and inequality; Klandermans, Roefs, and Olivier 2001 on political participation and civil society involvement; and see also the various chapters reported in Pillay, Roberts, and Rule 2006. One might also add to this list Thabo Mbeki (1998), who has often complained about the racially defined "Two Nations" in South Africa. For a most useful comparative analysis of the attitudes of South Africans with citizens of other African countries, see Bratton, Mattes, and Gyimah-Boadi 2005.

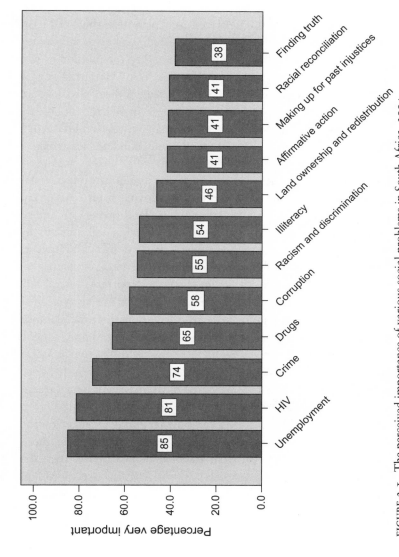

FIGURE 2.1. The perceived importance of various social problems in South Africa, 2004.
Note: The entries are the percentages of respondents rating the issue as "very important," the highest point in the response set offered.

These problems vary in the degree to which South Africans of different races adopt different views. At one extreme is the problem of making up for past injustices. Of the black respondents, 44% rate this as very important, in contrast to only 21% of whites who are as concerned. At the other extreme, racial differences are trivial on ratings of racism and discrimination and affirmative action, which is perhaps surprising.[3] On the former, 53% of Africans rate racism and discrimination as very important, but so too do 58% of whites, 62% of Coloured people, and 54% of those of Asian origin. Issues on which racial divisions are particularly stark include making up for past injustices, finding the truth about the past, land ownership and redistribution, and HIV/AIDS.

The findings on the importance of land ownership and redistribution are particularly compelling. First, the problem is *not* seen as among the most pressing for South Africa, although it is difficult to imagine that land problems could rival the big three: unemployment, HIV/AIDS, and crime. Only a minority of South Africans rate land ownership and redistribution as very important, although only a very small minority ascribe little if any importance to the problem (data not shown). However, as I have noted, racial differences on this item are stark. As Figure 2.2 shows, a majority of Africans rate land as very important, even if only one-quarter to one-third of the other racial groups are so concerned about this issue. It is particularly noteworthy that the three racial minorities (whites, Coloured people, and those of Asian origin) hold roughly similar viewpoints, while black South Africans are distinctive in ascribing greater importance to land issues in contemporary South Africa. Among South Africa's black majority, the most important issues are unemployment, HIV/AIDs, crime, drugs, corruption, racism and discrimination, illiteracy, and problems of land ownership and redistribution. Gender, class, and age differences of respondents regarding the importance attributed to the land problem are trivial.

Thus, these data reveal that black South Africans are more concerned about the past than others, and that an important instance of historical injustice is the land issue.

---

[3] It seems possible that black and white respondents ascribe the same importance to these issues, but for different reasons. For instance, whites may believe that affirmative action is an important social problem because it adversely affects them, whereas blacks believe that the policy is important for the economic advancement of the formerly disadvantaged.

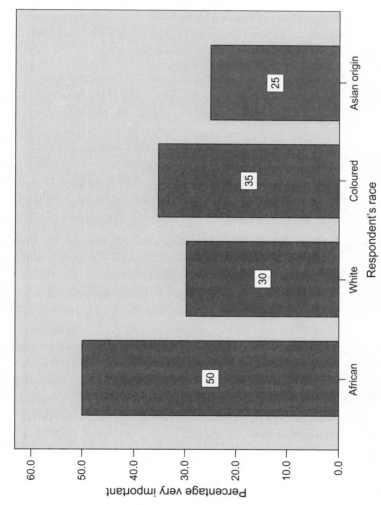

FIGURE 2.2. Racial differences in the perceived importance of land ownership and redistribution as a social problem.

Note: Cross-race difference of means (for the uncollapsed distribution): $\eta = .27$; $p < .000$. The entries are the percentages of respondents rating the issue as "very important," the highest point in the response set offered.

The Valuation Attached to Land in General

We anticipated these findings, in part since Africans were victimized the most by apartheid land policies, as well as owing to the conventional wisdom that Africans have a symbolic attachment to land in general that is stronger than that of other South Africans. We therefore put six statements regarding the valuation of land to the respondents in the form of five-point agree/disagree items. The statements are:

- Without having a piece of land, one is really not a complete person.
- Land is a symbol of all that has been taken away from Africans.
- I feel a special attachment to the place where my ancestors are buried.
- When times are tough, one can always survive if one owns some land.
- Land is special: Having land is more important than having money.
- If I had my choice, I would live on a piece of land that I could farm.

Is land important to South Africans, and do racial differences exist in the importance ascribed to land? Figure 2.3 provides evidence with which this question can be addressed.

Figure 2.3 reports the average number of statements endorsed by members of each of the four racial groups. The results are rather dramatic. On average, the black respondents agreed with 4.7 of these statements; in contrast, whites agreed with only 2.1. Coloured people expressed relatively strong commitments to land (mean = 4.0), while those of Asian origin are closer to whites in their views (mean = 3.0). The hypothesis that blacks attach unusual value to land is strongly supported by these survey data.[4] Again, gender, age, and class differences in the valuation of land are trivial.

---

[4] When this set of items is subjected to Common Factor Analysis, a strongly unidimensional factor structure emerges. The eigenvalue of the first extracted factor is 3.07, accounting for 51.1% of the common variance; the eigenvalue for the second factor is a mere .75 (explaining only 12.5% of the residual common variance). All items load roughly equally on the first factor, with the strongest loading associated with the statement on land making one a complete person (.68) and the weakest with the assertion about ancestors (.58). Cronbach's alpha is .81. Thus, the statistical analysis reveals that this set of items is unidimensional and that the index created from these items is highly valid and reliable.

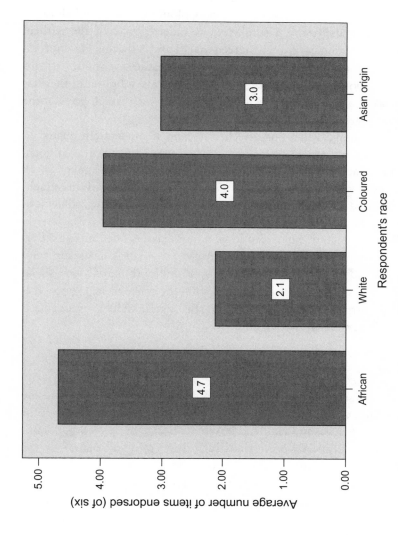

FIGURE 2.3. Racial differences in the symbolic value South Africans attach to land. *Note:* Cross-race difference of means: $\eta = .54$; $p < .000$.

One can see this interracial difference vividly in the data presented in Figure 2.4. The statement put to the respondents is: "Without having a piece of land, one is not really a complete person." Fully 78% of the black respondents agreed with this statement, while only one-third of the whites and about one-half of the Coloured people and those of Asian origin expressed a similar view. Indeed, 70% of the African respondents (data not shown) agreed that "Land is special: Having land is more important than having money." Land issues for South Africans are thus about more than just land; they are "a symbol of all that has been taken away from Africans" (a statement with which 70% of the Africans agreed).

The symbolic value one attaches to land is moderately related to the priority one assigns to land issues ($r = .27$). Thus, the conventional wisdom that Africans value land more highly than most other South Africans is confirmed by these data, and one consequence of this attachment to land is that greater priority is assigned to addressing problems of historical land injustices in South Africa.

With just a couple of exceptions, minor class, gender, or age differences exist in attitudes toward land. Among those of Asian origin, land is attributed more value by older people and by those of lower social classes. No such relationships exist within the other racial groups. It is perhaps surprising that, among Africans, class, gender, and generational differences are so slight.

THE SANCTITY OF PRIVATE PROPERTY

A key issue in the debate over land redistribution has to do with the importance of respecting private property rights. Ntsebeza (2007), for instance, believes (and Hall and Ntsebeza, 2007, 11, agree) that South Africa's constitutional protections for private property rights – in the context of the country's colonial and apartheid past – make the redistribution of land virtually impossible. His argument is as follows: Respect for property rights is inevitably tied to market definitions of the value of property; the state seems to have insufficient resources to purchase land at market value prices; current property owners have profited from unjust enrichment and state subsidies, and therefore current market values must be discounted for the unfairness of the past; since agreement between buyers and sellers on these various points is extremely

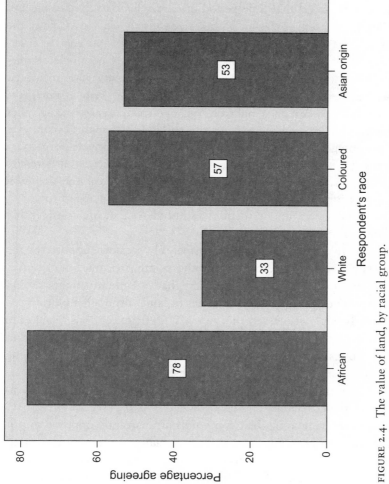

FIGURE 2.4. The value of land, by racial group.

Note: The statement read: "Without having a piece of land, one is really not a complete person." Cross-race difference of means (for the uncollapsed distribution): $\eta = .44$; $p < .000$.

unlikely, the state must confiscate private property; and the property seized can be used not just for public purposes but for private purposes that serve the public good.[5] In at least one clear respect (if not in others), Ntsebeza is in conflict with land legislation: He rejects the notion that land claims today are bounded by events subsequent to 1913. Instead, Ntsebeza would extend that time period, it seems, back to the seventeenth century (a proposal with which Walker 2007, 136, disagrees). Thus, the land issue may simply be a concrete manifestation of more general differences over the sanctity of private property and, if so, may reflect something of a (mini) "clash of cultures." Consequently, we measured generalized commitments to private property. The various statements shown in Table 2.1 pit a right of land ownership against some other consideration. Note that the data column labeled "Support" represents the percentage of respondents who favor the right of private property.

First, I note that on most items, quite substantial racial differences exist (as documented by the eta statistics).[6] Notably, the common pattern is for whites, Coloured people, and those of Asian origin to hold similar views among themselves but views that are considerably different from those of Africans.

In general, Africans express considerably weaker support for the sanctity of private property than do other South Africans. For example, blacks are much more likely to assert that community rights should trump individual rights when it comes to land (although a plurality of Coloured people also assert this view). With no exceptions, blacks are always more weakly committed to private property rights than other racial groups in South Africa. Perhaps most unsettling is the finding that more than one-third of the black respondents agree that all white-owned land in South Africa ought to be taken away without compensation by the government.

But at the same time, blacks are not intransigently opposed to private property rights. For instance, a large majority (71.1%) assert that farmers must receive compensation if their land is seized by the government for purposes of land reform. A plurality of Africans opposes

[5] Obviously, many observers disagree with this viewpoint. For the purposes of this research, it is not necessary to judge the efficacy of this policy position.

[6] Based on their research in Benin, Duch and Palmer (2004, 448) suggest that support for private property rights is a universal, "instinctual" value. Such seems not to be the case in South Africa.

TABLE 2.1. *Support for Private Property Rights,* 2004

Policy/Race	Oppose[a]	Uncertain[a]	Support[a]	Mean	Std. dev.	N
Farmers must receive compensation[b]						
African	15.6	13.3	71.1	3.76	1.13	1,538
White	3.2	3.2	93.7	4.49	.76	1,354
Coloured	8.2	8.5	83.4	3.98	.88	733
Asian origin	4.1	5.9	90.0	4.16	.74	458
Take white land without compensation[c]						
African	35.9	21.2	42.9	3.03	1.27	1,530
White	5.0	7.2	87.8	4.47	.90	1,347
Coloured	10.8	16.3	72.9	3.87	.98	731
Asian origin	6.2	10.9	82.9	4.13	.87	451
Reduce property rights of owners[d]						
African	60.5	18.2	21.3	2.40	1.18	1,534
White	17.2	12.1	70.7	3.79	1.11	1,346
Coloured	58.4	11.1	30.5	2.62	1.21	728
Asian origin	41.5	13.5	45.0	3.11	1.22	459
Community land rights more important than individual rights[e]						
African	63.8	18.6	17.6	2.32	1.14	1,532
White	19.5	21.0	59.5	3.56	1.06	1,345
Coloured	48.2	16.6	35.2	2.82	1.15	736
Asian origin	27.3	17.6	55.2	3.37	1.12	455
Recognize tenure rights if have lived on land for a long time[f]						
African	73.4	15.6	11.0	2.01	1.08	1,533
White	25.3	13.9	60.8	3.50	1.25	1,341
Coloured	76.3	9.4	14.3	2.15	1.03	734
Asian origin	37.0	16.7	46.3	3.13	1.20	454

(continued)

TABLE 2.1 *(continued)*

Policy/Race	Oppose[a]	Uncertain[a]	Support[a]	Mean	Std. dev.	N
Number of pro-private property statements endorsed[g]						
African	–	–	–	1.63	1.09	1,545
White	–	–	–	3.69	1.30	1,358
Coloured	–	–	–	2.34	1.21	738
Asian origin	–	–	–	3.17	1.24	459

[a] These are percentages, calculated on the basis of collapsing the five-point Likert response set (e.g., "agree strongly" and "agree" responses are combined), and they total to 100%, across the three columns, except for rounding errors. The means and standard deviations are calculated on the uncollapsed distributions. Higher mean scores indicate greater support for rights of private property.

[b] Interracial difference of means: $p < .001$; $\eta = .32$.

[c] Interracial difference of means: $p < .001$; $\eta = .50$.

[d] Interracial difference of means: $p < .001$; $\eta = .46$.

[e] Interracial difference of means: $p < .001$; $\eta = .44$.

[f] Interracial difference of means: $p < .001$; $\eta = .51$.

[g] Interracial difference of means: $p < .001$; $\eta = .60$.

Note: The statements read: "Farmers must receive fair compensation if their farms are taken away by the government for land reform." (Agree) "All white-owned land in South Africa ought to be taken away by the government, without any compensation to anyone." (Disagree) "In a country with so much poverty, the property rights of the wealthy must be reduced." (Disagree) "When it comes to land, the rights of the community are more important than the rights of individual land owners." (Disagree) "If someone has lived on a piece of property for a long time – say 10 years – then that person must be recognized as having the right of ownership to the property." (Disagree)

the expropriation of white-owned property. Just from these frequencies alone, one might conclude that support for private property rights among blacks is not strong, but that several conflicting currents run through black public opinion.

A few surprises can also be seen in the data on white attitudes. For instance, nearly one-fourth of whites agree that the tenure rights of people who have lived on a piece of property for a long period of time ought to be recognized. Thus, whites are not necessarily dogmatically attached to private property rights.

As noted, white and Indian opinion are frequently similar, although on some issues (e.g., whether to reduce the rights of wealthy land owners), important differences exist. The views of Coloured South Africans are less supportive of private property in general, with a majority of Coloured respondents endorsing property rights on only two of the five statements (in contrast to five out of five for whites, and three out of five for those of Asian origin).

The last portion of this table reports the number of statements to which the respondents gave pro–private property rights replies. Dramatic cross-race differences are apparent here. For instance, the average black respondent endorsed 1.6 of these statements; the average white respondent favored private property rights on 3.7 of the statements. As is often the case on land issues, South Africans of Asian origin are relatively closer to whites, while Coloured South Africans are relatively closer to blacks. I reiterate, however, that interracial differences in support for the rights of private property are substantial indeed. These data may not suggest a "clash of cultures," but without a doubt, different racial groups in South Africa value private property to significantly different degrees.[7]

ALLOCATING BLAME FOR LAND INJUSTICES

Who is to blame for the land problems in South Africa today?[8] We began our investigation of this issue with the following preface: "Today, most productive land in South Africa is in the hands of white people. Most black people are quite poor and own little land. We are interested in your views about how this came to be. For each of the following factors please indicate how much you believe this inequality in South Africa today is a result of the following."

[7] The property rights items have marginal reliability (Cronbach's alpha = .60; mean interitem correlation = .23), in part owing to degenerate variance on the first item in the table (farmer compensation). This item is also the most weakly correlated with the other statements, and it has the smallest loading on the first unrotated factor extracted in a Common Factor Analysis. That analysis reveals two significant dimensions, although the eigenvalue of the second factor, at 1.04, just barely exceeds 1.00. I have kept the farmer compensation item in the index of support for private property rights, even though it is virtually a constant and therefore has little impact on the analysis. I have calculated an index of support for private property rights that is simply the mean of the responses to these five items. Not surprisingly, differences across the racial groups are enormous, with the set of racial dummy variables able to explain 43% of the variance in this attitude.

[8] A vast literature on blame attributions exists. For research on blame in the South African case, see Gibson and Gouws 1999.

Among black South Africans, the most widely accepted factor accounting for land inequality is the advantages whites still hold as a result of the apartheid past: 77% of blacks consider this to be either an important or very important cause of land injustice. Coloured people hold similar views (80%), as do those of Asian origin (63%). Whites, as usual, are the exception: Only 34% attribute land inequality to the apartheid past. It is difficult indeed to understand how the majority of whites do not connect contemporary land inequality with the country's history of apartheid.[9]

But black views are complicated; they see multiple causes of the land problem. A majority of blacks rate the following factors as important causes of land injustice: that there are white advantages from the apartheid past (77%), that blacks have been unable to recover from colonialism and apartheid (73%), that whites are ruthless in terms of being willing to do anything to get what they want (65%), that blacks are captives of traditional ways (62%), that blacks are too divided among themselves (62%), and that black people are less well educated than whites (57%). Thus, black attributions for the causes of land injustice include advantages from the past enjoyed by whites and disadvantages from the past from which blacks still suffer. Indeed, it is stunning to note that 41% of the black respondents lay blame on the factor that "white people are more intelligent than black people," as do 40% of whites, 46% of Coloured people, and 38% of those of Asian origin (see Figure 2.5). The interracial difference is slightly statistically significant, but is largely trivial. It is not precisely clear how to understand the responses to this last statement, but it is plausible that blacks believe that apartheid deprived them of education, making them less "intelligent" today, which accounts in part for the disparities in the ownership of land in contemporary South Africa. In general, blacks see almost *four times as many* very important causes of land inequality as do whites, surely reflecting the greater salience of the issue to them, as well as the adoption of a more

---

[9] This viewpoint is well illustrated by the comments of a white female in one of our focus groups. She exclaimed (emphasis added): "On the one hand, I feel these dispossessions happened long ago and I mean they cannot now blame the owners of the houses for what the government did at that time. I mean it is just like this apartheid, when it came into effect, they cannot blame us now because it was implemented. *We had nothing to do with it.*"

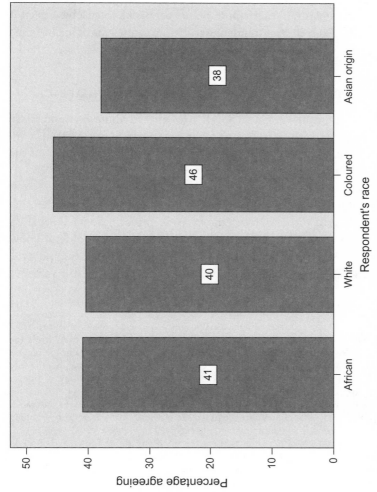

FIGURE 2.5. Attributions of blame for contemporary land inequality – intelligence.
Note: The causal factor to account for the unequal distribution of land in contemporary South Africa is: "White people are more intelligent than black people." Cross-race difference of means (for the uncollapsed distribution): $\eta = .05$; $p = .010$.

47

contextualized and historical perspective on contemporary land inequality.[10]

No gender or age differences exist in attributions of blame for land inequality. However, in addition to the racial differences, at least a modest influence of social class can be observed. Those of a higher social class are more willing to attribute blame to blacks themselves, even if they do not differ in their tendency to blame whites and the country's apartheid past. On this issue, at least, class overshadows race.

THE HISTORY OF LAND INJUSTICE IN SOUTH AFRICA

As I have noted, most black South Africans attribute contemporary land injustices to the past. But to what degree are South Africans cognizant of their past? To what degree are they knowledgeable about the history of land injustice in the country?

We asked the respondents a series of questions about South African history.[11] One question asked: "Do you know approximately when the last racially motivated forced removal took place in South Africa?"[12] Nearly one half (46%) of all South Africans admitted they did not know the answer to the query, including 46% of black South Africans and 55% of white South Africans. The correct answer to this question (the 1980s[13])

---

[10] When factor analyzed, these blame attributions produce a two-dimensional structure. The first factor allocates blame to whites and the apartheid past, while the second factor is defined primarily in terms of the perceived shortcomings of blacks. These two factors are, however, strongly correlated ($r = .62$), indicating that they are nothing more than slightly different emphases in an overall ideology of blame. South Africans are strongly divided by race in terms of blaming whites and the apartheid past ($\eta = .58$), with vast differences between whites and blacks, but racial differences on whether blacks are themselves to blame are considerably more muted ($\eta = .24$), as already suggested by the data reported in Figure 2.5.

[11] For quite valuable assistance on framing the questions about knowledge of South African history, I am indebted to Chris Willemse and to Christopher Saunders (University of Cape Town, history department). For an earlier report on South Africans' knowledge of their history, see Macfarlane 2003.

[12] The question was accompanied by a showcard with categories for each decade from the 1910s to the 1990s. A tiny proportion of respondents volunteered that they believed that no forced removals had taken place in South Africa.

[13] As a result of the constitution of 1983 (and other preparatory legislation), blacks were no longer considered to be citizens of South Africa and were to be expelled to the so-called Bantustans. This scheme of ethnic cleansing – never entirely implemented – required the relocation of massive numbers of black people.

was selected by 10% of the Africans, 14% of the whites, 11% of Coloured people, and 10% of those of Asian origin. Aside from those who did not know the answer to this question, the modal response among blacks was the 1960s (12%). Among those blacks with an opinion, 29% thought that the last forced removals took place in the 1950s or earlier, and another 22% chose the 1960s as the date. Few in South Africa appreciate how recent forced removals are in their country.

This ignorance about the country's land history is vividly reinforced by the data in Figure 2.6, which show the percentage of each racial group who correctly identified (from a list of three answers) the term "Bantustan."[14] These figures will likely startle many. Only about one-third of each racial group knows what a Bantustan is. Also surprising is that interracial differences are trivial. For South Africans of all races, the turbulent events of the ethnic cleansing of the 1980s (and earlier) seem to have been entirely forgotten.

In light of these data, it is therefore not surprising that only 16% of black South Africans can define the term "black spot" (again, from a list of three alternatives).[15] The figures for whites, Coloured people, and those of Asian origin are 25%, 34%, and 25%, respectively.

The respondents were also asked to estimate about how many people were forced to move under apartheid. In terms of scoring the accuracy of their replies, the correct answer is the largest number on the list of possible answers we provided: three million people or more.[16] Among

---

[14] The choices available to the respondents (and the percentage of respondents selecting that answer) were: (1) A Bantustan is a form of tribal leadership found in some rural areas of South Africa (16.8%); (2) a Bantustan is an area where black people were expected to live under apartheid (34.5%); and (3) a Bantustan is a farm owned and managed exclusively by black people (7.6%). A total of 39.2% of the respondents admitted to not knowing the answer to this question.

[15] The choices available to the respondents (and the percentage of respondents selecting that answer) were: (1) "Black spot" refers to land of a very high quality that was reserved for white farmers under apartheid (10.7%); (2) "black spot" refers to pockets of strong black opposition to the apartheid system (17.7%); and (3) "Black spot" refers to a nonwhite community living within an area designated for white people by the apartheid government (19.7%). A total of 51.9 % of the respondents admitted not knowing the answer to this question.

[16] As I have noted, the Surplus People Project (1983) estimates that 1.29 million people were evicted from farms, and 614,000 were resettled during the abolition of "black spots" and homeland consolidation processes (see Turner and Ibsen 2000 for details). Villa-Vicencio and Ngesi (2003, 283; see also Platzky and Walker 1985) put the figure at approximately 3.5 million blacks removed from designated white areas between 1963 and 1985, a figure that is widely accepted among scholars.

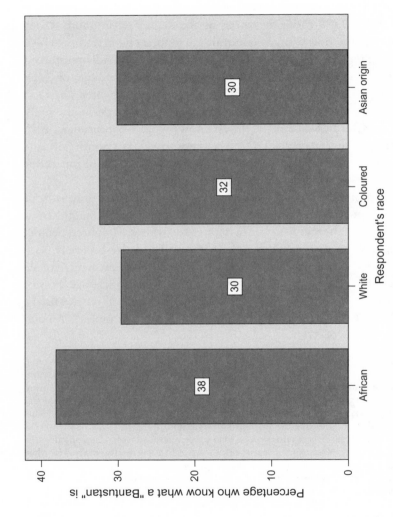

FIGURE 2.6. Knowledge of the meaning of the term "Bantustan."
Note: The correct definition of Bantustan is: "A Bantustan is an area where black people were expected to live under apartheid." Cross-race difference (for the uncollapsed distribution): $\chi^2 = 106.7; p < .000$.

blacks, 19% answered the question correctly, as did 12% of whites, 21% of Coloured people, and 20% of those of Asian origin. Virtually no respondents said that "none" had been forced to move under apartheid, although sizable proportions of each group put the number at under half a million people. As before, very large proportions of respondents (and more than half of whites) told us they do not know how many South Africans were forced to move under apartheid.

South Africans may feel aggrieved about historical land justices, but clearly those views are not grounded in any meaningful understanding of South African land history. Indeed, when we added a fifth question asking in which decade the Nationalist Party government first introduced apartheid as the official policy of South Africa to the four land questions to create an index of knowledge about the past, we got the results shown in Figure 2.7. The entries in the figure indicate the number of correct answers to the five questions about South African history. All four racial groups show similar, and dismal, levels of knowledge of their country's history, with, on average, each group getting about one out of five questions correct. Interracial differences are generally small, but Coloured South Africans score slightly better than any other group. It is noteworthy that the mean score for blacks is lower than that for any other group. *Indeed, 41 percent of black South Africans got none of these items correct!* Only a single black respondent (out of 1,550) got all five items correct. Whatever the source of perceptions of land injustice, it is clearly not grounded in specific knowledge of the land abuses of the past.

An analysis of the variance in knowledge of South African land history supports several conclusions. First, gender differences are trivial. Second, substantial class differences exist, with those of higher social class having a considerably better grasp of South African history. This class difference persists even with a control for level of education: In the multivariate equation, both class and education make independent contributions to historical knowledge. Third, age influences knowledge, with older South Africans being considerably more knowledgeable about history, even controlling for level of education, class, and so on. This finding, however, should not be exaggerated. The least knowledgeable age group is those under twenty, who, on average, got 0.72 of the five historical questions correct. The most knowledgeable age group is those in their fifties. However, this group,

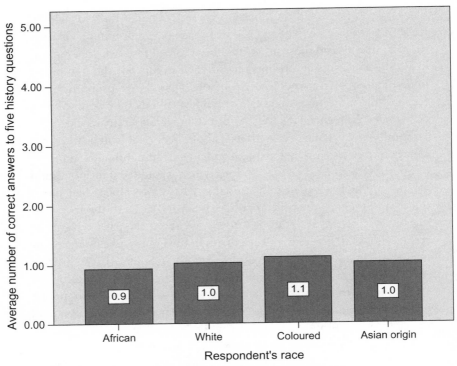

FIGURE 2.7. Knowledge of South African land history.
Note: Cross-race difference of means: $\eta = .07$; $p < .000$.

on average, got only 1.14 of the five history questions correct. Age differences exist, but they are relatively minor in the context of fairly widespread ignorance of South African land history. Finally, in the multivariate equation, whites have significantly less knowledge of history than blacks, although Coloured people and those of Asian origin do not differ significantly from blacks in their knowledge of the past.[17] Generally, however, these differences pale in comparison to the overall finding that knowledge of the country's apartheid past is limited, at best.

---

[17] I also note that knowledge of land history is unrelated to the two factors assessing blame for land inequality in contemporary South Africa – casting blame apparently does not require historical knowledge of the sort about which we asked – although there is a slight relationship between the valuations of land and the extent of historical knowledge.

THE EXTENT OF LAND GRIEVING

If the sense of land injustice is not based on an understanding of the country's history, perhaps it is based on more specific knowledge of one's own circumstances and history. To what degree did apartheid victimize South Africans, in general and specifically with regard to land? Such a question is difficult to answer, especially with data collected after the fall of apartheid, since myriad subtle injuries may have been inflicted on the population, perhaps even without its awareness. Indeed, perhaps the greatest damage of apartheid was in what it did *not* do, in the sense that the system failed to make available to the entire population the considerable benefits of wealth, industrialization, and modernization more generally (see Gibson 2003a). To ask people about the injuries they experienced is therefore to document only the tip of what may be a formidable underlying iceberg. With this important caveat, I now turn to the data from our surveys.

In 1996, we asked a representative sample of South Africans whether they had ever been subjected to a forced removal.[18] Our 2001 and 2004 surveys repeated this question.[19] The results, for the various racial groups, are reported in Table 2.2.

Care must be taken in comparing these figures, since they are based on substantially different numbers of respondents.[20] Nonetheless, the surveys produce several consistent and substantively significant findings. First, somewhat fewer than one in five Africans claim to have been subject to a forced residential change, and this figure remains relatively constant across the surveys. Second, as entirely expected, virtually no whites were similarly subjected to forced removals. Third, Coloured South Africans experienced forced removals at about the same level as Africans, although the 1996 figure (based on a relatively small sample) suggests that the problem is actually *more* acute within the Coloured community. Finally, although the figures for

[18] For substantive details on this survey, see Gibson and Gouws 2003.

[19] Details on the 2001 survey can be found in Gibson 2004a. In general, the methodology of that survey was very similar to that employed by the 2004 Land Reconciliation Survey.

[20] The consequence of this is that fairly small differences for the African subsample can be statistically significant, whereas fairly large differences for the sample of those of Asian origin are not significant. Note as well that in 2004 a substantial number of respondents replied to these questions by saying they had never lived under apartheid (because they are too young or because they lived elsewhere).

TABLE 2.2. *Forced Residential Changes, 1996–2004*

% forced to move	Respondent's race			
	African	White	Coloured	Asian origin
1996	15.9 (1,968)	1.4 (491)	24.2 (248)	18.6 (269)
2001	17.2 (2,002)	2.1 (986)	16.3 (485)	22.0 (245)
2004	18.6 (1,341)	0.9 (1,280)	16.6 (679)	12.5 (432)

Note: Entries are the percentages of the total number of respondents (*N*, shown in parentheses) reporting that they were forced to move their residence under apartheid.

South Africans of Asian origin bounce around a bit across the surveys, forced residence changes also seem to have affected a substantial number of people.

From these data, we see that the problem of forced residential changes is far more common than many might have expected. Moreover, the question asked about only one aspect of the land problem in South Africa. In 2003 and 2004 surveys, we devoted substantially more attention to trying to understand the extent to which South Africans have experienced several types of land injustices.

A forced residence change is only one form of land victimization. In both the Reconciliation Barometer of 2003[21] and my Land Reconciliation Survey of 2004, we asked representative samples of South Africans about their grievances on various land matters, with the results shown in the top portion of Table 2.3 ("historical experiences"). The percentages reported represent those asserting that the problem "definitely" or "probably" applies to the respondent or his or her immediate family. Of course, responses to these questions represent subjective assessments of land grievances rather than objective, verified instances of land victimization.[22] These results represent land grievances as they exist in the minds of South Africans, not as they have been documented in a court of law.

[21] The 2003 data are taken from an ominbus (M.Bus) survey conducted by Markinor. The Institute for Justice and Reconciliation (IJR) commissioned a portion of this survey to address issues of land reconciliation. For details on the methodology of the survey, see http://www.ijr.org.za/politicalanalysis/reconcbar/First%20Round%20 Research%20Report.pdf (accessed 7/12/2005).

[22] For a study in South Africa of perceptions of having been a victim of crime, see http:// www.polity.org.za/html/govdocs/reports/crime297.html (accessed July 16, 2003). See also Wilsem 2004.

TABLE 2.3. *Land Experiences and Circumstances, 2003 and 2004*

	Respondent's race			
	African	White	Coloured	Asian origin
Historical experiences				
Believe land or land rights were unfairly taken from me or my immediate family in the past				
2003	29.8	4.6	30.9	30.0
2004	38.1	3.5	42.5	28.2
Was subject to a forced removal				
2003	19.9	3.5	27.1	24.1
2004	29.6	2.6	34.8	20.8
Deprived of benefits, such as water rights or mineral rights				
2003	18.6	1.6	5.9	5.9
2004	39.7	3.9	19.1	9.3
Experienced any of these harms				
2003	39.4	6.0	35.5	34.7
2004	54.5	6.6	49.9	33.3
Believe I have a right to the land on which I live, even though I do not legally own it.				
2003	34.1	5.7	32.5	14.7
2004	44.5	6.8	38.5	12.4
Believe that others might file claim of ownership to my land				
2003	17.0	4.6	11.3	11.2
2004	23.0	5.8	10.6	5.9

Note: Entries are the percentages asserting that the statement "definitely" or "probably" applies. Approximate numbers of respondents in 2003: African, 2,000; white, 937; Coloured, 391; and Asian origin, 170. Approximate numbers of respondents in 2004: African, 1,536; white, 1337; Coloured, 708; and Asian origin, 456. The question stem read: "As a result of the history of our country, many South Africans believe that they have been unfairly deprived of land or land rights that is rightfully theirs. We are interested in whether you or your immediate family is involved in any of these issues. Do any of the following apply to you?"

Several startling findings emerge from this table. Perhaps the most dramatic is that in 2004, over half (54.5%) of black South Africans assert some sort of land grievance. If the black population of South Africa is approximately 21,731,000 people, then this represents roughly 11,844,000 black adult South Africans who claim to have been victimized in one way or another on a land issue.[23] Also noteworthy is the finding that Coloured people (49.9%) are roughly as likely to assert some sort of historical land injustice, and even one-third (33.3%) of the respondents of Asian origin report suffering a land grievance. The land issue is clearly not one that is confined to the African portion of the population. It is noteworthy but not surprising that whites report few such experiences; only a very small percentage of the white respondents claim any sort of land harm from the past.[24] All told, an enormous portion of the South African population (35.4%) expresses some sort of historical land grievance.

The general claim that land was unfairly taken is a common grievance among blacks, Coloured people, and those of Asian origin. Because the claim is indeed general, this finding may not be surprising. But it is perhaps revealing to note that reported forced removals were *more frequent* among Coloured people than among blacks,[25] and that Asian South Africans also experienced high rates of forced removals. Conversely, claims of water rights, mineral rights, and so on are more prevalent among black South Africans than the other groups, no doubt because blacks are more likely to reside in rural areas of South Africa. These data suggest that the meaning of the land issue varies somewhat within different racial communities in South Africa, with Africans asserting problems of mineral rights, and so on, in addition to ordinary land claims.

Among black and Coloured respondents, land grieving increased rather substantially between the 2003 and 2004 surveys. This most likely reflects the fairly widespread publicity about land issues in the South African mass media (e.g., the Constitutional Court decision that a small group of black South Africans were illegally deprived of their rights to proceeds from diamond mining[26]). Note especially the nearly

---

[23] These population projections are of course rough estimates and should therefore be used only to indicate the order of magnitude of the various groups.

[24] White land grievances may be associated with interracial marriages, whites who were removed from black resettlement areas, or whites who believe themselves "forced" to move by an influx of black residents to their area.

[25] An obvious (and infamous) example of this is the forced removal of Coloured people from District 6 in Cape Town. On this tragic episode in South African land policy, see Field 2001.

[26] See *Alexkor Limited and the Government of the Republic of South Africa v. the Richtersveld Community and Others* CCT 19/03, decided October 14, 2003.

20% increase in the number of black South Africans believing them-selves to have been deprived of the benefit of their land, such as water and mineral rights. This ominous finding suggests that, ironically, the more attention paid to land issues in South Africa, the more likely people are to develop a sense of victimhood and entitlement, with political consequences that might become highly destabilizing.

The second portion of Table 2.3 reports contemporary rather than historical grievances. Nearly half of the African respondents (and nearly as many of the Coloured people) assert at least some form of tenure insecurity. This problem is not so common among those of Asian origin and is rare among whites. Nor do many whites believe that putative claims on their own land exist.[27] Indeed, worry about the land claims of others is most common *among Africans* (23.0%), and one in ten Coloured South Africans are similarly concerned. This compares with about 6% of both the white respondents and respondents of Asian origin. To reiterate, these data reflect perceptions of tenure insecurity, rather than any verified, objective vulnerability. Once more, awareness of these problems among blacks became more widespread between 2003 and 2004.

Figure 2.8 reports the percentage of the population within each of the provinces asserting some sort of land grievance. These provincial figures are of course not terribly stable in that they are based on sample sizes that vary considerably and that are in each instance fairly small. Nonetheless, the data reveal that land grievances are considerably more widespread in four provinces: the Free State, Limpopo, and the Eastern and Northern Capes. Land grievances are perhaps slightly less common in KwaZulu Natal and the North West.

One might suppose that land grieving is concentrated among older South Africans, but that is not so. Figure 2.9 reports the percentages of South Africans expressing any land grievance according to age group (in 2004). While those in their forties are the most likely to express

---

[27] This statistical finding is strongly reinforced by the discussions I observed in a white focus group conducted in preparation for this survey. The whites seemed to have no understanding whatsoever of any potential vulnerability of their property to land claims. When this subject was introduced to them during the focus group discus-sions, the level of anxiety of the members of the group increased palpably as they began to think more systematically about the historical land claims of blacks in South Africa.

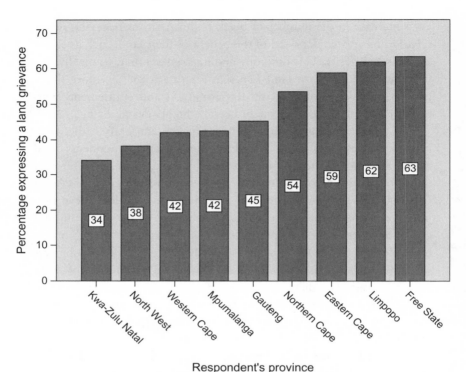

FIGURE 2.8. The prevalence of land grieving within each province, 2004.

a land grievance, the differences across the age groups are not large, and except for those in their twenties, roughly one-half of South Africans of every age believe they have been harmed. This finding obviously indicates that a sense of land victimization has been transferred from one generation to the next.

It is perhaps noteworthy that land grieving does not vary according to the size of place of residence. Grievances are equally common in metropolitan and rural areas. Nor do gender or class differences in grieving exist.[28]

---

[28] However, the difference in land grieving between male and female Coloured people is significant, with 54.7% of the Coloured men expressing a grievance, compared with only 45.3% of Coloured women. A slight, but statistically insignificant, difference also exists between Asian men and women.

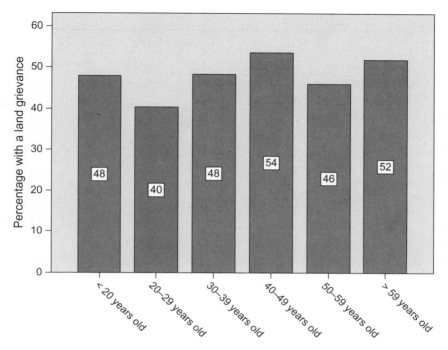

Age categories, 2004

FIGURE 2.9. Land grieving by age, 2004.
Note: N = 4,028. Gamma = .09.

Claiming

Claiming in South Africa is decidedly less common than grieving (see Table 2.4). While 54.5% of the African respondents report some sort of grievance in 2004, only 18.8% have laid any type of claim on the basis of their grievance. Claiming is even less common among Coloured people and those of Asian origin. Quite in contrast to the data on grieving, the prevalence of land claiming did not change much between 2003 and 2004.

Among Africans, the four types of claims occur with approximately equal frequency. It is perhaps noteworthy that almost one in ten Africans has had a dispute with a traditional leader over land rights. Fully 12% of the African respondents assert that they have made a claim to a governmental agency. This figure represents approximately 2,608,000 black South Africans. Among Coloured people and those of Asian origin, claims against traditional leaders are obviously practically nonexistent,

TABLE 2.4. *Claiming for Land Grievances, 2003–2004*

	Respondent's race			
	African	White	Coloured	Asian origin
Claiming and disputing				
Have made a claim before a government agency				
2003	12.0	2.3	8.4	4.7
2004	12.0	1.2	7.2	4.0
Have made a claim before a nongovernmental agency (such as a church)				
2003	11.2	1.6	8.4	4.7
2004	8.7	1.8	3.3	4.2
Have made a claim to the owner of the land				
2003	10.6	3.5	3.1	2.4
2004	9.6	2.5	2.6	2.2
Have had a dispute with traditional leaders over my rights to the land				
2003	11.5	2.4	3.1	0.0
2004	8.7	1.2	2.5	1.1
Have had any of these claims or disputes				
2003	20.9	5.2	9.7	5.3
2004	18.8	3.6	10.0	7.1

Note: Entries are the percentages asserting that the statement "definitely" or "probably" applies. Approximate numbers of respondents in 2003: African, 2,000; white, 937; Coloured, 391; and Asian origin, 170. Approximate numbers of respondents in 2004: African, 1,521; white, 1,338; Coloured, 718; and Asian origin, 450. The question stem read: "As a result of the history of our country, many South Africans believe that they have been unfairly deprived of land or land rights that is rightfully theirs. We are interested in whether you or your immediate family is involved in any of these issues. Do any of the following apply to you?"

and claims against government and other organizations are considerably less common than among black South Africans.[29] Even among blacks, no evidence of class, gender, or age differences in claiming can be found.

The Potential of Unclaimed Land Grievances

A simple cross-tabulation of land grievances with land claims provides some estimate of the degree to which the land issue has consequences for South Africa. Figure 2.10 reports the percentages of respondents in 2004 asserting a land grievance who have not pursued any claim in response to the grievance. Since very few whites have asserted any grievances at all, I have excluded them from this portion of the analysis.

The data reveal that a substantial majority of black people with land grievances, and large majorities of grieving Coloured people and those of Asian origin, have made *no land claim whatsoever.* There are surely many reasons for the lack of claiming (and one should not assume that all claims result in satisfaction), but only a minority of South Africans who believe they hold a valid claim have sought any sort of restitution for land injustice. *Thus, it seems that the land restitution process (the closing date for which occurred years ago[30]) has not addressed the land grieving problem in South Africa and the issue of land injustice still holds great political potential.* The conclusion takes on special immediacy in light of the findings that land grieving became more widespread between 2003 and 2004, while land claiming did not.

---

[29] I resist making a comparison between these survey data on claiming and official claims for restitution registered with the Land Claims Commission. These survey data do not specify the precise nature of the claim, and in any event, these are the subjective assertions of South Africans rather than verifiable legal actions (on the difficulty of validating land claims, see Walker 2000). The purpose of the survey is to examine feelings of land grieving and claiming as they are perceived by ordinary people, and nothing more. In terms of the political consequences of land issues, what people believe and assert is likely more important than what may actually be true.

[30] In July 2005, discussions of reopening the restitution application process resurfaced. According to Groenewald (2005), 60,000 elderly people in Gauteng have organized and are asking that the application process be reopened. Furthermore, in the Eastern Cape, about half a million people apparently feel aggrieved over historical land issues, even though they have made no formal claim for restitution. These people lost their land under the "betterment" scheme of the apartheid government in the 1960s (a policy of "forced villagerisation"), but they were actively discouraged from applying for restitution by the provincial land claims office (Groenewald 2005). Early indications are that there is little chance that the government will accede to these demands.

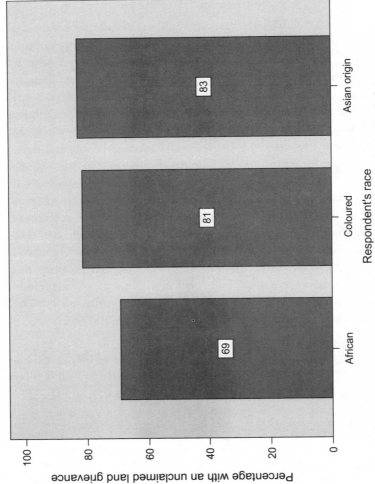

FIGURE 2.10. Percentage of land grievers who have not filed a land claim, 2004.

Among black South Africans, women and younger people are slightly more likely to assert an unclaimed grievance, while residents of villages and rural areas are somewhat less likely. None of these differences, however, is substantial.

Knowledge of the land claims process is not particularly widespread among any racial group in South Africa. The greatest awareness is, not surprisingly, among blacks, but only 42.3% of the black respondents claim "some" or "a great deal" of information about the process. This figure dips to 31.7% among those of Asian origin. Roughly 20% of each racial group claims to know nothing at all about claims procedures.

Not unexpectedly, a strong relationship exists between self-professed knowledge of the land claims process and holding an unclaimed grievance. This relationship for Africans is shown in Figure 2.11. Not surprising is the finding that nearly all (92%) of grieving South Africans who know nothing about the claims process have an unclaimed grievance. In contrast, about half (52%) of those professing to know a great deal about land claims asserted a grievance for which they have not claimed. Those knowing something about the process and those knowing not very much have failed to claim at roughly equal (and large) rates. This reasonably strong relationship indicates that lack of knowledge of the claims process itself is an insufficient explanation of why some grieving Africans have not advanced a formal land claim.

Thus, this survey has discovered that land grievances are widespread and perhaps growing. But most who grieve have not lodged a formal land claim. Such unrequited expectations, on an issue brimming with both symbolic and material salience, have great political potential, should leaders attempt to mobilize land discontent in the country.

POLICY ATTITUDES

To this point, I have established that land issues are fairly serious in South Africa, affecting a substantial portion of the population. A variety of policy initiatives have been proposed to address various aspects of these land problems. To what degree do South Africans support such policies?

Table 2.5 reports attitudes toward a panoply of land policies.[31] Several general aspects of the data stand out. First, strong interracial

---

[31] Bertus de Villiers provided most useful help on the formulation of the land policy questions.

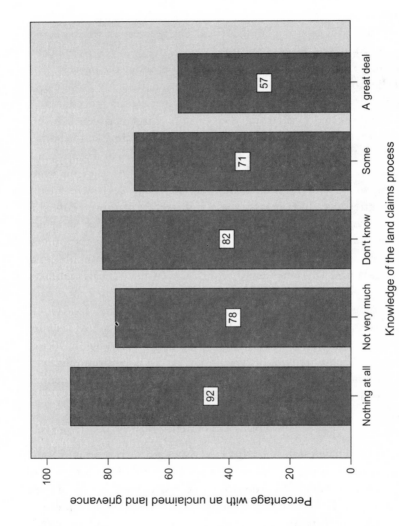

FIGURE 2.11. Unclaimed land grievances as a function of knowledge of the land claims process, Africans, 2004.

Note: Gamma=.37, *p* < .000. *N* = 808.

TABLE 2.5. *Support for Various Land Policies, 2004*

Policy/Race	Support[a]	Uncertain[a]	Oppose[a]	Mean	Std. dev.	N
Returning land to those who had it taken away from them during apartheid[b]						
African	90.9	5.7	3.4	4.42[b]	.78	1,542
White	36.1	28.2	35.7	2.93	1.12	1,303
Coloured	89.2	6.8	4.0	4.28	.78	734
Asian origin	68.2	22.3	9.6	3.73	.94	449
Returning land to those who had it taken away from them by the original white settlers in South Africa[c]						
African	83.2	11.8	5.0	4.23[c]	.88	1,545
White	17.3	30.9	51.8	2.49	1.03	1,295
Coloured	75.0	17.1	7.9	3.96	.90	733
Asian origin	56.5	29.5	14.0	3.50	.94	451
Taking land from those who unfairly got property in the past[d]						
African	73.2	16.7	10.1	3.96[d]	1.03	1,528
White	28.8	32.6	38.6	2.78	1.10	1,304
Coloured	60.5	19.3	20.2	3.54	1.09	734
Asian origin	45.0	31.0	24.2	3.21	1.00	449
Giving farm workers rights of ownership to the houses in which they are currently living[e]						
African	77.7	15.0	7.2	4.11[e]	.96	1,536
White	33.7	23.0	43.3	2.82	1.15	1,320
Coloured	87.6	9.5	2.9	4.20	.74	734
Asian origin	56.0	23.1	20.9	3.41	.97	451
Forcing large land owners to sell some of their property to the government so that it can be given to landless people[f]						
African	71.0	15.1	14.0	3.88[f]	1.11	1,532
White	22.9	22.9	54.2	2.51	1.15	1,323
Coloured	61.5	17.8	20.7	3.55	1.09	735
Asian origin	54.1	18.1	27.8	3.28	1.17	453

(continued)

TABLE 2.5 *(continued)*

Policy/Race	Support[a]	Uncertain[a]	Oppose[a]	Mean	Std. dev.	N
Taxing white property owners at a higher rate than black property owners[g]						
African	49.3	22.8	27.9	3.40[g]	1.26	1,523
White	4.5	7.5	88.0	1.63	.85	1,340
Coloured	26.6	22.5	50.9	2.72	1.15	733
Asian origin	10.1	21.1	68.7	2.20	.96	454
Increasing taxes on everyone to pay for the distribution of land to the poor[b]						
African	45.8	25.2	29.0	3.24[b]	1.24	1,515
White	16.9	15.4	67.7	2.19	1.13	1,328
Coloured	30.2	27.3	42.6	2.81	1.11	733
Asian origin	17.1	17.8	65.1	2.29	1.10	456
Preventing squatting by strictly enforcing the law[i]						
African	61.4	21.5	17.1	3.65[i]	1.12	1,532
White	84.7	9.9	5.4	4.23	.88	1,336
Coloured	74.3	15.1	10.6	3.94	.99	735
Asian origin	84.9	9.9	5.3	4.26	.91	456
Providing more protection to land owners against squatters[j]						
African	64.9	23.4	11.7	3.74[j]	1.05	1,527
White	85.3	9.5	5.2	4.27	.91	1,332
Coloured	80.1	14.5	5.5	3.99	.82	733
Asian origin	85.0	9.0	5.9	4.19	.89	455
Giving land only to those who know how to use it productively[k]						
African	62.1	17.7	20.2	3.64[k]	1.21	1,526
White	65.5	16.4	18.1	3.66	1.11	1,326

Coloured	61.0	17.0	22.0	3.50	1.06	735
Asian origin	45.6	22.0	32.4	3.14	1.20	453

Requiring that any policy about land and land claims treat men and women equally[j]

African	83.2	12.3	4.5	4.22[l]	.88	1,526
White	79.7	13.5	6.8	3.97	.87	1,326
Coloured	88.5	9.0	2.5	4.22	.73	731
Asian origin	79.0	16.6	4.4	3.95	.80	452

Forcing tribal leaders to give each tribal member individual legal ownership of specific plots of land[m]

African	67.2	19.1	13.6	3.77[m]	1.10	1,525
White	41.3	34.2	24.7	3.18	1.11	1,306
Coloured	40.7	42.9	16.5	3.32	.94	728
Asian origin	36.0	35.3	28.6	3.02	1.00	447

[a] These are percentages, calculated on the basis of collapsing the five-point Likert response set (e.g., "agree strongly" and "agree" responses are combined), and they total to 100%, across the three columns, except for rounding errors. The means and standard deviations are calculated on the uncollapsed distributions. Higher mean scores indicate more support of the policy.

[b] Interracial difference of means: $p < .001$; $\eta = .58$.

[c] Interracial difference of means: $p < .001$; $\eta = .63$.

[d] Interracial difference of means: $p < .001$; $\eta = .43$.

[e] Interracial difference of means: $p < .001$; $\eta = .52$.

[f] Interracial difference of means: $p < .001$; $\eta = .46$.

[g] Interracial difference of means: $p < .001$; $\eta = .57$.

[h] Interracial difference of means: $p < .001$; $\eta = .37$.

[i] Interracial difference of means: $p < .001$; $\eta = .26$.

[j] Interracial difference of means: $p < .001$; $\eta = .24$.

[k] Interracial difference of means: $p < .001$; $\eta = .14$.

[l] Interracial difference of means: $p < .001$; $\eta = .15$.

[m] Interracial difference of means: $p < .001$; $\eta = .26$.

differences in attitudes exist (see the eta coefficient, reported in the table footnotes), especially between blacks and whites. On some policies (e.g., the first two listed in the table), interracial differences are enormous. Second, most of these policy ideas are endorsed by a majority of blacks and, by extension, a majority of South Africans. Nonetheless, variability exists within the black majority in the degree of enthusiasm for each of these policies.

Nearly all black South Africans support the idea of returning land to those who had it taken away during apartheid, as do nearly all Coloured people, and a large majority of those of Asian origin. Whites, however, are strongly divided on this issue, with a large percentage unable to form an opinion on the matter. Perhaps many white respondents need the concrete details of any such plan to return land in order to form an opinion. Opinions about returning land taken by the original settlers in South Africa are even more polarized, with a majority of whites opposing this idea, but large majorities of Africans and Coloured people supporting it. The responses to these two questions reflect fundamentally different views of the land problem in South Africa between blacks and whites.

The fourth item in the table concerns the tenure rights of farm workers. Again, blacks and Coloured people strongly support this policy, as do a majority of those of Asian origin, while only one-third of whites would grant ownership rights to farm workers.

More modest racial differences exist on policy proposals regarding squatters. A majority of blacks and large majorities of whites, Coloured people, and those of Asian origin support preventing squatting by strictly enforcing the law. Although blacks are more divided on squatting than on other issues, it is noteworthy and politically significant that only a small minority of blacks opposes strict enforcement of squatting laws.

Current South African policy on land redistribution is based on the "willing seller/willing buyer" principle.[32] A majority of blacks, Coloured people, and those of Asian origin support going further

---

[32] It appears that the South African government is currently rethinking its stance toward this policy.

than existing policy to force landowners to sell some of their property to the government for purposes of redistribution. A majority of whites oppose expanding the policy. However, as the next two policy statements demonstrate, support for a tax increase – for white property owners or for everyone – is not widespread. Nearly all whites oppose taxing white property owners at a higher rate, but so too do a majority of Coloured people and those of Asian origin. More support exists for an across-the-board tax increase, but among no group is there a majority favoring increasing taxes to deal with land inequities.

The smallest interracial differences are found on whether land ought to be distributed only to those who know how to use it productively. Except for those of Asian origin, solid majorities, including among blacks, support this policy. Similarly, large majorities with rather small interracial differences support treating men and women equally when it comes to land claims and policy.

Finally, a strong majority of blacks believe that tribal leaders ought to be forced to give each tribal member individual ownership rights to land. Members of the other three racial groups are more divided on this, but largely because substantial proportions do not hold an opinion on the issue.

With a few exceptions, it is possible to classify each of these policies in terms of whether they support the broad redistribution of land in South Africa and/or whether they encroach on individual property rights. Those favoring redistribution would approve of all of the policies except that of giving land only to those who know how to use it productively. Squatting is also difficult to classify, since squatting affects many poor blacks as even poorer emigrants move into poor areas (and recall that a majority of blacks support strict enforcement of anti-squatting laws). The first seven policies in the table can therefore be used to create an index indicating support for the broad redistribution of land in South Africa.[33] Interracial differences on the index are

---

[33] This index is highly reliable, with a Cronbach's alpha of .79. Index scores are entirely uncorrelated with support for policy on squatters, and only weakly correlated with support for giving land only to productive users, but moderately correlated with attitudes toward the individuation of tribal land and gender equality in land policy. When factor analyzed among all South Africans, only one significant factor emerges, with factor loadings ranging from .72 (returning land taken by settlers) to .39 (increasing taxes on everyone).

enormous ($\eta = .66$). While 18.9% of the black respondents support all seven policies, practically none of the whites do. Indeed, 30.8% of the whites support *none* of the seven policies. Support for redistribution is strongest among blacks, followed by Coloured people, those of Asian origin, and, last by far, whites. Figure 2.12 shows these results by reporting the average number of items endorsed (out of seven) for each of the racial groups.

Thus, South Africans are deeply divided on policy solutions for the land problem. Perhaps not surprisingly, blacks are strongly supportive of redistributive policies, while whites are not. Class, gender, and age differences are trivial.

Principles Undergirding Land Policy

Another way in which land policy can be considered is to determine what criteria people think ought to serve as the underpinnings of such policy. We asked the respondents: "At the moment, there are many different factors that might influence land policy in South Africa. Would you say that land policy should give high importance, some importance, not very much importance, or no importance to making up for land injustices in the past?" Their responses are reported in Table 2.6.

South Africans of every race believe it quite important that land policy be based on strictly following the law. No doubt influenced by the lawless land grabs in Zimbabwe and elsewhere, the percentages of blacks, whites, Coloured people, and those of Asian origin favoring strictly following the rule of law are 80% or higher. And it is noteworthy that large proportions of respondents rate this as a factor of highest importance.

At the other extreme, South Africans of different races are divided on whether having suffered in the past should have much influence on land policy. Two-thirds of blacks think that having suffered should matter, whereas only 17% of whites are so inclined. Coloured people hold views similar to blacks, while those of Asian origin are closer to the view of whites. One can also see this strong racial difference in the orientations toward the past in the first item in the table, although in this formulation whites are considerably more sympathetic to ensuring that land policy makes up for past injustices.

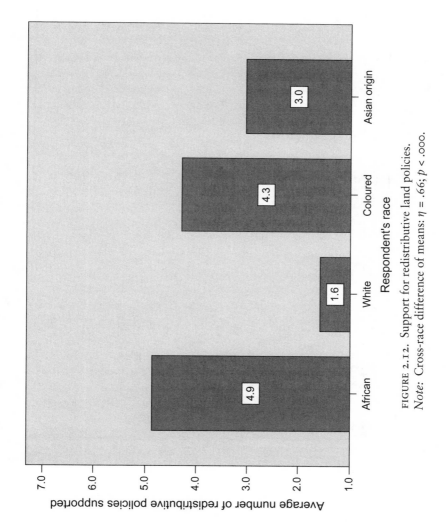

FIGURE 2.12. Support for redistributive land policies.
Note: Cross-race difference of means: $\eta = .66$; $p < .000$.

TABLE 2.6. *Criteria on Which Land Policy Ought to Be Based*

Policy/Race	Some importance (%)	High importance (%)	Some or high importance (%)
Making up for past injustices[a]			
African	40.6	35.9	76.5
White	36.7	9.6	46.4
Coloured	42.7	42.3	85.0
Asian origin	48.1	15.3	63.4
Reduce unequal access to land[b]			
African	37.0	38.3	75.2
White	38.4	15.0	53.4
Coloured	44.3	34.4	78.7
Asian origin	41.3	17.0	58.3
Ensuring hardest workers get more[c]			
African	35.5	28.4	63.9
White	31.1	13.3	44.5
Coloured	32.0	20.1	52.1
Asian origin	25.5	7.4	32.9
Strictly following the law[d]			
African	40.6	41.0	81.6
White	33.0	47.5	80.5
Coloured	33.1	53.7	86.8
Asian origin	42.5	37.0	79.4

Ensuring those suffering most get more[e]

African	33.8	33.4	67.1
White	13.1	3.6	16.7
Coloured	34.0	21.5	55.5
Asian origin	29.2	9.2	38.5

Taking away land unfairly acquired[f]

African	37.1	32.7	69.9
White	28.9	7.5	36.4
Coloured	38.0	27.3	65.3
Asian origin	37.6	11.9	49.5

Note: Entries are the percentages of all respondents answering the question who gave the particular reply. The third column is simply the sum of the first two columns (except for rounding errors). The criteria are: "Making up for land injustices in the past"; "Making certain that unequal access to land is reduced"; "Making certain that the hardest workers get the greatest amount of land"; "Making certain that land reform strictly follows the law"; "Making certain that those who suffered most under apartheid get the greatest amount of land"; "Making certain that those who acquired land unfairly under apartheid do not get to keep it."

[a] Interracial difference of means: $p < .001$; $\eta = .38$.
[b] Interracial difference of means: $p < .001$; $\eta = .29$.
[c] Interracial difference of means: $p < .001$; $\eta = .25$.
[d] Interracial difference of means: $p < .001$; $\eta = .10$.
[e] Interracial difference of means: $p < .001$; $\eta = .46$.
[f] Interracial difference of means: $p < .001$; $\eta = .34$.

As shown in the last item in the table, blacks and Coloured people are more likely to adopt the view that contemporary land policy ought to be based on retribution for the sins and crimes of the past.[34] Indeed, one finding that stands out starkly in these data is that black and Coloured South Africans are particularly concerned about issues of the past when it comes to formulating contemporary land policies (even if none of the criteria related to the past ever receives the highest importance rating from a majority of these groups).

The views of most South Africans on land policy reflect a mixture of contemporary and historical criteria. In the present, most ascribe great importance to following the rule of law, most applaud the objective of reducing land inequality, and most believe that the greatest benefits ought to go to the hardest workers. As for the past, South Africans are more strongly divided, with whites in particular generally unwilling to assert that past injustices should shape contemporary land policies.

The various criteria reported in Table 2.6 can be classified as largely emphasizing present or past factors in formulating land policy. Three of the criteria about which we asked the respondents concern contemporary considerations: following the rule of law, reducing current land inequality, and rewarding those who work the hardest. These are all criteria on which land policies might be based with total disregard to the country's apartheid and colonial past. Citizens emphasizing these factors are focusing on contemporary criteria for formulating land policy in the country. Other criteria about which we asked directly concern the past, as in basing land policy on making up for past injustices, ensuring that those who suffered most in the past get more land today, and taking land away from those who acquired it unfairly.

On the basis of two simple summated indices representing concern with the present and concern with the past, the data show very strong interracial differences regarding the past and less strong differences

---

[34] As Ntsebeza (2007, 124) notes: "It is hard to imagine how any process of land re-distribution that downplays this history can hope to gain legitimacy, in particular in the eyes of those who were robbed of their land." And: "The starting point in [the debate over property rights and the willing buyer, willing seller approach to land reform] should be whether a comprehensive land redistribution programme in South Africa can take place if it ignores colonial conquest, land dispossession and the fact that commercial farming triumphed as a result of the naked exploitation of African labour."

regarding the present, with eta statistics of .49 and .26, respectively.[35] Black South Africans are substantially more likely to assert the importance of criteria grounded in the past (mean = 3.7), followed closely by Coloured people (mean = 3.6). Those of Asian origin are less concerned about the past (mean = 3.0), and whites are the least concerned of all (mean = 2.5).

SUPPORT FOR THE RULE OF LAW

The analysis of the criteria South Africans think ought to drive land reconciliation policy showed that there was wide support among all racial groups that the rule of law ought not to be suspended in order to facilitate land reform. Beyond that specific question, it is also useful to consider whether South Africans support the rule of law more generally. The Land Reconciliation Survey addressed this question.

Few people are likely to reject the rule of law in principle. Survey questions that ask people whether they agree that rulers ought not to act arbitrarily or capriciously or that citizens should be free to ignore the law are unlikely to be of much use in tapping popular commitments to the rule of law.

Instead, the difficult test of support for the rule of law involves the juxtaposition of law and some other valued principle. Questions are most useful when they force people to weigh the relative value of two principles;[36] only when supporting the rule of law involves some cost can we begin to gauge how valuable the rule of law is to people.[37]

Consequently, the Land Reconciliation Survey asked people to agree or disagree (on a five-point Likert scale, ranging from agree strongly to disagree strongly) with statements pitting the rule of law against another value. In two questions, the other value was expediency. The statements are: "In times of emergency, the government ought to be able to suspend

---

[35] I do not necessarily contend that contemporary and historical criteria are locked in zero-sum tension in the minds of most South Africans. Indeed, there is a reasonably strong connection between preferring that policy be based on the past and that it be based on the future ($r > .5$).

[36] For a similar analysis of the relative value Americans ascribe to security and liberty, see Davis and Silver 2004 and Davis 2006.

[37] A considerable body of research examines mass support for the rule of law. In the South African case, see Gibson 2004a, 2008 and Gibson and Gouws 1997; on Russia, see Gibson 2003b; on Europe, see Gibson and Caldeira 1996; and on the United States, see Gibson 2007. Tamanaha (2004) provides a most useful theoretical analysis of the concept of rule of law.

law in order to solve pressing social problems." "Sometimes it might be better to ignore the law and solve problems immediately rather than wait for a legal solution." Another statement paired the rule of law with fairness: "Even if laws are not always fair, it is more important that government actions follow the law than that they be fair."

Some of those who oppose the rule of law do so on grounds of pragmatism, arguing that the rule of law can be unnecessarily rigid and confining. Law must be flexible if it is to be effective. We therefore asked the respondents their opinions of the following statement: "It's all right to get around the law as long as you don't actually break it."

Finally, many believe that elections provide legitimacy to governments and the laws they make. Conversely, law made by a government one opposes and did not vote for may not be deemed worthy of support. We tested this idea with the following statement: "It is not necessary to obey the laws of a government that I did not vote for."

Considerable variability exists in the replies of the respondents to these statements. At one extreme, only one-fourth of South Africans disagree with the statement that bending a law is acceptable; the vast majority approve of getting around the law. A similar minority disagrees that emergencies justify the suspension of the rule of law.[38] On the other hand, two-thirds of the respondents agree that legality should trump fairness, and a majority reject the idea that one is not obliged to follow laws created by an opposition government. Across the set of five statements, the average number of responses favoring the rule of law is 2.2, which seems to indicate fairly limited commitments to legal universalism.[39]

---

[38] The responses to this item are particularly revealing since the apartheid government in South Africa often ruled via states of emergency, albeit states that were legally declared via legitimate apartheid institutions and procedures.

[39] For reasons that are not entirely obvious (but which may be associated with acquiescence bias), the statement contrasting legality and fairness does not perform as expected. That is, the item correlates negatively with responses to each of the other four statements. In addition, this statement generated "don't know" or "uncertain" responses among 20.9% of the respondents, the highest of any item in the set. Apparently, many South Africans could not imagine the circumstance under which law and justice conflict. Of the remainder, the vast majority agreed with the statement, rendering it of little value in terms of differentiating among respondents. Consequently, I have excluded this item from the calculation of an index of overall support for the rule of law. With this item excluded, the average number of the remaining four items endorsed is 1.6, which is still consistent the conclusion that support for the rule of law in South Africa is not widespread.

It rarely makes a great deal of sense, however, to think of "South African public opinion" as a unified whole. Racial differences on almost all issues are enormous, and therefore these data must be reconsidered from the point of view of the four major racial communities in South Africa. Consequently, Figure 2.13 reports the average number of rule-of-law statements endorsed by members of each of the four racial groups.

Interracial differences in support for the rule of law in South Africa are substantial (for the difference of means across the races, $\eta = .29$, $p < .001$). Black South Africans endorse significantly fewer of the rule-of-law statements, especially compared with white South Africans. Both Coloured South Africans and South Africans of Asian origin are also substantially more committed to the rule of law than blacks. The data also indicate that whites are significantly more supportive of the rule of law than the other two racial minorities in the country, although the difference is not nearly as great as that between black and white South Africans.

Consider, for instance, these interracial differences with regard to the statement that "it's all right to get around the law so long as you don't actually break it." Here we see that Africans are much less supportive of the rule of law as compared with the other two racial groups, with only 19% of the African respondents asserting that one should not try to manipulate the law in this manner. This figure stands in sharp contrast to the 51% of the whites holding pro–rule-of-law attitudes. Coloured people are twice as supportive of the rule of law as Africans, as are (roughly) those of Asian origin. These findings strongly reinforce the general conclusion that Africans express considerably less support for the rule of law than the three racial minorities in the country.

Of course, law has rarely served the interests of black South Africans, so it is perhaps not surprising that support for the rule of law would be so limited. Conversely, whites, as a fairly small minority of the South African population, no doubt look to law as a means of protection from abuse by the majority (and the same may be true of Coloured people and those of Asian origin). Whatever the causes of these differences, however, these data provide unsettling evidence of the willingness of a large percentage of the black majority to suspend law in order to achieve other goals.

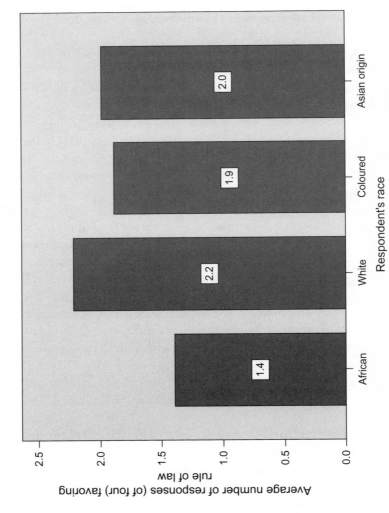

FIGURE 2.13. Interracial differences in support for the rule of law.
Note: Cross-race difference of means: $\eta = .29$, $p < .001$.

LAND ACTIVISM

To this point, I have focused primarily on the attitudes South Africans hold toward aspects of the land issue. But land is an issue that has stimulated many South Africans to protest activities, so we therefore asked about engaging in "different forms of political action that people can take when it comes to land issues." Figure 2.14 reports their replies.

Political activism on any issue characterizes only a very small proportion of every mass public. Thus, we should not be surprised to see that the percentages of South Africans reporting engaging in these sorts of land activism is fairly small. Only 3.0% of all South Africans have refused to pay rates or levies in connection with a land dispute; 5.2% reported having complained to government about some land issue. Considering all six types of activities, a total of 13.9% of South Africans have taken some sort of action on land issues. However, members of the various racial groups were active to different degrees: Some land activism was pursued by 16.1% of blacks, and 4.7%, 8.6%, and 2.6% of whites, Coloured people, and those of Asian origin, respectively. Thus, activism is remarkably common among black South Africans. Activism is completely unrelated to gender, class, and age.

To what degree is land activism concentrated among those with a land grievance or a land claim? Figure 2.15 reports the relationships. The top portion of Figure 2.15 demonstrates that among those asserting a land grievance, 21.2% engaged in some form of land activism, in comparison to only 7.4% among those with no land grievance. The relationship between land claiming and activism is even stronger; 30.7% of those with a land claim engaged in some sort of land protest behavior. These relationships are reasonably strong and indicate that a significant number of South Africans are taking political action in pursuance of their sense of land injustice. These data represent further evidence (if any is still needed) of the intensity of the land issue.

SUMMARY AND CONCLUSIONS

This chapter has traveled a considerable distance, addressing many aspects of South Africans' attitudes and behaviors on various dimensions of the land problem. It is perhaps useful, therefore, to begin

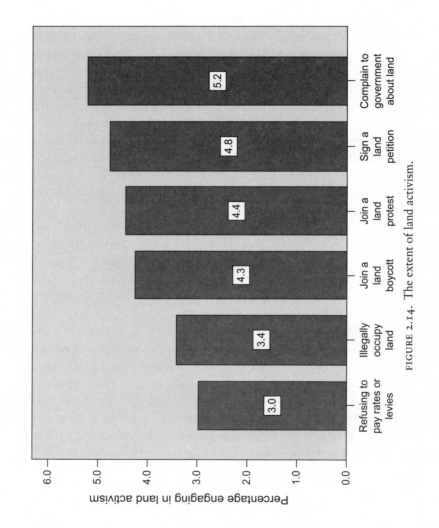

FIGURE 2.14. The extent of land activism.

80

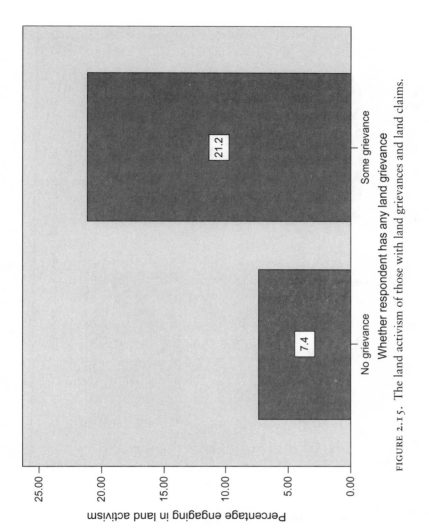

FIGURE 2.15. The land activism of those with land grievances and land claims.

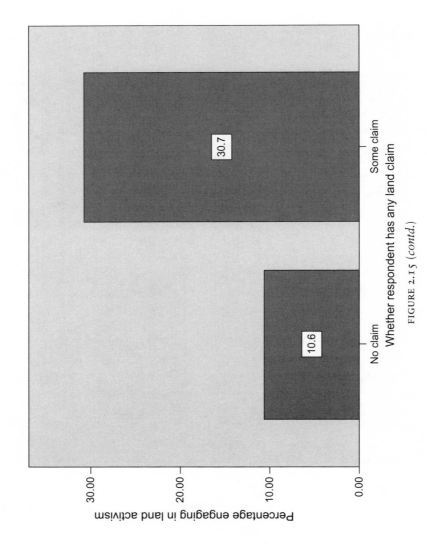

FIGURE 2.15 (contd.)

thinking about the implications of these findings by reviewing the empirical conclusions unearthed to this point.

- Land is not the most pressing issue for most South Africans, but it is an issue of considerable importance, especially to Africans.
- Land issues are important to blacks in part because they assign a deep symbolic significance to land. Blacks more than any other South Africans express a strong attachment to land, which renders land more than a "simple" economic issue.
- South Africans of different races are also quite divided in how much they value private property, with the black versus white divide being particularly stark. Perhaps this finding signals nothing more than that those who own all the property value property the most, but, whatever the cause of the interracial differences, the basic value framework for land policy varies considerably across groups in South Africa.
- Views about the causes of contemporary land inequality are complex, representing a mixture of blame on the apartheid past and on blacks and whites today. Whites emphasize the shortcomings of blacks. Blacks seem to believe that inequality today is a function of inequities from the past, which is consistent with their general willingness to take the past into consideration in judging the present.
- Perhaps one reason why whites are so insensitive to the crimes of the past is that they are remarkably ignorant of South African land history. Their contemporary judgments therefore are insensitive to the historical context of colonialism and apartheid in South Africa. Blacks, Coloured people, and those of Asian origin are little more informed about the specific details of the past, even if they weight past injustices heavily in their contemporary judgments.
- Blacks are concerned about historical land injustices in part because a large proportion of the black population (more than half) views itself as holding a land grievance rooted in the past. If anything, the proportion of the black population feeling aggrieved is growing. Only a small proportion of these South Africans have lodged formal land claims. These unsated land grievances hold the potential to become a major destabilizing force in South African politics.
- The policy preferences of blacks and whites on matters of land differ enormously. Blacks favor redistributive policies; whites

resist. The interracial gulf in land policy preference is as great as any found in these data.

- Land issues are unusually powerful in motivating political activism in South Africa. The normally passive citizenry has demonstrated a relatively high degree of protest activity over land issues.

What do all of these empirical findings actually mean for land issues and South African politics? Caution must be exercised in answering this question since, as I have noted, politics is about far more than the preferences of ordinary people. But perhaps the single most important conclusion from this analysis is that land issues are terribly important to black South Africans, and they are practically invisible to white South Africans. Blacks feel aggrieved; they have been willing to take political action on behalf of those grievances; and grievances may be growing in number rather than declining. And perhaps unfortunately, land has taken on symbolic importance for black South Africans, indicating that economic solutions alone may be insufficient.[40] Land issues have all of the characteristics required to become volatile and destabilizing, should effective political leadership emerge to mobilize the discontented.

What can be done to reduce the chances that land issues will threaten the consolidation of democracy in South Africa? Several possibilities suggest themselves. First, South Africans of all races are remarkably ignorant of the country's history of land injustices. Whites in particular need to understand the magnitude of the land injustices committed against blacks, Coloured people, and those of Asian origin, as well as the recency of such abuses. Whites should also be encouraged to understand that land has symbolic meaning for black people, beyond material considerations.

Black expectations seem to be escalating, and unsatisfied expectations are always politically dangerous. How might such expectations be managed? A constant refrain from Nelson Mandela and others

---

[40] In an earlier analysis of how South Africans feel about amnesty, Gibson (2002) showed that the retributive justice shortfall created by amnesty could be ameliorated by distributive justice (compensation), but that procedural and restorative justice also played a powerful compensatory role. Giving victims voice (procedural justice), coupled with apologies (restorative justice) goes a long way with South Africans in making up for the failure to extract retribution from those admitting gross human rights abuses. Perhaps a similar sort of approach could be taken to compensate for the injustices of the past.

during the 1990s was to encourage South Africans not to expect too much, too soon. On the other hand, democracy is now more than a decade old in South Africa, as the many critics of the pace of land reform regularly observe. Were government to appreciate fully the priority of this issue for so many black South Africans, perhaps greater resources would be devoted to land restitution and redistribution.[41] A mixture of speeding up land reform, while simultaneously explaining frankly the limits of such policy, seems to be in order.

Finally, this analysis seems to justify the need for continuous monitoring of public opinion on land issues. I have documented some rather dramatic changes between 2003 and 2004; further volatility in opinions seems inevitable, especially as it becomes clear that some groups are being handsomely rewarded for their land claims. Such opinion monitoring should pay careful attention to the size of the population with dashed expectations. Land is a tinderbox issue; with just a few well-placed sparks, a serious conflagration could ignite in South African politics. Especially as South Africa moves into a post-Mandela, post-Mbeki era, land will likely remain one of the most volatile political issues.

---

[41] There are many issues of land policy that extend far beyond the purview of this report. For instance, it is often argued that simply giving land to people, without support for training, infrastructure, capital, etc., is bound to fail, especially in highly competitive and demanding areas such as farming. Whether such arguments are correct is not an issue that can be addressed through an analysis of public opinion.

3

Group Identities and Land Policy Preferences

The overarching theory employed in this research has to do with how individuals relate to groups. Social Identity Theory (SIT) has been developed over the past several decades to explain these group attachments. The essential insights of the theory are that:

People receive psychological value from associating themselves with groups.

Group identities come to shape how people view the world.

Group identities can lead to concerns for fellow members of one's group that extend beyond acquaintances. Group identities can also connect individuals to group histories.

These sociotropic concerns for group justice structure how people perceive and act on issues such as land reconciliation.

The purpose of this chapter is to provide an overview of this theory and to examine the survey evidence on the ways in which South Africans identify with groups. Most important, I test the hypothesis that land policy preferences reflect these group identities. In the end, it seems that policy preferences reflect symbolic considerations associated with groups more than they reflect individual-level instrumentalism, and this is especially so among those who adopt particular types of group identities.

IDENTITIES AND GROUP HISTORY

Attitudes, beliefs, and actions regarding land issues are likely shaped by at least two major forces. On one hand, land preferences may reflect individual self-interests. Those who suffered from land policies of the past may simply seek restorative justice: the righting of the wrong that they experienced. In addition, those without land today may, whatever their histories, seek redistributive justice: land on which to live and work. *Egocentric instrumentalism* therefore provides one accounting of why people think and act as they do, even if such an account is neither terribly complex nor interesting. Preferences on land issues may reflect little more than individual self-interests, according to this hypothesis.

Social scientists have found that self-interestedness is typically not a very powerful explanation of individual attitudes and actions (e.g., Funk 2000, Kinder 1986). It is worth quoting at length a particularly exhaustive review of this literature by Wolpert and Gimbel (1998, 241–242):

Although it is widely assumed that citizens adopt policy preferences that further their private interests, a vast body of empirical research reveals that self-interest exerts little influence over mass preferences (for a review of the literature, see Sears and Funk, 1990). White parents whose children are affected by a desegregation plan are no more likely than other whites to oppose busing (Sears et al., 1979, 1980); those with poor health insurance are no more likely to support national health insurance than the fully insured (Sears et al., 1980); those vulnerable to the military draft do not have distinctive preferences on the draft (Lau et al., 1978); those with relatives and friends serving in Vietnam were no more likely to oppose the Vietnam War than others (Lau et al., 1978); the unemployed do not support job programs more than the employed (Lau and Sears, 1981); parents of children in public schools do not support aid to education more than others (Sears and Citrin, 1985); whites adversely affected by affirmative action are no more likely to oppose preferential hiring than other whites (Kinder and Sanders, 1987; Kluegel and Smith, 1983; Kinder, 1986); vulnerability to crime does not produce distinctive attitudes on law and order policies (Sears et al., 1980; Kleck, 1996); and working women are no more likely than homemakers to support the ERA or affirmative action for women (Sears and Huddy, 1990). Similarly, on issues such as bilingual education (Huddy and Sears, 1989), immigration (Stein et al., 1997), English as an official language (Huddy and Sears, 1989; Citrin et al., 1990a, 1990b), inflation (Sears and Citrin, 1985), and the energy crisis (Sears et al., 1978), tangible personal interests fail to produce distinctive policy attitudes.

On most political controversies, understanding preferences requires more than understanding whether or not an individual benefits directly from the policy.

Theories of symbolic politics have been developed as an alternative to theories of rational self-interest, and a rich literature on the importance of symbols in politics exists. Largely associated with the work of David Sears, symbolic politics theory asserts that people acquire "affective responses to particular symbols" (Sears 1995, 120), and these influence the way people react to the daily flow of political events, issues, individuals, and groups. Symbols are thus important because they "often evoke and mobilize human emotions" (1995, 113). Grounded in emotion, attitudes toward political symbols seem to be more stable, more generally applicable, more likely to be readily accessible, and, as a consequence, more likely to provide a frame for understanding a variety of political issues. When symbolic attitudes are evoked, political judgment is less likely to be strictly associated with interest maximization: "the symbolic politics process is characterized by generally unthinking, reflexive, affective responses to remote attitude objects rather than by calculations of probable costs and benefits (whether personal or not)" (Sears 1995, 120). As Sides and Citrin (2007, 479) further explain: "Symbolic politics theory emphasizes the potency of values and identities on opinion formation, arguing that the role of these 'ideal interests' frequently overrides the influence of material concerns."

A considerable body of research assesses whether symbolic attitudes or rational self-interests provide the most useful view of policy preference formation. For instance, Sears (1995) and many others have juxtaposed these two explanations of citizen preferences and have generally found that symbolic attitudes are more influential. As a more recent example, Sides and Citrin (2007, 477) report an investigation of "the empirical validity of 'rational' and 'symbolic' theories of attitudes toward immigration," and conclude that the material interests of people have much less influence on immigration attitudes than do their symbolic attitudes (in their case, national identities). Specifically: "Public opinion is not insensitive to the economic consequences of immigration, but more important are deeply held symbolic attitudes, such as beliefs about cultural unity or homogeneity" (Sides and Citrin 2007, 501). Exceptions to the general finding that self-interest is a poor predictor of political preferences can certainly be found (e.g., Wolpert and Gimbel 1998, Bobo and Tuan 2006; see also Schneider and Jacoby 2007), but, typically, self-interests are not as influential as symbolic attitudes in shaping land preferences.

People are often motivated by sociotropic, or group, concerns. Even without direct interests involved, individuals may care about fairness to their group. Mutz and Mondak (1997) refer to this as "sociotropic fairness," defining the concept as "people's concerns with whether economic gains and losses have been distributed equitably among the nation's many groups" (Mutz and Mondak 1997, 288). Of course, one can readily substitute anything of value for their "economic gains and losses"; indeed, sociotropic fairness may refer to the distribution of justice, historical and contemporary, among the citizens of a nation (as Mutz and Mondak recognize). Thus, preferences on land issues may be defined by concerns about *sociotropic justice:* the tendency to judge policy in terms of how it affects one's group rather than one individually. In this sense, groups matter "because identification produces a *symbolic* interest in the group's well-being" (Mutz and Mondak 1997, 303, emphasis added).[1] Consequently, a central purpose of this analysis is to test the relative influence of instrumental and symbolic concerns in structuring policy preferences on land redistribution.

The most significant finding from the mountain of data reported in Chapter 2 is that nearly all land preferences are overwhelmingly associated with one's racial group. But what does race mean? Race may stand as a proxy for self-interest since a reasonably strong correlation is likely to exist between one's racial group and the degree of victimization under

---

[1] I of course recognize that, in the original formulation of these concepts (Kinder and Kiewiet 1979), sociotropic interests were conceptualized largely in self-interest terms under something akin to a "linked fate" explanation (e.g., Dawson 1994): To the extent that one's group profits, one also benefits. However, Mutz and Mondak describe this sense of sociotropic justice not so much in direct self- or group-interest terms but rather as an interest in seeing that all groups in society (including one's own) are treated fairly (which can include the desire for acknowledgment that one's group was treated unfairly in the past). In this sense, the theory is related to Tyler's relational theory of procedural justice (see Tyler and Lind 1992) in which citizens learn about their value in society through the treatment their group is perceived to receive. See also Bobo and Tuan (2006), who argue that self-interest must be understood within the context of social structures (in the South African context, colonialism and apartheid) determining intergroup relations, and therefore that self-interest and group interests may coincide.

apartheid and colonialism. But race may also stand for identity, a sense of attachment to one's racial group and thereby a sense of connectedness (or "linked fate"; see Dawson 1994) with other members of the group. The connection to a group's past – and the historical injustices it experienced – is therefore provided by identification with a group: To hold sociotropic justice concerns requires some degree of identification with a group.[2] Because nominal group membership is insufficient to capture the full effects of identity processes, I turn now to more comprehensive and complicated theories of group membership and identity. Fortunately, a considerable body of theory is available.

SOCIAL IDENTITY THEORY AND SOCIOTROPIC JUSTICE

One of the truisms of modern politics is that groups are important, in many different respects. From the point of view of the individual citizen, policy preferences are often formed in reference to groups. As Grant and Rudolph have noted: "In essence, individuals' attitudes toward particular policies are shaped by the perceived impact of those policies on political friends and foes" (2003, 456). Groups are powerful reference points in politics, in part because they provide a means of forming preferences on issues in which the citizen has no direct material involvement or interests. Women around the world care, for instance, about the plight of Afghan girls simply owing to shared membership in a group defined by gender. It is not surprising therefore that so much attention has been given to the role of groups in preference formation (e.g., Sniderman et al. 1989).

Many researchers conceptualize groups fairly simply in terms of "likeability heuristics": whether one likes the group or not (Brady and Sniderman 1985). Grant and Rudolph (2003), for instance, demonstrate that attitudes toward restrictions on campaign contributions depend in

---

[2] Many scholars acknowledge that group identifications can transform politics from a process of rational choice to one of symbolic politics (see Horowitz 1985; Johnson and Schlemmer 1996; and Friedman 2004 for South African applications), and many (e.g., Ferree 2006) note a tension between these two forms of thinking about politics. At least in terms of voting, however, Mattes (1995), Mattes, Taylor, and Africa (1999), Mattes and Piombo (2001), and Ferree (2006) have concluded that most South Africans rely on instrumental rather than symbolic factors while choosing which political parties to support with their votes. Voting, however, may be a relatively easy context within which instrumental behavior is possible.

part on whether one likes or dislikes the group under consideration. But political psychologists have moved beyond simple likeability to consider how definitions of ingroups and outgroups shape the way people think about issues.

There is more to group politics than simple nominal membership in a group. Groups most likely acquire their potency when membership is associated with some sort of identification with the group, and even with the development of various psychic benefits from group identification. People may, for instance, derive some degree of self-esteem from thinking of themselves as members of a particular group. In political contexts in which groups are highly relevant, people may come to understand much if not most of politics as having to do with how benefits and costs are allocated across groups.

Are groups relevant within the context of South African land politics? Perhaps in no other country in the world are groups – racial, ethnic, and linguistic – of as much importance as they are in South Africa. Apartheid defined – legally, socially, and politically – individuals by their racial group: black, white, Coloured, and Indian. One's group designation had a great deal to do with one's public life under apartheid. Consequently, it is not surprising that group identities survived the fall of apartheid and continue to influence politics in contemporary South Africa.

However, our earlier research on political intolerance in South African politics (Gibson and Gouws 2003; Gibson 2004, 2006) alerts us to the fact that group identities are only conditionally relevant. That is, the significance of identities for politics seems to vary over time, perhaps in relationship to the overall salience of groups in the politics of a polity. Moreover, earlier research has demonstrated that group membership per se is not politically significant; instead, it is the collateral attitudes sometimes associated with membership that seem to influence perceptions and judgments of politics. Group membership is of course relatively obdurate; the attitudes associated with such groups can indeed change over time.

This more nuanced view of the importance of group attachments suggests the possibility that policies may also vary in the degree to which they implicate groups and their identities. From the viewpoint of this research, I hypothesize that land is an issue implicating group identities – owing to the group-based injustices of the past rather than

individual dispossessions – and therefore I expect to find significant relationships between land policy preferences and group attachments and
ideologies. Specifically, I hypothesize that the historical injustices of land
dispossessions in South Africa are likely to implicate identity concerns,
and hence that group identities will structure the ways in which people
view the issue.[3]

MEASURING GROUP IDENTITIES

We began consideration of group attachments by putting the following
question to the respondents in the survey: "People see themselves in
many different ways. Using this list, which *one* of these best describes you? Please take a moment to look at all of the terms on the
list." Table 3.1 reports the replies to this question.

Among black South Africans, the modal identity is "African," which
is preferred by a margin of almost two to one over "black." Nonetheless,
the identities of Africans are broadly mixed, with many respondents
identifying with their ethnic/language group rather than their racial
group. Among whites, the modal identity is "South African," although
many whites think of themselves as either "Christians" or "Afrikaners."
Regarding the latter, it is noteworthy that those identifying as Afrikaners
are twice as common as those identifying as "English." Coloured people
are most likely to associate with the term "Coloured," although this
characterizes less than one-third of the Coloured respondents. Roughly
12% of Coloured people identify themselves as "Afrikaners," no doubt
referring primarily to their language group. South Africans of Asian
origin are more likely to think of themselves as "South African" than
"Indian," and quite a sizable percentage define themselves in religious
terms (Christian, Moslem, and Hindu). In general, these data document
considerable pluralism in primary group identities, with no single
association being adopted by more than one-third of the respondents.

---

[3] For instance, Nicholson, Pantoja, and Segura (2006) take a similar approach in distinguishing between more rational criteria such as policy agreement between the candidate and the voter for deciding how to cast one's vote, versus more symbolic factors,
such as whether the candidate speaks the language of the voter (no matter how poorly).
Among those with low information about politics, symbolic factors have a disproportionate influence. This distinction parallels my distinguishing between instrumental
considerations and symbolic factors in land policy preference formation.

TABLE 3.1. *The Distribution of Primary Positive Social Identities, 2004*

Primary identity	% all South Africans	% within racial group[a]			
		African	White	Coloured	Asian origin
African	22.2	26.8	2.7	5.3	0.9
South African	18.1	13.9	33.4	21.8	30.7
Black	10.6	14.5			
Zulu	9.3	13.5			
Xhosa	8.0	11.0			
Christian	5.6	1.3	20.7	17.5	10.5
Afrikaner	4.1		20.9	12.5	
North Sotho–Sepedi	3.3	4.5			
South Sotho–Sesotho	3.1	3.6			
Coloured	2.6			30.7	
Tswana	2.4	3.6			
Tsonga–Shangaan	2.1	2.9			
Siswati–Swazi	1.7	2.2			
English	1.6		9.7		
Venda	1.0	1.4			
White	0.9		6.2		
Other	0.8		2.4		1.3
Moslem	0.8			6.6	7.5
Indian	0.6				24.1
Boer	0.4		3.2		
Brown	0.4			3.0	
Hindu	0.4				12.9
Asian origin	0.3				11.6
% "*South African*"[b]	38.0	33.2	55.1	44.4	57.3
N	4,095	1,543	1,361	737	456

[a] χ^2 for differences across race = 6199.1; $p < .001$.

[b] Percentage of respondents claiming "South African" identity as a primary *or* secondary identity.

Note: Within the racial groups, only percentages greater than or equal to 1.0% are shown. For "All South Africans" the "other" category includes any group identity that was selected by less than 1.0% of any of the racial groups. The modal response within each racial group is highlighted in the table.

The Benefits of Group Identities

The data provide strong evidence that these identities are significant for South Africans. Across all respondents, 86.7% rated their group identity as "very important," the highest point on the response set scale. Considerable intergroup differences exist in the importance of these identities, ranging from only 58.5% of those claiming to be "English" rating that identity as very important to the 92.2% asserting an African identity as very important. The contrast in the importance of group attachments between English and Afrikaans identities is striking. But in general, South Africans of every type ascribe considerable significance to their group attachments.

The interview pursued this issue further by inquiring about the psychic benefits the respondents derive from these identities. We asked whether they received any security, self-importance, or self-esteem as a result of their group identifications.[4] Roughly 70% of the respondents claimed to derive each of these psychic benefits, with 56% of the respondents asserting strong benefits of all three types. The measure of benefits received is fairly strongly correlated with the rated importance of the respondent's identity ($r = .32$). Clearly, group identities provide useful psychological benefits to most South Africans.

Group and National Identities

Table 3.1 also reports the percentages of respondents claiming a South African national identity. The second row in the table (in italics) identifies those who claim a national attachment as their primary identity; toward the end of the table, the percentages claiming a national identity as either primary or secondary are reported. Only among whites and South Africans of Asian origin do we find a majority of respondents asserting a national identity. Moreover, when compared with data from 2001 (see Gibson 2004a), this 2004 survey reveals marked declines in national identities within each of the racial/ethnic/linguistic groups. Across all South Africans, the percentage selecting a "South African"

---

[4] The question stem read: "People have different sorts of feelings as a result of being a member of a group. Which of the following characteristics describes how you feel about being a [member of the group]?" The feelings asked about were security, importance, and feelings about self-worth.

identity declined from 51.9% to 38.0% in 2004. Although comparisons between the two surveys must be made with caution[5], the evidence here is sufficiently strong and consistent in support of the conclusion that the prevalence of national identities has declined significantly between 2001 and 2004.[6]

Because an important part of nation building is the development of national attachments, we pursued this question further, putting two propositions to all of the respondents: "It makes me proud to be called a South African." "Being a South African is a very important part of how I see myself." More than 90% of the respondents agreed with the first statement, with 61.4% agreeing strongly. Regarding the second proposition, 89.3% of the respondents agreed with the statement, with just over half agreeing strongly. Only a tiny proportion of the respondents rejected these statements. Most South Africans strongly embrace their national identities, and from this evidence, it seems that national attachments and group identities may not be in conflict with one another. That is a question these data allow me to pursue further.

The conventional hypothesis is that the more one identifies with a subgroup the less one will identify with the nation-state (e.g., Sidanius et al. 1997). The best way in which to test this hypothesis is to examine *within each identity group* the strength of that group identity and the responses to the national identity statements. The data in Table 3.2 report the correlations necessary to test this hypothesis. The first row of data indicates the correlations with the average response to the two patriotism questions for those who selected "South African" as their primary group identity. The table reports the correlations ranked by the number of respondents selecting each identity. Caution must be

---

[5] In general, it is difficult to draw conclusions about identity across different studies since vastly different measures have been used by different scholars. Rarely do scholars investigate anything more than psychological membership in a group, as in, for example, the psychological benefits (e.g., self-esteem) one derives from group membership. As Ferree dramatically understated it (2006, 807): "These are not ideal measures of identity." In the case of this study, the measures are identical but some differences in the nature of the samples exist, and of course, different survey research firms conducted the surveys. So-called house effects can be particularly large on open-ended questions.

[6] One possibility accounting for this change may be that racialized policies such as Affirmative Action and Black Economic Empowerment have provided incentives for South Africans to think of themselves in terms of their racial rather than national group.

TABLE 3.2. *The Relationship Between Group and National Identifications*

Identity asserted	Correlation between strength of group identity and national identity index	% agreeing with both statements	N
South African	.23***	87.3	963
African	.19***	87.9	489
Christian	.22***	84.2	475
Afrikaner	.17***	81.4	374
Black	.09	78.6	229
Coloured	.27***	92.9	226
Zulu	.07	92.3	208
Xhosa	−.01	88.9	170
English	.16	75.0	136
Indian	.11	88.2	109
White	.06	69.0	85
Moslem	.03	76.2	84
North Sotho–Sepedi	−.16	79.7	69
Hindu	.43***	88.9	62
South Sotho–Sesotho	.00	80.4	56
Asian origin	−.04	85.5	55
Tswana	.32*	66.7	55
Other	.44	77.4	52
Boer	−.12	86.7	46
Tsonga–Shangaan	−.06	86.4	44
Siswati–Swazi	−.03	79.4	34
Venda	−.17	87.0	24
Brown	.45*	95.8	24

Note: Correlations are shown for groups with 10 or more identifiers.
***$p < .001$, **$p < .01$, *$p < .05$ (two-tailed test).

exercised in interpreting some of these coefficients, since for some identities they are based on relatively small numbers of respondents.

The data require that the hypothesis be unequivocally rejected. For nearly every group, the more one identifies with the group, *the more likely one is to hold a strong national identity.* For instance, consider those who selected "African" as their primary group identity. The greater the importance of this identity, the more likely one is to assert that being South African makes him or her proud and the more important is a South African identity. The magnitude of the correlations varies across identity, but in no instance is there a statistically significant or even nontrivial negative correlation between group identities and national identities.[7] These data are important because they indicate that national and group identities are not locked in a zero-sum tension with each other. Indeed, quite the contrary is true. South Africans seem entirely capable of holding multiple identities simultaneously and without apparent conflict.

It seems possible that the opposite of group or national identity is in fact social isolation or atomization: the failure to identity with any group. Identity may reflect an enduring psychological attribute of individuals, with those able to identify with one group being better able to identify with other groups as well. Of course, I do not contend that this tendency toward joint identities applies to all groups, as for instance, with groups that are in direct political conflict with one another. But in South Africa, identifying with the nation is *not incompatible* with identifying with one's own group. In this sense, "tribalism" seems not to be inimical to asserting a strong national identity.

I must note, however, that all of these relationships are weaker than those observed in 2001 (see Gibson 2004a). For instance, in 2001, the correlation between one's strength of Zulu identity and national pride was on the order of .4; in the 2004 survey, the correlation is an insignificant .07. Because both surveys demonstrate very high levels of agreement with both statements, perhaps the 2004 correlations are depressed by degenerate variance affecting statistical measures of association and rendering cross-time comparisons problematical.[8] Nonetheless, on their face, these data suggest that group and national identities have become less closely intertwined (as national identities have become less common).

The group attachments reported in Table 3.1 are subject to some more theoretically inspired categorization. Let us consider black South Africans first, since they constitute the easiest case.

---

[7] Note that there are three negative coefficients exceeding .10: among blacks, for North Sotho/Sepedi and Venda identifiers, and among whites, for those referring to themselves as Boers. It seems explicable that Boers identify less with the nation as a whole, but it is not clear why that would be true of the black ethnic groups.

[8] Moreover, since the correlations reported in this table (and in 2001) are based on relatively small numbers of cases, the standard errors of the coefficients are quite large.

TABLE 3.3. *Identity Classifications*

Nominal race	National	General racial group	Ethnic/linguistic group
African	South African	African, Black, Brown	North Sotho/Sepedi, Siswati/Swazi, South Sotho/Sesotho, Tsonga/Shangaan, Tswana, Venda, Xhosa, Zulu, Ndebele, Shona
White	South African, African, Black	Asian, White, European	Afrikaner, Boer, English, Venda, Xhosa
Coloured	South African, African, Black	Asian, Brown, Coloured	Afrikaner, Boer, English, South Sotho, Xhosa
Asian origin	South African, African, Black	Asian, Indian	Afrikaner, Boer

Other: Christian, Hindu, Moslem, Jewish, other religions.

About 14% of the black respondents classified themselves primarily as South Africans. Another 41% asserted an identity in terms of a general racial category – either "African" or "black." For 43% of the respondents, the identity was defined in terms of a specific ethnic/linguistic group – e.g., Zulu, Xhosa, North Sotho. Nearly all respondents answered this question in terms of identities falling within these three categories.[9] (See Table 3.3 for the full classification scheme.) I am not suggesting that individuals do not have multiple layers of identity, but for a (slim) plurality of blacks, a specific ethnic/linguistic group provides their primary group identity.[10]

Whites, Coloured people, and those of Asian origin are more difficult to classify, largely owing to the fairly widespread use of religious

[9] Less than 2% of the respondents mentioned an identity not in these three categories. The most common of these was "Christian" ($N = 20$).
[10] For instance, those holding these various types of identities differ little in terms of their national patriotism.

groups to define primary identities. For instance, as noted above, about one-fifth of whites claim a "Christian" identity, which obviously is not easily categorized within this scheme. Coloured and Asian South Africans also claimed Hindu and Moslem identities, which are of course especially difficult to classify (as are the few people who claimed "Jewish" as their primary attachment). As a result, the "other" category balloons for whites, Coloured people, and those of Asian origin to 22.0%, 24.8%, and 32.1%, respectively.

Nonetheless, these data reveal that the three racial minorities are considerably more likely to assert a national identity as primary than are blacks. For instance, the figure among blacks is 14.0%; among whites, 36.2% assert a South African national identity. Very few whites (7.6%) claim a racial identity, although one-third (34.1%) assert an ethnic identity (mostly "Afrikaners"). The modal response for blacks was an ethnic attachment (43.0%), for whites it was a national identity (36.2%), for Coloured people and those of Asian origin, an ethnic identity (33.8%, and 35.8%, respectively). These identities differ little in terms of their self-proclaimed importance to the respondents; all are quite important.[11] For ease of communication, I will refer to these as national identities, racial identities, and ethnic identities, even though I do not ascribe much substance to the words "racial" and "ethnic." In the analysis below, these identity categories play a significant role.

Connecting Identities to Politics

Earlier research in South Africa (e.g., Gibson and Gouws 2001) has discovered that identities per se are not particularly consequential for politics; instead, it is the associated beliefs attached to those identities that render group attachments politically relevant. We have explored that possibility in the 2004 survey, replicating the earlier analysis. Table 3.4 reports the replies to our queries.

South Africans clearly believe that their group attachments are important, as most clearly revealed in the responses to the third item in the table ("group fate affects me"). Very large majorities of every racial

---

[11] Across the three types of identities, insignificant differences exist in the ascribed importance of the identity, with the range being from 91% among those asserting a national identity to 86% among those claiming an ethnic identity.

TABLE 3.4. *Attitudes Toward Groups and Social Identity*

Item/Race	Agree (%)	Uncertain (%)	Disagree (%)	Mean	Std. dev.	N
My group is best[a]						
All South Africans	73.0	11.7	15.2	2.14	1.09	4,025
African	75.6	11.5	12.9	2.06	1.06	1,530
White	66.4	12.1	21.5	2.34	1.15	1,279
Coloured	69.5	10.8	19.6	2.30	1.07	719
Asian origin	52.1	17.0	30.9	2.77	1.09	448
Support my group's view[b]						
All South Africans	75.8	11.6	12.6	2.11	1.04	4,059
African	76.5	12.9	10.6	2.05	1.03	1,531
White	71.2	10.2	18.6	2.30	1.05	1,335
Coloured	80.1	7.8	12.1	2.12	.92	739
Asian origin	75.3	9.3	15.5	2.33	.92	453
Group fate affects me[c]						
All South Africans	81.1	9.6	9.3	1.94	1.00	4,046
African	81.1	9.8	9.2	1.92	1.02	1,526
White	82.2	9.2	8.6	1.97	.90	1,329
Coloured	86.7	7.0	6.3	1.90	.81	730
Asian origin	82.3	6.4	11.3	2.10	.92	452
Group should stand together[d]						
All South Africans	83.5	8.8	7.6	1.84	.97	4,052
African	84.7	9.2	6.2	1.78	.94	1,527
White	77.1	9.5	13.3	2.09	1.05	1,320
Coloured	88.4	5.0	6.5	1.82	.85	736
Asian origin	81.8	6.0	12.2	2.04	.97	452
Can't get much without group[e]						
All South Africans	46.4	22.4	31.1	2.79	1.26	4,008
African	47.4	22.1	30.4	2.77	1.29	1,518
White	40.8	23.5	35.7	2.89	1.17	1,295
Coloured	49.8	22.5	27.7	2.73	1.09	708
Asian origin	42.7	20.9	36.3	2.91	1.16	453

Item/Race	Agree (%)	Uncertain (%)	Disagree (%)	Mean	Std. dev.	N
Fate has to do with politics[f]						
All South Africans	52.3	20.2	27.6	2.67	1.24	3,995
African	56.1	21.9	21.9	2.54	1.21	1,506
White	41.3	14.8	43.9	3.03	1.27	1,307
Coloured	47.5	15.6	36.9	2.88	1.21	710
Asian origin	35.3	16.2	48.6	3.21	1.23	451

[a] Interracial difference of means: $p < .001$; $\eta = .18$.
[b] Interracial difference of means: $p > .001$; $\eta = .07$.
[c] Interracial difference of means: $p < .001$; $\eta = .04$.
[d] Interracial difference of means: $p > .001$; $\eta = .07$.
[e] Interracial difference of means: $p < .01$; $\eta = .02$.
[f] Interracial difference of means: $p < .001$; $\eta = .16$.

Note: The percentages are based on collapsing the five-point Likert response set (e.g., "agree strongly" and "agree" responses are combined), and total to 100% across the three columns (except for rounding errors). The means and standard deviations are calculated on the uncollapsed distributions. Lower mean scores indicate more agreement with the statement. The items read: "Of all the groups in South Africa, [MY GROUP] is best." "Even though I might sometimes disagree with the standpoint/viewpoint taken by [MY GROUP], it is extremely important to support [MY GROUP'S] point of view." "What happens to [MY GROUP] in South Africa will affect my life a great deal." "When it comes to politics, it is important for all of [MY GROUP] to stand together." "Unless you are a member of a group like [MY GROUP] it is very difficult to get much out of South African politics." "The well-being of [MY GROUP] has more to do with politics than it does with our own hard work."

group agree with this statement. Nearly all South Africans also believe that their group should "stand together." Indeed, preferences for strong "group solidarity" can be seen throughout these data. For instance, the second proposition in the table asserts that individuals should subordinate their individual interests to the interests of the group. A large majority of South Africans proclaim the importance of following the group's view, even when it differs from the individual's view. Variability across racial groups in the responses to this proposition is not substantial ($\eta = .07$), with only a somewhat larger percentage of Coloured respondents and a somewhat smaller proportion of whites asserting greater importance for the group than the individual. Overall, the data in Table 3.4 reveal considerable perceived political significance of these group identities. In contrast to nearly all other empirical findings from this survey, racial differences in these perceptions are quite unimportant. South Africans of every race recognize the political significance of groups.

We also asked the respondents to assess some propositions about the undesirable attributes of groups:

> "The way South Africa is right now, if one group gets more power it is usually because another group is getting less power."

> "The trouble with politics in South Africa is that it is always based on what group you are a member of."

> "If people don't realize we are all South Africans and stop thinking of themselves as Xhosa or Afrikaans or Zulu or whatever, South Africa will have a very difficult political future."

Table 3.5 reports the responses to these propositions. The data in this table reveal considerable antigroup sentiment among all South Africans. Consider the last statement first. Large majorities of each racial group assert that people should stop thinking of themselves in terms of narrow groups and instead think in terms of a larger South African identity. Similar antigroup sentiment is revealed in the responses to the other two statements. And in comparison to many if not most of the findings in this book, interracial differences in how people think about groups in the abstract are trivial. It seems from the various data presented here that many South Africans continue to think of themselves in terms of groups, but that many also would prefer that this not be so.

The Dimensionality of Group Identifications

When these various identity items are factor analyzed (Common Factor Analysis, with oblique rotation), four dimensions emerge.[12] The first factor is defined by the four group solidarity items, with the strongest loading associated with the statement about the importance of the group standing together. The second factor indicates the psychic benefits derived from one's group identity, with the three indicators strongly loading on the factor. The third factor concerns the political relevance of groups and is defined by the two statements about groups and

---

[12] The eigenvalue of the fifth extracted factor is a trivial .84.

TABLE 3.5. *General Attitudes Critical Toward Groups*

Item/Race	Agree (%)	Uncertain (%)	Disagree (%)	Mean	Std. dev.	N
Group power is zero-sum[a]						
All South Africans	75.3	14.6	10.1	2.09	.98	4,046
African	75.1	16.0	8.9	2.05	.98	1,521
White	73.1	11.2	15.8	2.27	1.03	1,333
Coloured	76.2	10.1	13.8	2.19	.93	734
Asian origin	69.1	13.7	17.2	2.37	.98	452
Politics is always based on groups[b]						
All South Africans	65.7	19.6	14.6	2.31	1.02	4,062
African	65.6	20.5	13.9	2.28	1.03	1,528
White	63.0	19.7	17.2	2.40	.99	1,334
Coloured	74.1	13.6	12.3	2.24	.89	732
Asian origin	65.2	16.0	18.8	2.40	1.00	457
Stop thinking of selves in group terms[c]						
All South Africans	76.8	11.1	12.1	1.99	1.08	4,071
African	76.5	12.2	11.3	1.98	1.09	1,535
White	71.1	11.5	17.4	2.19	1.09	1,339
Coloured	80.1	7.8	12.1	1.98	1.02	734
Asian origin	75.1	8.7	16.2	2.11	1.07	459

[a] Interracial difference of means: $p < .001$; $\eta = .11$.

[b] Interracial difference of means: $p < .001$; $\eta = .07$.

[c] Interracial difference of means: $p < .001$; $\eta = .09$.

Note: The percentages are based on collapsing the five-point Likert response set (e.g., "agree strongly" and "agree" responses are combined), and total to 100% across the three columns (except for rounding errors). The means and standard deviations are calculated on the uncollapsed distributions. Lower mean scores indicate more agreement with the statement. The items read: "The way South Africa is right now, if one group gets more power it is usually because another group is getting less power." "The trouble with politics in South Africa is that it is always based on what group you are a member of." "If people don't realize we are all South Africans and stop thinking of themselves as Xhosa or Afrikaans or Zulu or whatever, South Africa will have a very difficult political future."

politics. Finally, the fourth factor is comprised of the three antigroup variables. In general, the factor structure is extremely clean and clear, with each item loading on its hypothesized dimension. Because oblique rotation was employed, the factors are themselves intercorrelated;

the strongest relationship is between the group solidarity factor and the factor assessing the political relevance of groups ($r = -.46$). Furthermore, those who derive psychological benefits from their group membership are likely to believe in the need for group solidarity, to see groups as politically relevant, and to reject the statements about the undesirable qualitites of group-based politics.

Racial differences on these four indices are moderate (and of course statistically significant). Africans are considerably more likely than others to derive psychic benefits from their identities, are the most likely to advocate group solidarity, are the least likely to hold antigroup attitudes, and are the most likely (but only slightly so) to judge groups to be relevant to South African politics. I should note, however, that race accounts for no more than 14% of the variance in these various indices, so in contrast to substantive land attitudes, racial differences on the identity variables are somewhat muted.

Strong group attachments can be defined as deriving benefits from group membership, believing in the need for group solidarity, recognizing the political relevance of groups, and rejecting antigroup propositions. To derive a measure of the overall strength of one's group identity, I have simply taken the mean of the four indices.[13] This measure is related to the ascribed importance of one's group attachment within each racial group, although the relationship is weak among Africans.

Summary

There can be no doubt that group identities are important in South Africa for blacks, whites, Coloured people, and those of Asian origin. The importance of these associations is documented by the finding that people derive a series of psychic benefits from their identities. Given that group conflict has shaped much of the politics of the country for at least the last century or so, this finding should not surprise anyone.

---

[13] When factor analyzed in a second-order analysis, the four factors reveal a strongly unidimensional structure.

This analysis also reveals that race alone provides only a limited understanding of group politics in South Africa. Only 14.5% of black South Africans select "black" as their primary group identity, with another 26.8% selecting "African." Only 6.2% of whites identify as "white." Among Coloured people, less than one-third (30.7%) accept the designation "Coloured," and among those of Asian origin, only 24.1% think of themselves primarily as "Indian." Thus, within each racial grouping, great variability exists in the group attachments that people define for themselves.

National identities are fairly widespread, even if they may be declining somewhat in contemporary South Africa. Large majorities of South Africans derive a sense of pride from associating with their country. Most important, and contrary to some earlier existing findings, group identities are not inimical to national identities. Indeed, I have suggested that a generalized propensity to identify with groups may exist, and that therefore the antithesis of identifying with groups or nations is social atomization. Being South African and being Zulu or Xhosa or even Afrikaans does not detract from identifying as a South African.

Finally, racial differences are smaller on these identity items than on most questions in the survey. All groups in South Africa draw benefits from their identities, in part because nearly everyone recognizes the political significance of groups in the politics of the country, even while many may wish this were not so. Not many South Africans believe that groups can be ignored in contemporary politics. People do differ in their perceptions of the need for group solidarity – and that difference is important, as I will demonstrate later in this book – but individual differences are much stronger than group differences.

In the analysis that follows, I focus on three aspects of identity: (1) the degree of inclusiveness of the group to which the respondent is primarily attached, (2) the psychic benefits the person derives from the membership, and (3) the associated beliefs about groups – belief in the need for group solidarity, beliefs about the political relevance of groups, and antigroup attitudes. I do not further consider the simple importance individuals attach to their group identity since this is virtually a constant, with all respondents assigning a great deal of importance to their primary group membership. Nor do I pay much attention to patriotism, since it too is virtually a constant, with nearly all South Africans expressing a considerable degree of affection for their country. I define strong group identities as deriving large psychic benefits from group membership, asserting the need for group solidarity, believing that groups are highly relevant to contemporary South African politics, and rejecting antigroup ideas.

CONNECTING IDENTITIES TO LAND POLITICS

How might these group attachments shape attitudes toward land? As I noted in Chapter 2, interracial differences in land policy preferences are substantial: When the index of redistribution/restitution is regressed on a set of racial dummy variables, a whopping 37% of the variance can be explained. However, as always, race provides a particularly unsatisfying explanation of policy attitudes. What specifically is it about the beliefs, experiences, and attitudes of the various racial groups that actually accounts for the differences in policy preferences? Do group identities have anything to do with explaining variation in support for redistributive land policies, or instead are policy preferences instrumentally rational?

The Instrumental Hypothesis: Experiences Under Apartheid

Racial groups in South Africa differ mightily in terms of how they fared under apartheid, and perhaps these experiences provide some explanation of land policy attitudes. For instance, a rational South African would favor land redistribution if he or she would profit from it and would oppose it if direct or indirect costs were involved. Several indicators of the degree to which the respondent would benefit from land redistribution/restitution are included in this analysis:

Whether the respondent is a squatter (i.e., living on land owned by others without their permission).
Whether the respondent claims to have a historical land grievance. This is a subjective response that has not been verified; it is simply the assertion of the respondent.
Whether the respondent has filed a formal claim for land restitution.
More generally, the degree to which the respondent claims to have suffered injuries under the apartheid system.

The degree to which the respondent views his or her own land as being currently at risk.

In this analysis, I control for the respondent's social class, under the hypothesis that redistribution/restitution will be paid for in part from the government treasury, and hence from taxes on the people, with the wealthy paying more.[14] Table 3.6 reports the results from this analysis.[15]

The first thing to note from this table is that historical experiences and grievances provide only a weak explanation of land policy attitudes, especially among black and white South Africans (see the R^2 statistics). Among blacks, those with historical land grievances are more likely to favor redistribution; however, those who have made claims for land restitution are somewhat *less likely* to favor redistribution. Perhaps claimants fear that opening up the process of redistribution in general would be harmful to their specific claims. Again, however, I note that these relationships are actually weak and that self-interestedness is simply not a very useful explanation of policy attitudes (as it rarely is; see Funk 2000). And despite growing class differences among black South Africans, social class provides no predictive ability when it comes to land policy preferences.

Among whites, the relationships are also weak. The positive but small coefficient linking social class with policy preferences indicates that whites of higher social class tend to favor *more* redistribution, although the relationship really is quite weak. The data also reveal a slight tendency for those claiming greater injuries from apartheid to be more supportive of redistribution. But since few whites claim injuries from apartheid, these relationships are feeble indeed.

Among Coloured people, policy attitudes reflect to some degree the extent of land grievances: Those who claim to have been subjected to more historical land injustice are more likely to favor redistribution. A weak social class effect (in the hypothesized direction) is documented

---

[14] According to an OLS analysis, 38% of the variance in social class is associated with race, with whites being dramatically better off than blacks, while South Africans of Asian origin and Coloured people are somewhat better off than blacks. Seekings and Nattrass (2002) assert that the class cleavage is quickly overtaking the race cleavage in contemporary South African politics.

[15] See the Appendix to this chapter for the measurement of these constructs.

TABLE 3.6. *The Influence of Instrumental Considerations on Land Policy Preferences*

Race/Criterion	r	b	s.e.	β
African				
Whether respondent is a squatter	.03	.03	.02	.03
Has historical land grievances	.12	.02	.00	.14***
Number of land claims	−.05	−.02	.01	−.11***
Number of harms from apartheid	.07	.00	.00	.04
Fears that others might claim my land	.07	.00	.00	.02
Social class	.04	.01	.01	.06*
Intercept		.71	.01	
Standard deviation − dependent variable		.15		
Standard error of estimate		.15		
R²				.03***
N		1,455		
White				
Whether respondent is a squatter	n/a	n/a	n/a	n/a
Has historical land grievances	.04	.00	.01	.01
Number of land claims	.05	.01	.01	.03
Number of harms from apartheid	.10	.03	.01	.10***
Fears that others might claim my land	.04	.00	.01	.02
Social class	.11	.03	.01	.11***
Intercept		.31	.02	
Standard deviation − dependent variable		.17		
Standard error of estimate		.17		
R²				.02***
N		1,233		
Coloured				
Whether respondent is a squatter	n/a	n/a	n/a	n/a
Has historical land grievances	.20	.02	.01	.18***
Number of land claims	.07	−.00	.01	−.01
Number of harms from apartheid	.09	.00	.00	.01
Fears that others might claim my land	.11	.01	.01	.04
Social class	−.08	−.02	.01	−.09*

Race/Criterion	r	b	s.e.	β
Intercept		.60	.01	
Standard deviation – dependent variable		.14		
Standard error of estimate		.14		
R²				.05**
N		673		
Asian origin				
Whether respondent is a squatter	n/a	n/a	n/a	n/a
Has historical land grievances	.18	.02	.01	.12*
Number of land claims	.19	.04	.01	.16**
Number of harms from apartheid	.18	.02	.01	.13**
Fears that others might claim my land	.08	−.01	.01	−.06
Social class	.04	.01	.01	.03
Intercept		.44	.02	
Standard deviation – dependent variable		.15		
Standard error of estimate		.15		
R²				.07***
N		438		

Note: n/a coefficient cannot be calculated owing to insufficient variance in the variable. Significance of standardized regression coefficient (β): ***$p < .001$, **$p < .01$, *$p < .05$.

in the multivariate equation, but, while statistically significant, the coefficient is nearly trivial.

The greatest purchase on land policy preferences is found among those of Asian origin. Support for redistribution is greatest among those who have lodged a claim to land, who assert greater injuries from apartheid, and who claim more historical land grievances. Asian land claimants support redistributive policies, whereas, as was documented above, black land claimants do not. Social class does not differentiate among the policy preferences of South Africans of Asian origin.

The most general conclusion from this analysis is that there appears to be far more to land redistribution attitudes than self-interested instrumentalism. It seems that many blacks favor redistribution even though they do not assert injustices from the past; many whites oppose redistribution even though they would not be directly harmed by such policies. The politics of land in South Africa may have more to do with a generalized sense of injustice than a specific claim to compensation for injuries from the past.[16]

THE LARGER SYMBOLIC CONTEXT OF LAND

From the analysis marshaled to this point, evidence has been produced showing that land policy preferences are not driven by instrumental concerns; instead, they may have more to do with the larger symbolic issues of historical injustices under colonialism and apartheid. In order to consider the connection between support for redistribution and symbolic concerns, this section of the analysis assesses whether land preferences are connected to more abstract and diffuse values, as well as to more specific beliefs about and knowledge of the past. The attitudes I consider are (1) the valuation one attaches to the symbol of land, (2) whether private property rights are deemed sacrosanct, (3) general support for the rule of law, (4) willingness to blame whites for contemporary land inequality, (5) willingness to blame blacks for contemporary land inequality, and (6) knowledge of South African land history. Each of these concepts was explicated and operationalized in Chapter 2. For the multivariate analysis, I hypothesize that greater support for redistributive policy is associated with: greater symbolic valuation attached to land, the sanctity assigned to private property rights, willingness to blame whites for contemporary land inequality, willingness

---

[16] In research such as this, debates always emerge about whether self-interest is adequately captured by the measures employed. If one takes a quite broad view of self-interest, then interests are always implicated and the theory is tautological. For example, I could be said to profit from the murder of my wife because, by society punishing the murder, it reaffirms and reinforces the norm that murder is improper, thereby giving me solace and perhaps even reducing the chances of murder – even my murder – happening in the future, which is of course to my benefit. In the instance of land interests in South Africa, given that there is a formal claims process by which South Africans can assert their grievances – and given that the survey measures treat grieving and claiming in extremely broad terms and without requiring verification – the indicators of interests are unusually valid. Note as well that these conditions are, according to Citrin and Green (1990, 22), among those most likely to generate an influence of self-interest: "the critical elements in this regard [the conditions under which self-interests are influential] refer to the nature of the stakes and the ability of citizens to perceive the personal costs and benefits involved." Land restitution and retribution in South Africa clearly satisfy these criteria.

to blame blacks for contemporary land inequality, general commitments to the rule of law, and historical knowledge of land injustices in South Africa. Table 3.7 reports the regression results.

The analysis in the table supports a variety of conclusions. First, as reflected in the R^2 statistics, a considerable portion of the variance in land policy preferences can be accounted for by these attitudes. Obviously, the interconnections of these various indicators are reasonably strong.

Second, land policy preferences are fairly strongly connected to beliefs about the symbolic value of land and the importance of private property rights. An exception to this general finding is found among whites: How white South Africans feel about land as a symbolic issue is entirely unconnected to policy preferences. Among Africans, Coloured people, and those of Asian origin, however, the stronger the symbolic attachment to land, the greater the commitment to redistributive policies. The relationship is particularly noteworthy among those of Asian origin.

Among all four racial groups, the stronger the commitment to private property, the *less* likely one is to favor redistributive land policies. This finding is not, strictly speaking, a function of beliefs in the rule of law, since the effect of rule-of-law attitudes is statistically and substantively insignificant for all South Africans. It seems likely that the connection with private property reflects the position that those who currently hold property ought to be secure in their holdings, and therefore land redistribution should not take place. That rule-of-law attitudes are not important in explaining variation in support for redistributive policies may reflect the assumption of most South Africans that land redistribution will (and should) be implemented in accordance with the rule of law.

The findings regarding blame attributes are also interesting. Among all racial groups, the more one blames whites for contemporary inequities in land ownership in South Africa, the more likely one is to favor redistribution. This is not surprising. But among whites (and to a lesser degree, among those of Asian origin), policy attitudes also reflect the willingness to attribute blame to blacks themselves. To the extent that white people blame blacks for land inequality, they are unwilling to support redistributive land policies. Among blacks and Coloured South Africans, policy preferences are unconnected to beliefs about whether blacks themselves are to blame.

TABLE 3.7. *The Influence of Symbolic Values on Land Policy Preferences*

Race/Criterion	r	b	s.e.	β
African				
Symbolic value of land	.35	.25	.02	.27***
Sanctity of private property	−.33	−.26	.02	−.27***
Support for the rule of law	−.05	.01	.02	.01
Blaming whites for land inequality	.23	.17	.03	.19***
Blaming blacks for land inequality	.09	−.10	.03	−.06*
Knowledge of South African land history	.07	.01	.00	.03
Intercept		.55	.03	
Standard deviation − dependent variable		.15		
Standard error of estimate		.14		
R²				.22***
N		1,435		
White				
Symbolic value of land	.14	−.01	.02	−.01
Sanctity of private property	−.29	−.22	.03	−.22***
Support for the rule of law	−.06	.03	.03	.03
Blaming whites for land inequality	.26	.28	.03	.03
Blaming blacks for land inequality	.00	−.17	.03	−.19***
Knowledge of South African land history	.17	.02	.00	.13***
Intercept		.48	.03	
Standard deviation − dependent variable		.17		
Standard error of estimate		.15		
R²				.17***
N		1,183		
Coloured				
Symbolic value of land	.31	.16	.03	.20***
Sanctity of private property	−.31	−.19	.04	−.20***
Support for the rule of law	−.14	−.10	.03	−.06
Blaming whites for land inequality	.32	.22	.04	.28***
Blaming blacks for land inequality	.19	−.04	.04	−.05
Knowledge of South African land history	.05	.00	.01	.03

Race/Criterion	r	b	s.e.	β
Intercept		.55	.04	
Standard deviation – dependent variable		.14		
Standard error of estimate		.13		
R²				.22***
N		706		
Asian origin				
Symbolic value of land	.42	.24	.04	.31***
Sanctity of private property	−.39	−.24	.05	−.23***
Support for the rule of law	−.10	−.03	.04	−.03
Blaming whites for land inequality	.22	.16	.05	.20***
Blaming blacks for land inequality	.08	−.10	.05	−.11
Knowledge of South African land history	.06	.01	.01	.06
Intercept		.51	.05	
Standard deviation – dependent variable		.15		
Standard error of estimate		.13		
R²				.26***
N		434		

Note: Significance of standardized regression coefficient (β): ***$p < .001$, **$p < .01$, *$p < .05$.

In general, support for redistribution does not require knowledge of South African land history: The relationship between knowledge and policy preferences is trivial for Africans, Coloured people, and South Africans of Asian origin. Among whites, however, those who know more about the past are more likely to support redistributive policies. The relationship is weak but is statistically significant.[17]

Finally, when the instrumental variables from Table 3.6 are added to the equation shown in Table 3.7, none of the coefficients for the symbolic attitudes changes in any substantively meaningful way. However, among Africans, Coloured people, and South Africans of Asian origin, the coefficient for grievances exceeds .10, although for none

---

[17] Interestingly, little relationship exists within any group between knowledge of South Africa's land history and willingness to blame either blacks or whites for contemporary land inequality. Nor do I find any interesting interactive effects of land knowledge.

does the coefficient exceed .14 (and the coefficient for whites is trivial, as it should be). Thus, in an equation with both instrumental and symbolic variables, the overwhelming influences on land policy attitudes are the symbolic measures. Instrumentalism provides very little explanation of why some South Africans seek land redistribution and others do not.

The analysis to this point has not incorporated hypotheses about the role of group identities in the formation of policy preferences. Before doing so, it is first necessary to consider how historical and contemporary injustices shape land policy preferences.

Adding the Past to the Equation: Historical versus Contemporary Explanations of Land Attitudes

I begin considering historical explanations of land attitudes by investigating what criteria the respondents believe ought to govern land policy. We asked the respondents: "At the moment, there are many different factors that might influence land policy in South Africa. Would you say that land policy should give high importance, some importance, not very much importance, or no importance to making up for land injustices in the past?" As I noted in Chapter 2, the views of most South Africans on land policy reflect a mixture of contemporary and historical criteria. In the present, most ascribe great importance to following the rule of law, most applaud the objective of reducing land inequality, and most believe that the greatest benefits ought to go to the hardest workers. As for the past, South Africans are more strongly divided, with whites in particular generally unwilling to assert that past injustices should shape contemporary land policies.

To what degree is support for redistributive land policies a function of these various policy criteria? As expected, these factors fairly strongly predict substantive policy positions, accounting for 15 to 25% of the variance in land attitudes (see Table 3.8). Among black South Africans, favoring redistributive policy is most closely connected to the belief that land ought to be taken away from those who acquired it unfairly ($\beta = .22$), to the desire to ensure that those suffering most under apartheid get more land ($\beta = .20$), and to the preference for reducing unequal access to land ($\beta = .19$). Thus, past injustices clearly and strongly influence contemporary policy preferences.[18]

White policy preferences also reflect concerns about past injustices. The strongest predictor of redistributive policy support is the criterion of making up for past injustices ($\beta = .27$), and past suffering and having land unfairly taken in the past are also important criteria for whites. In addition, and in contrast to black Africans, those more strongly emphasizing the rule of law are less supportive of redistribution. The rule of law thus seems to be a mechanism by which the inequities of the past are reinforced, at least among white South Africans.

The attitudes of Coloured people are shaped by the same factors structuring the attitudes of whites. For instance, Coloured people similarly emphasize past injustices, just as commitments to the rule of law undermine redistribution. In nearly all respects, white and Coloured South Africans emphasize the same criteria as the basis of contemporary land policy, despite their quite different treatment under apartheid.

South Africans of Asian origin are unique in the emphasis they would give to hard work ($\beta = .15$), with the tendency to justify land redistribution by the contemporary attributes of the beneficiaries. South Africans of Asian origin also place the strongest priority on restitution for land unfairly confiscated in the past, just as do black people.

The various criteria reported in Table 3.8 can be classified as primarily emphasizing present or past factors in formulating land policy. Three of the criteria about which we asked the respondents concern contemporary considerations: following the rule of law, reducing current land inequality, and rewarding those who work the hardest. These are all criteria on which land policies might be based with total disregard to the country's apartheid and colonial past. Citizens emphasizing these factors are focusing on contemporary criteria in formulating land policy in the country. The other criteria about which we asked directly concern the past, as in basing land policy on making up for past injustices, ensuring that those who suffered most in the

---

[18] One might expect the first item in this table ("Making up for past injustices") to be one of the best predictors of land policy preferences, and in fact the bivariate correlations are of moderate magnitude. Because responses to this item reflect a general viewpoint, the variable is strongly intercorrelated with the other independent variables, and, in the analysis for some groups, multicollinearity reduces the multivariate coefficient to insignificance.

TABLE 3.8. *The Influence of Present and Past Considerations on Land Policy Preferences*

Race/Criterion	r	b	s.e.	β
African				
Making up for past injustices	.23	.01	.01	.03
Reduce unequal access to land	.35	.10	.01	.19***
Ensuring hardest workers get more	.21	.01	.01	.02
Strictly following the law	.22	.02	.01	.04
Ensuring those suffering most get more	.34	.09	.01	.20***
Taking away land unfairly acquired	.37	.10	.01	.22***
Intercept		2.65	.07	
Standard deviation – dependent variable		.61		
Standard error of estimate		.54		
R^2				.23***
N		1,434		
White				
Making up for past injustices	.35	.12	.02	.27***
Reduce unequal access to land	.24	.03	.02	.07*
Ensuring hardest workers get more	.10	−.02	.01	−.05
Strictly following the law	−.01	−.08	.02	−.15***
Ensuring those suffering most get more	.32	.11	.02	.19***
Taking away land unfairly acquired	.28	.07	.02	.14***
Intercept		2.04	.07	
Standard deviation – dependent variable		.66		
Standard error of estimate		.59		
R^2				.21***
N		1,154		
Coloured				
Making up for past injustices	.27	.10	.02	.19***
Reduce unequal access to land	.22	.04	.02	.08
Ensuring hardest workers get more	.20	.02	.02	.04
Strictly following the law	.07	−.08	.03	−.13***
Ensuring those suffering most get more	.27	.06	.02	.16***
Taking away land unfairly acquired	.25	.07	.02	.16***
Intercept			2.86	.10
Standard deviation – dependent variable		.58		
Standard error of estimate		.54		
R^2				.15***
N		709		

Race/Criterion	r	b	s.e.	β
Asian origin				
Making up for past injustices	.32	.04	.03	.09
Reduce unequal access to land	.31	.04	.03	.08
Ensuring hardest workers get more	.30	.07	.02	.15***
Strictly following the law	.29	.04	.03	.07
Ensuring those suffering most get more	.34	.02	.03	.04
Taking away land unfairly acquired	.43	.13	.02	.27***
Intercept		2.11	.10	
Standard deviation – dependent variable		.60		
Standard error of estimate		.52		
R^2				.25***
N		427		

Note: Significance of standardized regression coefficient (β): ***$p < .001$, **$p < .01$, *$p < .05$.

past get more land today, and taking land away from those who acquired it unfairly.

On the basis of two simple summated indices representing concern with the present and concern with the past, very strong interracial differences exist regarding the importance of the past, and less strong differences regarding the present are found in the data, with eta statistics of .49 and .26, respectively.[19] Black South Africans are substantially more likely to assert the importance of criteria grounded in the past (mean = 3.7), followed closely by Coloured people (mean = 3.6). Those of Asian origin are less concerned about the past (mean = 3.0), and whites are the least concerned of all (mean = 2.5).

Table 3.9 reports the results of regressing policy preferences on the indices of past and contemporary criteria. Several aspects of the results are noteworthy. First, a moderate degree of variance can be explained by these simple equations, ranging from 13% among Coloured people to 22% among those of Asian origin and blacks. Second, the intercepts

---

[19] I do not contend that contemporary and historical criteria are locked in zero-sum tension in the minds of most South Africans. Indeed, there is a reasonably strong connection between preferring that policy be based on criteria grounded in the past and that it be based on contemporary factors ($r > .5$).

TABLE 3.9. *Reliance on Contemporary and Historical Justice Criteria in Forming Land Redistribution Preferences*

Race/Criterion	r	b	s.e.	β
African				
Historical injustices	.44	.89	.07	.34***
Contemporary injustices	.37	.48	.08	.18***
Intercept		2.95	.05	
Standard deviation – dependent variable		.61		
Standard error of estimate		.54		
R^2				.22***
N		1,527		
White	.41	1.24	.08	.47***
Historical injustices	.14	−.28	.08	−.11***
Contemporary injustices				
Intercept		2.20	.04	
Standard deviation – dependent variable		.66		
Standard error of estimate		.60		
R^2				.18***
N		1,254		
Coloured				
Historical injustices	.36	.88	.11	.35***
Contemporary injustices	.22	.02	.12	.01
Intercept		2.99	.07	
Standard deviation – dependent variable		.58		
Standard error of estimate		.54		
R^2				.13***
N		726		
Asian origin				
Historical injustices	.45	.75	.13	.33***
Contemporary injustices	.40	.44	.14	.18**
Intercept		2.46	.06	
Standard deviation – dependent variable		.59		
Standard error of estimate		.52		
R^2				.22***
N		445		

Note: Significance of standardized regression coefficients (β): ***$p < .001$, **$p < .01$, *$p < .05$.

across the four groups vary, indicating that not all interracial variation can be accounted for with these two indices. Third, for all four groups, the criteria based in the past best predict policy preferences, with standardized regression coefficients ranging from .33 among those of Asian origin to .47 among whites. Those who care more about the past are more likely to favor redistribution. But, fourth, different patterns of influence characterize the various groups. Among blacks and those of Asian origin, both contemporary and historical factors are important in showing redistributive preferences, although historical factors bear considerably more weight. Among Coloured people, only the past matters, with contemporary injustices receiving very little weight.

Finally, a quite interesting pattern emerges among whites. Historical injustices are the influential criteria, no doubt reflecting the fact that the variation among whites ranges from discounting the past among the majority to according it weight among a relatively small minority. But more significant is the negative (and statistically significant) coefficient for contemporary injustices. One might be tempted to attribute this to the unwanted effects of multicollinearity between the two independent variables (although the relationship is not markedly higher among whites as compared with the other racial groups), but instead this might represent a substantively meaningful relationship. After taking into account the past, whites are likely to oppose redistributive policy the more they judge contemporary factors to be important. In some sense, the past and present are locked in a weak zero-sum relationship. Perhaps this reflects the view among many whites that "the debt to blacks has been paid" through transition and transformation, Black Empowerment, and Affirmative Action and that, after the payment, further redistribution is not justified. If white South Africans could be made to focus more on the past, then support for redistributive policy would follow, but few whites are willing to deal with the past. Instead, whites emphasize the present, and these criteria lead to the opposition to redistribution. Thus, it is not surprising that so few whites support redistributive land policies.

How one feels about the land issue depends to considerable degree on whether past injustices are deemed relevant. A basic fact of land politics is that whites do not want to address the past; blacks do.

SOCIAL IDENTITIES AND LAND POLICY PREFERENCES

The first step in my analysis of social identities is simply to assess whether the various aspects of identity directly influence land policy preferences and/or the weight attached to present and past criteria in forming these preferences. Table 3.10 reports the results. Because the nature of group identities differs within the nominal race groups, I consider these relationships separately for blacks, whites, Coloured people, and those of Asian origin.[20]

Among black South Africans, several aspects of group identities are indeed associated with support for redistributive land policies. Those ascribing greater importance to group solidarity are considerably more likely to support redistribution. Similar but weaker relationships are found with the rejection of antigroup sentiment and the adoption of an ethnic identity (as compared with the excluded group, those selecting a national identity). A weak negative relationship exists with the political relevance indicator: Those who believe groups are relevant to politics are somewhat *less* likely to support redistribution. Not much emphasis should be given to this finding, however, since it is weak, and since the political relevance index is strongly correlated with the group solidarity measure. In general, whether black South Africans support redistributive land policies depends to some degree on the strength of their attachments to their national, racial, or ethnic group.

The findings for whites are quite different. Whereas group solidarity is associated with greater support among blacks for redistributive policies, whites who assert the need for solidarity are *less* likely to support redistribution. Relatedly, adopting an ethnic identity among whites (e.g., Afrikaans) is associated with opposition to redistribution; among blacks, the relationship is in the opposite direction. Identities are less influential in shaping white policy attitudes, but generally stronger group attachments produce less support for redistribution.

Coloured identities are not terribly important in shaping policy attitudes. As with Africans, belief in group solidarity is associated with

---

[20] The logic of analysis dictates that group identities be analyzed within race. For instance, claiming an ethnic identity does not necessarily have the same meaning for the black majority as it does for the racial minorities in the country. Consequently, in the analysis that follows, the identity variables are used as predictors within racial groups.

TABLE 3.10. *The Influence of Group Identities on Land Policy Preferences*

Race/Criterion	r	b	s.e.	β
African				
Group solidarity	.27	.27	.03	.28***
Psychic benefits	.05	−.01	.02	−.02
Political relevance of groups	.05	−.07	.02	−.12***
Rejection of antigroup sentiment	.23	.15	.03	.16***
Whether racial identity	−.02	.02	.01	.05
Whether ethnic identity	.06	.04	.01	.14***
Intercept		.45	.03	
Standard deviation − dependent variable		.15		
Standard error of estimate		.14		
R²				.11***
N		1,326		
White				
Group solidarity	−.15	−.11	.04	−.12**
Psychic benefits	−.02	.03	.02	.07*
Political relevance of groups	−.15	−.05	.03	−.07
Rejection of antigroup sentiment	−.15	−.08	.03	−.08*
Whether racial identity	−.04	−.05	.02	−.07*
Whether ethnic identity	−.10	−.04	.01	−.12***
Intercept		.52	.02	
Standard deviation − dependent variable		.16		
Standard error of estimate		.16		
R²				.06***
N		1,012		
Coloured				
Group solidarity	.15	.11	.05	.11*
Psychic benefits	.06	.00	.02	.01
Political relevance of groups	.05	−.01	.03	−.01
Rejection of antigroup sentiment	.15	.10	.04	.10*
Whether racial identity	−.01	−.01	.01	−.02
Whether ethnic identity	−.02	−.01	.02	−.03
Intercept		.51	.03	
Standard deviation − dependent variable		.15		
Standard error of estimate		.14		

(*continued*)

TABLE 3.10. *(continued)*

Race/Criterion	r	b	s.e.	β
R²				.03**
N		646		
Asian origin				
Group solidarity	.06	−.09	.06	−.10
Psychic benefits	−.07	−.03	.02	−.06
Political relevance of groups	.24	.19	.04	.31***
Rejection of antigroup sentiment	.05	−.01	.05	−.02
Whether racial identity	−.11	−.04	.02	−.13**
Whether ethnic identity	−.07	−.13	.12	−.05
Intercept		.52	.04	
Standard deviation – dependent variable		.15		
Standard error of estimate		.14		
R²				.09***
N		405		

Note: Significance of standardized regression coefficient (β): ***$p < .001$, **$p < .01$, *$p < .05$.

more support for redistribution. However, the inclusiveness of Coloured identities has little to do with land attitudes.

Finally, those of Asian origin are similar to whites in the sense that greater group solidarity is connected to less support for redistribution. However, the distinctive aspect of Asian identities is that those who believe that groups are highly relevant to South African politics favor more redistribution of land.

These various analyses have identified few consistent findings about the role of specific aspects of group identities in shaping policy preferences. Most of the results are idiosyncratic to the specific group. Identities seem to determine land policy preferences, but not in any uniform way. Nonetheless, based on the summary index of the strength of group attachments, the data indicate that stronger identities are related to a preference for redistribution among blacks, Coloured people, and those of Asian origin, whereas among whites, stronger identities lead to opposition to redistribution. In general, strong group identities seem to tie people more closely to the interests of their group.

A second way to think about the influence of identities on policy preferences involves the hypothesis that those more closely connected to their group are more likely to weight historical injustices more heavily in deriving their preferences about land redistribution. The social identity and group history hypothesis is that identities influence land attitudes by specifying the criteria that people consider important as determinants of land policy. The simple hypothesis is that, among those oppressed under apartheid, stronger group identities are associated with more concern about historical injustices in South Africa. Among whites, on the other hand, I expect exactly the opposite relationship: Stronger group identities should be associated with lack of concern about historical injustices. Relatedly, those with a strong national identity I expect to be less concerned about historical injustices.

The first empirical question to review is whether reliance on the past varies by race, and within race by inclusiveness of identity. As I noted above, moderate differences exist across races in the weight attributed to contemporary factors ($\eta = .26$), but large differences are found on the weight given to historical influences ($\eta = .49$). Black and Coloured South Africans attribute considerably more weight to historical injustices.

Is variation in the influence of the past related to the inclusiveness of one's group identity? Some modest but interesting relationships appear in the data (see Table 3.11). Among blacks, the greatest weight is assigned to past injustices by those adopting a less inclusive ethnic identity. Conversely, those least likely to emphasize the past are those with a national identity. The differences are not great, but they are statistically significant at the .01 level.

What makes this relationship interesting, however, is that it is reversed among whites and those of Asian origin. Within these two groups, those subscribing to a national identity are most likely to place greater weight on past injustices. Thus, among blacks, a national identity is associated with caring less about the past; among white and those of Asian origin, a national identity is associated with caring more about the past. For whites, a national identity seems to be associated with taking responsibility for the past; for blacks, the same identity means moving on to the future. Among Coloured people, no effects of different types of identity are observed. For most, how one weights historical injustices in contemporary land policy preferences is to some degree a function of one's group identity.

To consider the identity hypothesis more comprehensively, I next regressed the index of historical criteria on the various identity

TABLE 3.11. *The Importance of Past Injustices in Shaping Land Policy Preferences According to the Degree of Inclusiveness of Group Identities*

Race/Importance of the past	Primary identity		
	National	Racial	Ethnic
African[a]			
Mean	.63	.68	.70
Std. dev.	.23	.25	.23
N	215	632	657
White[b]			
Mean	.41	.32	.35
Std. dev.	.26	.23	.24
N	465	91	441
Coloured[c]			
Mean	.65	.65	.64
Std. dev.	.23	.24	.22
N	203	246	96
Asian origin[d]			
Mean	.55	.47	–
Std. dev.	.25	.27	–
N	143	156	–

[a] Intraracial difference of means: $\eta = .08, p < .01$.
[b] Intraracial difference of means: $\eta = .13, p < .001$.
[c] Intraracial difference of means: $\eta = .02, p > .05$.
[d] Intraracial difference of means: $\eta = .15, p < .05$.

variables. Among blacks, reliance on the past is significantly associated with rejection of antigroup sentiments, the value of group solidarity, and the adoption of an ethnic identity. Among Coloured people, reliance on the past is associated with the value attached to group solidarity and rejection of the political relevance of groups. For whites, those who do not perceive the need for group solidarity and who primarily identify with the nation rather than with an ethnic group are more likely to attribute importance to historical injustices. Finally, for South Africans of Asian origin, reliance on the past is associated with deriving few benefits from group attachments and with the adoption of a national rather than ethnic identity. So again, the findings are specific to group, even if identities do influence the degree to which individuals weight historical injustices in contemporary policy preferences. The summary index of identity strength is connected to this dependent variable in much the same way as it is directly connected to land policy preferences, although the relationships are weaker among Coloured people and those of Asian origin. For those oppressed under apartheid, group identities connect people to the past. The same is true of whites, although group identities lead to rejecting the past, rather than embracing it.

DISCUSSION AND CONCLUDING COMMENTS

The analysis reported in this chapter addresses three primary issues. First, what is the nature of the attachments South Africans hold with their nation and with their racial and/or ethnic group? Second, how much do South Africans support redistributive land policies, and what accounts for the variability in such support? Finally, to what degree do these identities connect individuals to the land injustices of South Africa's past? Do some South Africans judge present policy by the past, and does willingness to do so depend on the nature of one's group identifications?

In terms of group identities, several findings stand out. First, among all South Africans, group attachments are quite significant. Most derive psychic benefits from identifying as a member of a group, and most see both the need for group solidarity and the political relevance of groups in South Africa. An important corrective is that perhaps not all South Africans view group-based politics as desirable, even if all recognize that it is pervasive in the country today.

It is also perhaps worth emphasizing that the survey found a moderate decline in willingness to identify with the nation as a whole. I have speculated that this may be a function of public policies such as Affirmative Action that reward race-based thinking. When government policies categorize and allocate benefits to people by their race, it is perhaps not surprising that people come to think about themselves in more racialized terms.

In terms of support for redistributive land policies, several findings deserve emphasis. One of the principal findings of this research is that support for redistributive land policy is widespread in South Africa.

South Africans want land illicitly taken in the past to be returned to its rightful owners, be it land expropriated by the apartheid system or by tribal leaders. Across the population as a whole, support for virtually any scheme of land redistribution or retribution is widespread.

However, racial differences on land policy preferences are enormous. Nearly one-fifth of blacks support *all* of the policies about which they were queried; almost one-third of whites supported *none* of the policies. Land may well be one of the most racially polarized issues in all of contemporary South African politics.

But what does "race" mean in this context? This analysis demonstrates that race is not simply a synonym for individual self-interest. Using a variety of measures of direct self-interestedness in the land problem, I find that expectations of benefits (or costs) from land issues – at least as indicated by the measures included here – exhibit only the weakest connection to policy preferences. One need not expect to benefit from the policy in order to prefer redistribution. This finding is not surprising, inasmuch as self-interest typically provides a terribly incomplete explanation of politics.

Instead, race is important in South Africa because it stands for a variety of symbolic concerns. Indeed, perhaps the most important conclusion of this analysis is that the land issue in South Africa is about far more than land. It is not simply that those dispossessed under apartheid and colonialism want their land back; self-interest provides a remarkably poor explanation of support for redistributive policy preferences. Instead, land is a symbol of the country's repressive past. Land policy preferences are deeply embedded in race; but what that means is not so much based on interracial differences in the present as it is on interracial differences grounded in the past. Africans stress far more heavily historical criteria as a basis for contemporary land policy; attachments to land as a symbol – especially of the country's colonial and apartheid pasts – strongly determine support for redistribution. Because policy preferences are inextricably tied to symbolic attitudes, one need not have a direct stake in the redistribution of land in order to favor even fairly radical proposals. Symbolic politics provides a means of linking those without common instrumental interests to each other and to the group's past. Because that is so, the land issue cannot be easily negotiated (and certainly is unlikely to be resolved through cash payouts to a limited number of claimants), and the issue is likely to remain salient and volatile.

This analysis also documents a vast cultural divide between blacks and whites in South Africa. Consider the issue of support for private property rights. Black South Africans are dramatically less committed to private property rights than are whites. This analysis reveals broad and significant interracial differences on a variety of symbolic values, including the value one attaches to land and support for the rule of law. Perhaps the chasm between blacks and whites is bridgeable, but these data suggest that a considerable portion of the disagreement over land policy has to do with more fundamental, and perhaps even obdurate, orientations toward land and property.

Another highly significant, and related, finding is that black South Africans are far more willing to take the past into consideration than whites in formulating their contemporary positions on land issues. To the extent that whites can be encouraged to focus on the past, support for redistribution increases (although I note that *knowledge* of the country's land past has practically no impact on contemporary preferences). Among the black majority in South Africa, the contemporary land problem is closely associated with the past injustices of apartheid and colonialism. Because that is so, the issue cannot be easily negotiated. The simple truth of land politics in South Africa today is that most believe that past injustices must be rectified by redistribution, whereas the powerful white minority is unwilling to take the past into account. Without addressing past injustices, most believe the present cannot be just. Land is thus an issue not of egocentric instrumentalism, but instead of sociotropic justice.

Finally, the most important hypothesis of this chapter is that group identities connect individuals to the past. The findings here are certainly not as crisp as one might prefer. Different aspects of identity seem to be important within the different racial groups in South Africa. But in general, the hypothesis receives some significant support. Except for whites, those who identify more strongly with their group are more likely to support policies that are designed to compensate for the injustices of the past. For whites, the opposite relationship exists: Strong identities are associated with an emphasis on the present and a relative insensitivity to the injustices of the past. Thus, group identities seem to provide a bridge between the present and the past. The development of a national identity weakens this connection, but, as I have noted, national identities have become less common in contemporary South Africa. Nonetheless, how narrowly one identifies one's group, and especially how one feels about the value of group solidarity, influences how one feels about the injustices of the past, and consequently structures policy preferences in the present. And whether justice prevails in South Africa will have much to do with whether the country's democratic transition will be consolidated.

This chapter has focused on general preferences for policy on the redistribution of land in South Africa. Although general policy preferences are certainly an important part of politics, how these policies get played out and applied is also crucial. The next two chapters therefore examine applied land policy preferences, with particular attention to the role of context in shaping these preferences.

APPENDIX TO CHAPTER 3: MEASUREMENT

Social Class

Social class is measured by three indicators: (1) the range of consumer goods the respondent owns, (2) interviewer assessments of the respondent's living standard, and (3) interviewer assessments of the respondent's social class. An index was created via factor analysis.

Land Grieving

The question stem read: "As a result of the history of our country, many South Africans believe that they have been unfairly deprived of land or land rights that is rightfully theirs. We are interested in whether you or your immediate family is involved in any of these issues. Do any of the following apply to you?"

> Believe land or land rights were unfairly taken from me or my immediate family in the past
> Was subjected to a forced removal
> Believe I have a right to the land on which I live, even though I do not legally own it
> Deprived of benefits, such as water rights, mineral rights, etc.

The response set was:

1. Definitely applies to me
2. Probably applies to me
3. Probably does not apply to me
4. Definitely does not apply to me

Sense of Land Vulnerability

The same stem and response set for land grieving were used as a preface on the land vulnerability question:

Believe that others might file claim of ownership to my land.

Land Claiming

For assessing land claims, the same stem and response set were also used: "And do any of the following apply to your circumstances?"

Have made a claim before a government agency
Have made a claim before a nongovernmental agency (such as church)
Have made a claim to the owner of the land
Have had a dispute with traditional leaders over my rights to land

Harms from Apartheid

Experiences under apartheid were assessed with the following questions (using a simple "yes/no" response set): "Here is a list of things that happened to people under apartheid. Please tell me which, if any, of these experiences you have had."

Required to move my residence
Lost my job because of apartheid
Was assaulted by the police
Was imprisoned by the authorities
Was psychologically harmed

Was denied access to the education of my choice
Was unable to associate with people of different race and colour
Had to use a pass to move about

Knowledge of South African History

We asked five questions about South Africa's history of land disposses-sions and apartheid.

"Now we would like to ask you some questions about South Africa's history. In which decade did the Nationalist Party government first introduce apartheid as the official policy of South Africa?"

1. 1910s
2. 1920s
3. 1930s
4. 1940s [correct]
5. 1950s
6. 1960s
7. 1970s
8. 1980s
9. 1990s

"Which of the following best defines the term 'black spot'?"

1. "Black spot" refers to land of a very high quality that was re-served for white farmers under apartheid.
2. "Black spot" refers to pockets of strong black opposition to the apartheid system.
3. "Black spot" refers to a nonwhite community living within an area designated for white people by the apartheid govern-ment. [correct]

"Which of the following best defines the term 'Bantustan'?"

1. A Bantustan is a form of tribal leadership found in some rural areas of South Africa.
2. A Bantustan is an area where black people were expected to live under apartheid. [correct]
3. A Bantustan is a farm owned and managed exclusively by black people.

"Under apartheid, many people were forced to leave their living places and move to other parts of the country. Do you know approximately how many people were forced to move under apartheid?"

1. None
2. Less than 100,000 people
3. Up to ½ million people
4. Up to 1 million people
5. About 1–2 million people
6. About 2–3 million people
7. 3 million people or more [correct]

"Do you know approximately when the last racially motivated forced removal took place in South Africa?"

1. 1910s
2. 1920s
3. 1930s
4. 1940s
5. 1950s
6. 1960s
7. 1970s
8. 1980s [correct]
9. 1990s

4

Applied Justice Judgments

The Problem of Squatting

In many cities throughout the world, governments are confronted with serious problems of "land grabbing" by poor people. As the landless poor flock to the urban areas, they often find that the only housing option available is to "squat": to occupy and live on a piece of vacant land. The slums of most cities in the world, and nearly all cities in the Third World, are brimming with squatters (see Neuwirth 2005, who estimates that there are more than one billion squatters in the world today).

Nowhere is this problem more acute than in South Africa.[1] With the crumbling of apartheid came the end of the much hated race-based restrictions on individual mobility. Consequently, the countryside has emptied as citizens have made their way to the cities in hopes of a better life. The first step toward this better life, however, is finding a place to live. For many, squatting is the only possibility. Squatting is not new to South Africa (e.g., Murray and O'Regan 1990; Field 2001), but the magnitude of the problem of urban land grabs is enormous, unprecedented, and growing. Virtually every piece of vacant land in South Africa's cities is at risk.

---

[1] In mid-2007, Robert Mugabe launched a new campaign ("Operation Murambatsvina") to rid Zimbabwe's cities of squatters, forcibly removing them to the countryside. It is possible that this policy could cause even further unrest in Zimbabwe, although some speculate that the president's motive is to diminish the supply of urban protesters should the economic and political situation deteriorate further.

Land grabbing is an extremely important problem for the homeless, for landowners, and for governments. But land grabbing also presents intriguing theoretical issues because it so clearly pits alternative conceptions of justice against each other. On the one hand, the sanctity of private (or state-owned) property may justify removing the squatters from their perches. On the other hand, the dire need of the squatters may make land grabbing fair, especially in the context of the historical injustices of apartheid and colonialism, and to evict people from their newly constructed homes is to consign them to live on the streets or worse. Squatting is classically an example of a clash of values (see Sniderman et al. 1996) – in this case, a clash of judgments of what is fair. An opportunity is therefore created to examine how *commonsense justice* works when competing justice values are at stake.

Understanding the dynamics of the issue of squatting requires dissecting how ordinary people think about justice and injustice, and especially conflicts among competing conceptions of justice. How do preferences get formed when justice considerations are in direct tension with each other? How do citizens adjudicate such conflicts when creating opinions about issues like landlessness and squatting? Can the unfairness of the past be reconciled with contemporary requirements of justice? And to what degree are conceptions of justice rooted in group attachments and social identity concerns, especially where race is such a salient aspect of land politics? These are the questions this chapter investigates.

The central focus of this chapter is on evaluations of an experimental vignette depicting a conflict between a squatter and a landowner. In analyzing how ordinary people reach conclusions about fair outcomes in such disputes, I explore the role of various types of justice – especially *distributive* and *procedural* – in shaping fairness judgments. Moreover, because South Africa is itself a multicultural context, this chapter analyzes how preferred theories of justice vary across the country's most important racial/ethnic/linguistic groups. Finally, I also investigate within-group differences, focusing on the role of group attachments and identities in structuring fairness judgments. Thus, the chapter's empirical strengths lie in the multicultural context in which the research is embedded, the realism and salience of the justice dispute on which I focus, and the power of the research design, combining both internal and external validity. Its theoretical strength lies in its integration of social identity theory with the psychology of justice.

THE PROBLEM OF SQUATTING AND ITS RELATIONSHIP TO
COMMONSENSE JUSTICE

As I argued in the introductory chapter to this book, extant research has shown that citizens typically evaluate justice claims using multidimensional frameworks. To understand the politics of such claims, one must be able to assess which justice domains are dominant, whether group identity concerns get activated, and how conflicts among justice domains are adjudicated. I turn now to applying these conclusions about justice to the issue of homelessness and squatting.

As in many countries throughout the world, the issue of land squatters in South Africa is politically significant and contentious (e.g., Huchzermeyer 2004). Squatting is caused by two dominant factors: (1) the massive influx of landless people from the countryside to the cities, and (2) the vast economic inequality in the country. The demand for urban housing is great, as poor South Africans stream to the cities in search of jobs and economic opportunity.[2] At the same time, the inequality in the country is so vast that large quantities of land are held by small numbers of people. Thus, the land issue is a classic example of distributive justice, pitting the have-nots against the haves.

But land is more than "just" an issue of economic inequality. Instead, overlaid on the inequality is the history of the injustices of colonialism and apartheid. The landless make claims to land not just out of their economic need, but also out of a sense of having been illegitimately dispossessed from their land since whites first arrived in South Africa. Thus, in addition to class conflict over land, group-based differences in how land issues are perceived and judged are likely to be profound. This sense of historical injustice interacts with contemporary inequality to create a volatile political brew.

The land issue is apposite for those studying the psychology of justice because different justice considerations are juxtaposed and conflict with one another. On the one hand, those who value the rule of law and the sanctity of private property have strong arguments against squatters. They say that land should not be expropriated without

---

[2] Squatting is not just an urban problem. More than 40,000 squatters are currently occupying the Modderklip farm, owned by a white South African, and the authorities will neither evict the squatters nor pay compensation to the land owner. The case continues in litigation. See, e.g., Fife 2004.

compensation, and certainly should not be expropriated without proper legal procedures. The advocates of this view point toward the lawless land grabs in Zimbabwe, where unseemly and disingenuous political motivations dominate the politics of land. The notion that the land of another can simply be taken by people in a democratic society seems entirely unfair, whatever the needs and motives of the landless.[3]

The advocates of the landless poor make different claims to justice, pointing to historical injustices initiated by the colonialists and perpetuated and exacerbated by the apartheid system.[4] Their claims are grounded primarily in theories of distributive justice (especially need, deservingness, and equality), although some also make claims based on retributive and restorative justice (redressing the injustices of the past). To them, a fair, postcolonial society would not allow millions of people to be homeless. Squatters therefore have justice – or at least one form of justice – on their side.

Owing to these historical injustices, squatting is an issue likely to stimulate group identity concerns. Indeed, any individual instance of squatting may be difficult to justify; it is primarily when the squatting issue is reconceptualized as a group demand for fairness that squatting acquires normative force. When identities are implicated, the criteria of justice change, emphasizing sociotropic rather than (or in addition to) egocentric concerns. Squatting thereby gets transformed into an issue of social status and group standing – in Tyler's phrase, into a relational or group value model of justice. Consequently, those with strong group identities are likely more willing to accept the justice claims of squatters.

Thus, the issue of squatting is one that implicates various justice considerations. Certainly distributive (and redistributive) justice is at issue in land squatting. Procedural justice considerations arise as well, especially in relation to the process of eviction. Retributive justice lurks

---

[3] I should mention in passing the connection between popular conceptions of land justice and larger issues of property rights institutions. To the extent that the justice requirements of ordinary people clash with property rights (and perhaps more generally with the rule of law), a series of important political and economic consequences follow. For a recent exploration of these various linkages, see North 2005, and especially Duch and Palmer 2004.

[4] One of the most militant organizations representing the landless poor is the Landless People's Movement. For their charter, see http://www.nlc.co.za/pubs2003/landlesscharter1.htm (accessed 3/31/2005).

in the background, as South Africans argue that land inequality is a function of historical injustices that must be redressed. Understanding how these various justice considerations get reconciled in the views of ordinary South Africans is therefore an issue of considerable theoretical and practical import.

Hypotheses and Experimental Vignettes

These questions of the nature of justice judgments are explored here via an experimental vignette. Vignettes are a particularly useful technology for incorporating the context of justice conflicts within survey research. These short stories can reveal processes of reasoning perhaps not even directly accessible to the respondents themselves. (They have been used widely in the past – e.g., Hamilton and Sanders 1992; Gibson and Gouws 1999; Gibson 2002; Duch and Palmer 2004.)[5] For the purposes of the questions addressed in this chapter, experimental vignettes – especially when embedded in a representative national survey – provide an optimal methodology.[6] The vignettes allow me to assess how South Africans apply various principles of justice to complex social issues like squatting.

The analysis reported here is an inquiry into how justice judgments are made in the context of squatting. Following the literature on distributive fairness, I focus on two distributive justice claims typically voiced by squatters: a claim of need and a claim of deservingness (see Miller 1991 on various criteria of distributive justice, and Smith 2002 on deservingness). I also hypothesize that the "need" of the landowner influences justice judgments. Finally, following the vast literature on proceduralism (e.g., Tyler et al. 1997), fairness judgments are hypothesized to be a function of the procedural justice extended to the squatter. The general

---

[5] Robinson and Darley assert (1998, 417) that we cannot ask people directly about their mental processes "[b]ecause psychologists have discovered that subjects often do not have mental access to the principles and processes they use to make decisions, and thus cannot accurately articulate those principles. Instead, researchers present subjects with various cases to judge, and infer their judging principles from the resulting patterning of responses between the different cases."

[6] Experiments with random assignment of subjects to treatments (like this experiment) have numerous advantages, including strong internal validity (i.e., confidence in causal inferences). When included within a representative survey, external validity (the ability to generalize the findings) is also maximized. On experimentation in political science, see Kinder and Palfrey 1993.

hypothesis tested is that when procedural and distributive justice are denied in squatting disputes, the outcome of such disputes will be judged to be more unfair. Because distributive and procedural justice elements are manipulated in the experimental vignette (and thus are at odds with each other), the analysis investigates how a mix of justice considerations influences judgments of fairness in squatting disputes.

Nearly all of the analysis that follows posits (and finds) that justice judgments are influenced by the race of the respondent. Race is strongly implicated in the vignettes presented to the respondents, but I defer consideration of that issue until the explication of the vignettes (below).

THE EXPERIMENT – THE SQUATTER VIGNETTE

Two experimental vignettes were included in the survey,[7] with one-half of the respondents (randomly selected) hearing a vignette about Patience, a squatter. Within this subsample, respondents were randomly assigned to one of 16 versions of the squatter vignette. The 16 renditions of the story were created from four dichotomous experimental variables, in a fully crossed $2 \times 2 \times 2 \times 2$ factorial design. Given face-to-face interviews with paper copies of the questionnaire in multiple languages, minor imperfections in the administration of the survey resulted in variability from as few as the 114 respondents who were read version 11 of the vignette to the 144 people hearing vignette number 1. Variability of this magnitude is of no practical consequence. As an upshot of the design, the four dichotomous independent variables are themselves orthogonal; the maximum observed correlation among the dummy variables representing the manipulations is $-.019$.[8]

---

[7] In general, the interviewers judged the respondents to have understood the vignettes "well," with 71.6% of the respondents so scored. This figure is higher than the 65.0% of the respondents who were judged to understand well the other questions in the survey. These ratings are to some degree grounded in reality, since they are correlated with the number of times the story was reread to the respondent ($r = .14$, $p < .000$). Only 7.0% of the respondents understood the vignettes less well than the other questions in the survey; 13.5% were judged to understand the vignettes better than the other questions.

[8] The vignette was subjected to extensive pretesting prior to going into the field, including a large pretest with South African college students, as well as the pretest of the full questionnaire (including the vignettes) with a sample of ordinary South Africans.

The vignette tells a story about a squatter, Patience, and her family. As I have noted, it is common in South Africa for squatters to set up housing on apparently vacant land. Land owners have become extremely vigilant and act with considerable speed to dislodge squatters, since allowing these encampments to become established creates legal and political capital for the squatters, rendering their eviction far more difficult.[9] Because squatters are routinely evicted in contemporary South Africa, all versions of the vignette conclude with Patience and her family being removed from the property.[10] This obviously limits the generalizability of the findings in the sense that the vignette tells us little about fairness judgments in the context of successful land grabs.[11] Nonetheless, the vignette depicts the outcome that was most common for squatters at the time of the survey.[12]

The squatter vignette sought to determine how various types of justice considerations affect judgments of the fairness of outcomes in disputes over land grabs. The specific hypotheses are drawn from diverse theories of fairness and justice.

Distributive Justice – The Subordinate Party's Need. The experiment asserted a conflict between a landless person, Patience (and her family), and a land owner. Clearly implied in the vignette is class conflict between land owners and the landless. The need of the squatter was varied from ordinary need to dire need (few if any squatters have low levels of housing need). The two versions of the vignette are:

> *Dire Need*: Patience and her family are squatters. They are squatting because they want to live in the city, but have no other place to live.

---

[9] The law on squatting in South Africa is highly fluid, reflecting the considerable litigation that is ongoing. The most recent national legislation on squatting (which repealed a great deal of earlier law) is the Prevention of Illegal Eviction from and Unlawful Occupation of Land Act, 1998.

[10] Note as well that since "negative events elicit more attributional activity than do positive events" (Skitka 2003, 287), all vignettes conclude with the eviction of the squatter.

[11] Some land grabs are indeed successful. One of the most stunning examples is the Imizamo Yethu squatter camp established in Hout Bay (a Cape Town suburb).

[12] An important principle of vignette development is verisimilitude. That is, vignettes seek to identify the relevant elements of political contexts, determine how they vary, conceptualize them in theoretical terms (e.g., fit the elements to theories of justice), and operationalize them in concrete terms meaningful to survey respondents (e.g., Gibson and Gouws 2003). Vignettes consequently require a considerable amount of contextual knowledge and understanding of political controversies.

Ordinary Need: Patience and her family are squatters. They are squatting because they think the place where they are currently living is too far away from the place where Patience works.

According to the first statement, Patience has no place to live; the second statement asserts that she has a place to live, but that it is inconvenient to her working place. Of course, if Patience is willing to give up her current living place to squat elsewhere, then her current place of living is probably not very adequate. Moreover, in the South African context, living too far away from one's workplace implies as much as two hours of travel time, each way, to and from work. The hypothesis tested is that when the squatter is presented as having a more substantial need for housing, evicting her will be judged to be more unjust.

Although the race of the squatter is not explicitly specified in the vignette,[13] both by name (Patience) and by circumstances (squatting), the squatter is undoubtedly understood by all respondents to be a black person. A major source of squatting in contemporary South Africa is the migration to the cities by rural blacks. Moreover, although the race of the land owner is *not* entirely unambiguous, the vignette suggests that the land owner is white. Land that is grabbed in contemporary South Africa is sometimes privately owned (which would most likely imply white ownership), but is more often publicly owned. In this vignette, however, the implication is clearly private ownership, and that the land owner has access to a security force. The ability to get a court-ordered eviction implies resources, and whites are more likely to have access to such resources. Thus, it is virtually certain that nearly all respondents understood the subtext of the vignette as one of interracial conflict. At least for black South Africans and perhaps for South Africans of every race, the respondents were judging the eviction of a black person

---

[13] Considerable thought was given to this issue when the vignettes were being constructed. I decided not to specify the race of the participants in the vignette because, had the races of the actors been explicitly stated, I believe it could have led to a priming or framing effect of race that might have overwhelmed all other aspects of the story (e.g., Druckman 2004). As presented here, race is implicit, but the conflict is between the landless and the land owner. This, I believe, mirrors South African politics: Race is omnipresent, even if race is not the most salient cleavage in any given conflict.

by a white land owner, which is a relatively common occurrence in contemporary South Africa. If this is so, then sociotropic and group identity concerns are likely to be activated (a hypothesis that is tested below).

Distributive Justice – Deservingness. I also hypothesize that squatters vary in the degree to which they deserve housing assistance. Thus, the vignette read:

> *High Deservingness*: Patience had earlier applied to the government to be given a place to live, but the government told her she must wait in the queue of land seekers, and that it is likely to take several months before the government can provide her some land.
>
> *Low Deservingness*: Patience had earlier applied to the government to be given a place to live, but the government told her she is not eligible for government assistance because she has not lived in the area long enough.

Of course, I do not necessarily assume that people judge Patience's ineligibility as appropriate and legitimate; instead, this hypothesis is directly tested via the manipulation check (below). Nonetheless, an important political issue in South Africa concerns the housing needs of newly arrived emigrants to the cities in contrast to those urban dwellers who have been patiently waiting for years to receive housing from the government.[14] Denying housing to the latter is expected to be judged as less fair than denying housing to the less deserving newcomer.

Distributive Justice – The Superordinate Party's "Need." The need of the land owner for the land is represented by whether or not the property is currently being put to use. It is common in South Africa to hear people proclaim that an owner does not "need" her or

---

[14] An excellent example of the significance of being in the housing queue can be found in the conflict between residents of Delft and Langa (both Cape Town townships). In July 2006, a fire in Langa led to the displacement of many of its residents. The City provided housing for them in Delft. This outraged Delft "backyard dwellers" (people who live in shacks in the backyards of houses), who felt they had prior rights to a home, leading some to threaten violence against the incoming Langa people. See Powell 2006a and 2006b. Clearly, to many, deservingness is defined in part by having waited patiently in the housing queue, and newcomers to the queue, even needy ones, do not deserve to be given housing priority.

his land because the land is not being *used*.[15] This distinction is captured in the following manipulation:

Low Land Owner Need: The land where Patience squats is several hectares, and it is not currently being used by the owner of the land.
High Land Owner Need: The land where Patience squats is several hectares, and it is currently being used by the owner of the land for his own purposes.

I hypothesize that when the land is not being used, evicting the squatter will be judged to be less fair.
Procedural Justice – Rule of Law. Finally, the vignette manipulated the means by which Patience is evicted from the property (recall that in all vignette versions Patience is in fact evicted).

Low Procedural Justice: The owner of the land objects to Patience living on his property, and he hires security people to evict Patience and her family from his land. Patience asks for some time to sort herself out, but the owner goes ahead and evicts Patience immediately.
High Procedural Justice: The owner of the land objects to Patience living on his property, and he goes to court to get an order to evict Patience from his land. Patience is given some time to sort things out, and then the police evict her from the property.

I acknowledge that this manipulation includes two components: the speed with which Patience is evicted and by whom she is evicted. The experiment was designed this way since these two factors are inextricably interconnected in South Africa, thus contributing to verisimilitude. When land owners resist squatters, they do so quickly,

---

[15] For instance, in one of the focus groups conducted for the purpose of questionnaire development in this survey the following exchange showing the importance of land use took place:
Moderator: What about the situation where you have land owners actually, well they don't use the land and then people come and squat and they ask them a fee, a sort of occupation fee? Do you think that practice is fair?
Participant: That is not fair but let us get back to the question. There is land that lies vacant for 15 years, you can't allow that. Why is it left vacant? What is the purpose? I mean, let us say, 10 kilometers from central Durban, why is the land lying vacant? What purpose does it serve? I mean whose land is it? And you can't leave huge stacks of land vacant, undeveloped, there is nothing on it. You find out what is going on.

before the squatter can acquire any rights, and they primarily imple-ment evictions with private security forces.[16] These evictions often involve the destruction of property (both the dwelling unit erected by the squatter and the squatter's personal property), and nothing is dignified about the process. Alternatively, if the process gets delayed and winds up going to court, police will probably be called to evict the squatters, typically with a certain amount of orderliness and re-spect. The manipulation check for this stimulus emphasizes whether Patience was given adequate time before the eviction, and thus focuses on whether she was treated with a degree of dignity during the ordeal.

Aronson et al. (1990) distinguish between experimental (the con-tent of the experiment being realistic to the subjects so that they take the task seriously) and mundane realism (the similarity of the experi-mental context and stimuli to events likely to occur in the real world – in short, verisimilitude). Obviously, this experiment has a great deal of mundane realism, since the entire context is grounded in highly salient and widely publicized land grabs. And in light of the intensity – and poignancy – of land conflicts (involving the agents of the post-apartheid state removing mainly black people from either white-owned or public land), I strongly suspect that the respondents felt their judg-ments on the vignette were important and worthy of thought, and thus the vignettes profit from experimental realism as well. And according to the assessments of the interviewers, the vignette was well understood by more respondents than the remainder of the questions in the interview.

The sixteen vignette versions are reported in the appendix to this chapter. The scenario expected to generate the least widespread per-ceptions of a fair eviction is:

Patience and her family are squatters. They are squatting because they want to live in the city, but have no other place to live. Patience had earlier applied to

---

[16] Such security forces are well known and notorious in South Africa. The front-page headline to the February 11–17, 2005, edition of the *Mail & Guardian* announced: "Jo'burg fires hated Red Ants." The subtitle read: "City council cuts ties with its notorious private army following allegations of bribery and corruption." The story itself is entitled "Red Ants fumigated." The Red Ants are a private security firm hired by the city to evict squatters. I suspect that few urban blacks are unaware of such agencies.

the government to be given a place to live, but the government told her she must wait in the queue of land seekers, and that it is likely to take several months before the government can provide her some land. The land where Patience squats is several hectares, and it is not currently being used by the owner of the land for his own purposes. The owner of the land objects to Patience living on his property, and he hires security people to evict Patience and her family from his land. Patience asks for some time to sort herself out, but the owner goes ahead and evicts Patience immediately.

The scenario expected to stimulate the most widespread perceptions of a fair eviction is:

Patience and her family are squatters. They are squatting because they think the place where they are currently living is too far away from the place where Patience works. Patience had earlier applied to the government to be given a place to live, but the government told her she is not eligible for government assistance because she has not lived in the area long enough. The land where Patience squats is several hectares, and it is currently being used by the owner of the land for his own purposes. The owner of the land objects to Patience living on his property, and he goes to court to get an order to evict Patience from his land. Patience is given some time to sort things out, and then the police evicts her from the property.

FAIRNESS JUDGMENTS: THE DEPENDENT VARIABLE

We asked the respondents to assess the fairness of the treatment Patience received during the eviction, based on a ten-point scale ranging from "completely unfair" to "completely fair."[17] The data reveal enormous racial differences in perceptions of the fairness of her treatment. While 83.0% of blacks view the outcome as unfair to the squatter, only 40.4% of whites assert that the eviction was unfair. A large majority of Coloured people also see unfairness (72.2%), as do a similar majority of those of Asian origin (68.3%).[18] This racial divide in assessments of

---

[17] For ease of interpretation, I have rescored this and the independent variables to vary from zero to one. Note that all statistical analyses are conducted on the continuous dependent variable; I report in the text a rough categorization of this eleven-point continuum only as an aid to the interpretation of the data.

[18] In contrast to many of the questions we asked in this survey, tiny numbers of respondents (10 or fewer) said they did not know whether the outcome was unfair. Clearly, the story depicted in the vignette was accessible and engaging to essentially all South Africans.

the fairness of the eviction is foreboding for South African politics since the black majority and the powerful white minority differ so profoundly.

Despite the opinion expressed in the vignette, a majority of each racial group in South Africa opposes squatting. When asked whether they support or oppose a policy to prevent "squatting by strictly enforcing the law," the percentages of respondents favoring such a policy range from 61.4% among blacks to 84.9% among those of Asian origin (and 84.7% among whites). Similarly, when asked whether the law should provide more protection to land owners against squatters, from 64.9% of blacks to 85.3% of whites gave a supportive reply. Across all racial groups, only 14.6% of the respondents oppose strict enforcement of squatting laws and even fewer (10.5%) oppose protecting land owners from those who would squat on their land. Thus, these data indicate that despite opposition in general to the redistribution of land through squatting, significant majorities of blacks, Coloured people, and those of Asian origin nonetheless view the treatment of Patience as unfair. Understanding this seeming paradox requires that we treat fairness as a multidimensional concept implicating varying types of justice.

The principal dependent variable for the remainder of the analysis is perceptions of how fairly the squatter was treated. I hypothesize that the eviction of Patience is thought to be most fair when her need and deservingness are low, when the land owner's need is high, and when the eviction is procedurally fair. Conversely, when Patience has high need and deservingness, when the land owner has low need, and when the eviction does not follow the rule of law, then Patience will be judged to have been unfairly treated. Thus, the purpose of the experiment is to partition the variance in these fairness judgments, apportioning components of the judgments to various theories of justice.

ANALYSIS

Perceptions of the Experiment

As I have noted, strong racial differences exist in judgments of fairness. To what degree are these differences a function of variation in perceptions of the experimental manipulations? To answer this question, I examined the indicators of how the vignette was perceived, assessing whether those perceptions varied according to the race of the respondent.[19]

As it turns out, moderate interracial differences in perceptions exist for three of the four manipulations: Only perceptions of the need of the landowner are independent of race (even if the difference of means test is statistically significant, given the large N). For instance, while 53.9% of the white respondents asserted that Patience received adequate time to vacate the property, only 26.1% of blacks and 27.1% of Coloured people agreed.[20] The objective realities portrayed in these stories were apparently filtered through the attitudes and experiences of the respondents, and these attributes are to a considerable degree connected to race. This finding is important since (as will be shown in the analysis below) the perceptions of the experiment have a substantial impact on fairness judgments.

Consequently, the analytical strategy I pursue involves regressing fairness judgments on (1) the dichotomous experimental manipulations,[21] (2) perceptions of the manipulations, (3) race dummy variables

[19] The questions asked: "Thinking back on the story, how badly do you think that Patience and her family needed housing?" The respondents were presented with a response set ranging from "(1). Needed housing" to "(10). Did not need housing." "Compared to other people needing a place to live, how much do you think Patience and her family deserve to be given a place to stay by the government?" The response set was: "(1). Deserve a place to live very much, (2) Somewhat deserve a place to live, (3) Does not deserve a place to live very much, (4). Does not at all deserve a place to live." "How certain are you that the land on which Patience and her family squatted was currently being used by the owner of the land?" The response was: "(1). Certain it was, (2). Probably it was, (3). Probably it was not, (4). Certain it was not." "When Patience and her family were evicted from the property, do you think they were given sufficient time to get sorted out before being forced off the land?" The response set was: "(1). Certain they were given sufficient time, (2). Probably were given sufficient time, (3). Probably were not given sufficient time, (4). Definitely were not given sufficient time."

[20] Note again that this categorization of the responses is for illustrative purposes only, and that the statistical analysis employs the full range of variability based on uncollapsed response sets.

[21] To test for interactive effects of the experimental manipulations, I regressed the dependent variable in a hierarchical fashion on (1) the direct effects of the four experimental variables, (2) all of the two-way interaction terms, (3) all of the three-way effects, and (4) the four-way interaction term. In each instance, the appropriate statistical test is the significance of the change in R^2 with the addition of the variable set (see Cohen et al. 2003). For all racial groups, none of the changes in explained variance brought about by adding the interaction terms achieves statistical significance. Thus, I conclude that the impacts of these variables can be captured by their linear manifestations.

(with Africans as the excluded category), (4) race X perceptions interactions, and (5) race X manipulations interactions. I initially consider
each of the justice hypotheses separately, but then consolidate the
results in a single integrated equation.[22]

Procedural Justice for the Squatter

The strongest finding in this analysis has to do with whether the
squatter was accorded procedural justice. Table 4.1 reports the
results.[23]

Many important conclusions emerge from the coefficients in this
table. First, the equation is quite successful in accounting for judgments
of justice, with 37% of the variance being explained. Second, the evidence in this table confirms that racial differences exist even in the
multivariate context. The big difference is between blacks and whites,
with whites considerably more likely to judge the outcome as fair to the
squatter (b = .21). The views of Coloured people and those of Asian
origin are essentially indistinguishable from those of Africans.

---

[22] Especially when interaction terms are included, putting all variables in a single equation becomes cumbersome. Moreover, the equation may suffer from model misspecification in the sense that the term refers as well to the inclusion of variables *not
connected* to the dependent variable (rather than limiting misspecification to the
failure to include relevant variables). Thus, my analytical strategy is to consider each
of the four manipulations separately, with an eye toward eliminating variables from
consideration in the single integrated equation.

[23] I present this analysis in an OLS format since regression includes all information
typically found in analysis of variance (mainly inferential statistics) as well as measures of the degree of association between the variables. Because the numbers of cases
differ substantially across the four groups, and since measures of statistical significance are extremely sensitive to sample size, my substantive conclusions are grounded
more in the assessment of regression coefficients than in tests of significance.

   To the extent that there are different degrees of variability in the variables of interest
here, comparing standardized coefficients can be misleading. (The standard deviations
range from .24 for the perceptions of squatter need variable to .50 for the dichotomous manipulations.) However, as shown in the tables, the variability in the dependent variable (the justice judgments) is often similar across the four groups, so
standardized coefficients may provide useful information in this sample. Unstandardized coefficients are also reported in the table and are especially useful for cross-
equation comparisons. Note as well that all variables, independent and dependent,
have been rescaled to a zero to one range.

TABLE 4.1. *Predicting Justice Judgments, Procedural Justice Manipulation*

	r	b	s.e.	β
Respondent race				
White	.43	.21	.03	.28***
Coloured	−.07	.04	.03	.05
Asian origin	−.00	.08	.03	.07*
Perception of the manipulation	.51	.31	.03	.35***
Race/perception interactions				
White	.50	.10	.04	.10*
Coloured	.10	.07	.05	.04
Asian origin	.08	.02	.06	.01
Experimental manipulation	.17	−.02	.02	−.04
Race/manipulation interactions				
White	.38	.05	.03	.06
Coloured	.03	.09	.04	.07*
Asian origin	.05	.06	.05	.04
Equation statistics				
Intercept		.14	.02	
Standard deviation – dependent variable		.35		
Standard error of estimate		.28		
R²				.37***
N		1,988		

Note: Significance of standardized regression coefficients (β): ***$p < .001$, **$p < .01$, *$p < .05$.

Perceptions of the manipulation also have a substantial impact on justice judgments. Those who believe that the squatter was given sufficient time to get her affairs in order are considerably more likely to judge the outcome as fair. As documented in the interaction terms, only trivial interracial differences exist in the importance of these perceptions for fairness judgments (with the nearly trivial possible exception of whites, who are slightly more strongly influenced by whether they perceive Patience to have received procedural justice). In general, these perceptions influence fairness judgments roughly similarly among all four racial groups.

The manipulation itself has a substantial direct effect on fairness judgments ($r = .17$), but, as expected, that influence is eliminated in the multivariate equation that includes perceptions of the manipulation. Finally, the manipulation had similar effects on the members of all four racial groups, with only the slightest hint of a stronger impact among Coloured South Africans.

Generally, race directly shapes judgments of justice, but, with minor exceptions, reactions to the procedural aspects of this vignette do not vary significantly by race. South Africans of every race assess fairness in substantial part on the basis of procedural justice considerations.

The Squatter's Need

I note first that the need manipulation in the experiment was subject to a ceiling effect (despite efforts to calibrate the squatter's need via several pretests). Although I found a statistically significant difference ($p < .001$) between the two versions of the need manipulation, the substantive difference is slight: 94.0% of those told of Patience's dire need judged her to be needy, whereas 90.5% of those hearing that Patience had only ordinary need thought her needy.[24] Squatters, by definition, have high need for housing, irrespective of other circumstances that exacerbate or ameliorate the need. Consequently, the direct effect of this manipulation is trivial, as are the effects of the race/manipulation interactions (see Table 4.2).

On the other hand, *perceptions* of the need of the squatter have a strong direct effect on justice judgments. The relationship is substantial among black South Africans ($b = -.50$: as need is perceived to increase, fairness declines) but is considerably diminished among all three racial minorities. For example, the coefficient for Coloured South Africans is $-.22$ ($-.50 + .28$), and similar but weaker effects are observed among the other two racial minorities. Thus, black South Africans are particularly sensitive to the perceived need of the squatter, even if that need seems to be largely defined by factors other than the context as manipulated in this experiment.

---

[24] For descriptive purposes only, I have created a categorical variable from the ten-point scale. The percentages reported are those who rate the squatter's need at greater than the scale midpoint (.5).

TABLE 4.2. *Predicting Justice Judgments, Squatter's Need Manipulation*

	r	b	s.e.	β
Respondent race				
White	.43	.16	.07	.22**
Coloured	−.07	−.11	.08	−.12
Asian origin	−.00	−.06	.10	−.06
Perception of the manipulation	−.32	−.50	.06	−.34***
Race/perception interactions				
White	.34	.20	.07	.23**
Coloured	−.08	.28	.09	.28***
Asian origin	−.02	.23	.11	.18*
Experimental manipulation	−.04	.01	.02	.02
Race/manipulation interactions				
White	.25	−.02	.03	−.02
Coloured	−.08	−.07	.04	−.06
Asian origin	.00	.00	.05	.00
Equation statistics				
Intercept		.66	.05	
Standard deviation – dependent variable		.35		
Standard error of estimate		.30		
R^2				.26***
N		1,988		

Note: Significance of standardized regression coefficients (β): ***$p < .001$, **$p < .01$, *$p < .05$.

Finally, I note that even with all else controlled, whites still perceive greater fairness in the treatment of the squatter ($b = .16$).

The Squatter's Deservingness

Deservingness also suffers to some degree from a ceiling effect, with only 6.3% of the respondents seeing Patience as not or not at all deserving of being given a place to stay by the government. But as with perceptions of need, perceptions of deservingness significantly influence fairness judgments. Moreover, the race/perception interactions indicate that all racial groups are similarly affected by their perceptions of deservingness. Thus, as with the squatter's need, deservingness influences justice judgments, although deservingness apparently includes

TABLE 4.3. *Predicting Justice Judgments, Squatter's Deservingness Manipulation*

	r	b	s.e.	β
Respondent race				
White	.43	.28	.06	.38***
Coloured	−.07	.02	.09	.02
Asian origin	−.00	.12	.12	.11
Perception of the manipulation	−.38	−.37	.06	−.27***
Race/perception interactions				
White	.29	.01	.07	.01
Coloured	−.09	.09	.09	.09
Asian origin	−.02	.03	.13	.02
Experimental manipulation	.00	−.01	.02	−.01
Race/manipulation interactions				
White	.29	.02	.03	.02
Coloured	−.06	.00	.04	.00
Asian origin	−.00	.01	.05	.01
Equation statistics				
Intercept		.57	.06	
Standard deviation – dependent variable		.35		
Standard error of estimate		.30		
R^2				.27***
N		1,988		

Note: Significance of standardized regression coefficients (β): ***$p<.001$, **$p<.01$, *$p<.05$.

much more than waiting patiently in the queue for government-supplied housing (see Table 4.3).[25]

As with the squatter's need, Coloured people and those of Asian origin differ little from black South Africans, but whites are far more likely to judge the squatter to have been fairly treated (b = .28).

[25] When perceived deservingness is regressed on the other three perceptual variables, the overwhelming (and exclusive) influence is from the variable measuring perceptions of the need of the squatter. Squatters who are more needy are perceived to be more deserving (r = .40; β = .39). Perhaps this finding reflects a limitation of experimentation. Experiments can easily force independent variables to be orthogonal to each other (as this experiment does with need and deservingness), but in the real world these two factors are so closely intertwined that ordinary people cannot readily disentangle them. It is also noteworthy that substantial relationships are observed even with the relatively small amount of variance in perceived need and deservingness.

The Land Owner's Need

The dominant finding regarding the need of the land owner is that the respondent's race strongly influences perceived fairness, but little else does (see Table 4.4). To a large degree, whites see the outcome as fair to the squatter, and it matters little whether the land is being used or not, or even whether the respondents perceive that the land is being used. Consequently, I exclude this manipulation from further consideration in this analysis.

Integrating the Equations

The manipulations, of course, are statistically independent of each other, and therefore including all variables in a multivariate equation

TABLE 4.4. *Predicting Justice Judgments, Land Owner's Need Manipulation*

	r	b	s.e.	β
Respondent race				
White	.43	.38	.03	.52***
Coloured	−.07	.06	.03	.07
Asian origin	−.00	.16	.04	.14***
Perception of the manipulation	.09	.03	.03	.04
Race/perception interactions				
White	.32	.02	.04	.02
Coloured	.00	.14	.05	.10**
Asian origin	−.00	−.07	.07	−.04
Experimental manipulation	−.00	.01	.02	.01
Race/manipulation interactions				
White	.24	−.06	.04	−.06
Coloured	−.03	−.04	.04	−.03
Asian origin	.02	.07	.05	.04
Equation statistics				
Intercept		.21	.02	
Standard deviation – dependent variable		.35		
Standard error of estimate		.31		
R²				.22***
N		1,988		

Note: Significance of standardized regression coefficients (β): ***$p < .001$, **$p < .01$, *$p < .05$.

will produce essentially the same statistical results as those reported in each of the above tables. However, the perceptual variables are not orthogonal, and therefore it is useful to estimate one additional equation. In this analysis, I include the race and manipulation dummy variables, the perceptual variables, and only the race/perception interactions for the need manipulation, since the analyses above indicate significant interactive effects only for this dimension. Table 4.5 reports the statistical results.

This equation explains an unusually large amount of the variance in fairness judgments (41%). In addition, the independent, direct effects of race that were documented in Tables 4.1 through 4.4 have now been

TABLE 4.5. *Predicting Justice Judgments, Fully Specified Model*

	b	s.e.	β
Respondent race			
White	.04	.06	.06
Coloured	−.09	.07	−.11
Asian origin	−.03	.08	−.02
Perceptions of the manipulation			
Procedural justice	.32	.02	.35***
Need	−.31	.05	−.21***
Deservingness	−.23	.03	−.17***
Race/perception interactions: need			
White	.21	.06	.24***
Coloured	.21	.08	.20**
Asian origin	.14	.09	.11
Experimental manipulations			
Procedural justice	.03	.01	.04
Need	.00	.01	.00
Deservingness	−.01	.01	−.01
Equation statistics			
Intercept	.61	.05	
Standard deviation – dependent variable	.35		
Standard error of estimate	.27		
R²			.41***
N	1,997		

Note: Significance of standardized regression coefficients (β): ***p < .001, **p < .01, *p < .05.

completely eliminated by being incorporated into the other variables in the equation (i.e., none of the race dummy variables is statistically significant). This means that the strong racial effects I have observed to this point can be accounted for by the substantive variables in the equation, which is pleasing, since race itself is always an atheoretical variable.[26]

Finally, each of the aspects of justice has an important influence on fairness judgments. The eviction of the squatter is thought to be more fair when she receives procedural justice and when her perceived need and deservingness are relatively low. Note, however, that the influence of the interactive coefficients is to mitigate the influence on need among whites and Coloured people and, to a lesser degree, those of Asian origin (i.e., the interactive coefficients are positive). This indicates that black South Africans place disproportionate emphasis on the need of the squatter for housing. South Africans of all races are influenced by the perceived deservingness of the squatter, just as they are influenced by whether the squatter received procedural justice. Thus, fairness judgments are a product of conflicting justice mandates: Because the squatter has legitimate needs and is deserving, she has a right to housing, but, in the context of widespread opposition to squatting in general, these characteristics get trumped when the squatter is denied the land through fair eviction procedures.

The causal conclusions that can be drawn from the analyses reported in these tables vary. For the procedural justice hypothesis, the manipulation was accurately perceived by the respondents, and the perceptions had a strong impact on justice judgments. Moreover, the manipulation itself had a direct effect on assessments of fairness. Consequently, one can have considerable confidence in the causal inference that how the squatter was treated influenced conclusions about fairness.

With the squatter need and deservingness hypotheses, the answer to the question of causality is less clear. The manipulations themselves did

---

[26] When measures of social class and level of education are added to the equation in Table 4.5, the changes in the coefficients are minuscule. For instance, the β coefficients for the three perceptual variables with education and social class controlled are: .35, −.22, and −.17. Thus, controlling for socioeconomic factors requires no changes whatsoever in the substantive conclusions one should draw from the analysis reported in Table 4.5.

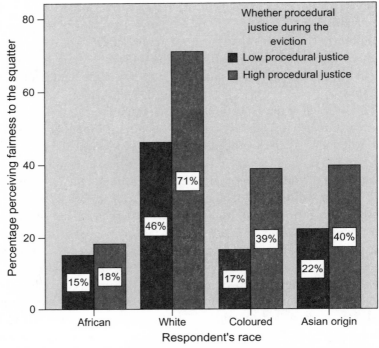

FIGURE 4.1. The effect of procedural justice on fairness judgments, by respondent race.

not have a direct effect on justice judgments, even though the perceptions did. I understand this as most likely reflecting a ceiling effect on the manipulations, even though variability in *perceived* need and deservingness is connected to justice assessments. Because the direct effect of the manipulation is insignificant, considerably less confidence in the causal inference connecting need and deservingness with justice is warranted, however (as is always the case with relationships grounded in post-hoc analysis).

Summary

The most important finding of this portion of the analysis is that it appears that extending procedural justice to the squatter adds legitimacy to the entire process of eviction, since it seems to acknowledge the legitimacy of the squatter's desire for housing. Because the squatter's need for housing is legitimate, she deserves fair treatment, even while it is also fair to deny her the land she sought to grab. Because the transgression of the squatter is to some degree legitimate, no moral imbalance is created by the land grab (see Robbennolt, Darley, and MacCoun 2003). Because the squatter can justify her behavior in terms of justice considerations, her transgression is quite unlike an ordinary criminal offense, and she therefore deserves fair treatment. When she receives it, evicting her is seen as fair.[27]

GROUP IDENTITIES AND PERCEPTIONS OF FAIRNESS

It remains to consider the degree to which justice judgments are grounded in the group identities of South Africans. For this portion of the analysis, I consider only the views of black South Africans. The logic of restricting the analysis to this group includes the following: (1) As I noted above, to most blacks, the vignette is undoubtedly understood as an interracial conflict between Patience (a black woman) and the land owner (a white man). Therefore, group identities may become activated and relevant. (2) Moreover, on many general land attitudes and experiences, blacks differ substantially from whites, Coloured people, and those of Asian origin. Although a majority of blacks hold what can be considered to be anti-squatter policy preferences, black opinion is more divided on issues of squatting than the opinions of the other groups.[28] (3) For blacks, it is reasonable to hypothesize that the whole issue of land grabs and especially evictions generates identity threats since, once again, indigenous South Africans are being denied by whites land that is their birthright.

---

[27] This finding comports with the relational theory of procedural justice as explicated by Tyler and his colleagues. Perhaps the most salient aspect of the procedural justice manipulation has to do with status recognition, which "refers to the quality of treatment that people experience in their interactions with group authorities – whether they are treated politely and with dignity, and whether respect is shown for their rights (i.e., aspects of experience that tell people about their standing in the group)" (Tyler and Blader 2000, 92).

[28] For instance, while 61.4% of blacks support strict enforcement of anti-squatter laws, the comparable figures for whites, Coloured people, and Asians are 84.7%, 74.3%, and 84.9%, respectively. And although 64.9% of blacks would provide land owners more protection against squatters, this is the position of 85.3% of whites, 80.1% of Coloured people, and 85.0% of those of Asian origin.

How might black identities be relevant to justice judgments? Gibson (2004b) has suggested that not all group identities are politically equivalent, especially in the South African case. Consequently, the basic group attachments of the respondents were measured with a question at the beginning of a section on group attitudes that asked simply: "People see themselves in many different ways. Using this list, which *one* of these best describes you? Please take a moment to look at all of the terms on the list."[29] The respondents' answers varied widely; fortunately, their replies are subject to some theoretically inspired categorization (for further details on this see Chapter 3, above).

As noted in Chapter 3, about 14% of the black respondents classified themselves primarily as South Africans. Another 41% asserted an identity in terms of a general racial category – either "African" or "black." For 43% of the respondents, the identity was defined in terms of a specific ethnic/linguistic group, for example, Zulu, Xhosa, North Sotho. Nearly all respondents answered this question in terms of identities falling within these three categories (less than 2% mentioned an identity not in these categories). Moreover, these identities are quite important to the respondents: In a follow-up question, 89% of black South Africans rated their chosen identity as very important (the most extreme point on the response set). As I noted above, I use the terms national identities, racial identities, and ethnic identities to refer to these self-selected group associations, even while ascribing little substance to the words "racial" and "ethnic."

Gibson (2004b) found that, in the South African case, those who identify with relatively narrow ethnic/linguistic groups and who believe strongly in the need for group solidarity are more likely to be intolerant of their political foes. Those identifying with large, heterogenous groups are not particularly intolerant, even when they believe strongly in the need for group solidarity.[30] Thus, in the case of political

---

[29] Much earlier research has been conducted on group identities in South Africa. See, for examples, Gibson and Gouws 2000, 2003, Jung 2000, and Gibson 2004a, 2004b, 2006. For useful recent reviews of social identity theory, see Brewer and Gaertner 2004 and Turner and Reynolds 2004.

[30] This is similar to Posner's (2004) finding in Zambia. Posner's analysis is particularly relevant because he posits that intergroup differences are neutralized in Zambia by the creation of a salient superordinate identity: Both Chewas and Tumbukas apparently think of themselves as "Easterners."

tolerance, these identities moderate the connection between ingroup sympathy and outgroup antipathy.

Is squatting a context that activates "identity-relevant concerns"? The "identity-threat hypothesis" states that "people should devote more thought and analysis to whether an encounter was fair or unfair if the encounter threatens rather than affirms the perceiver's currently activated identity and associated goals and values" (Skitka 2003, 287).[31] In the case of these justice judgments, perhaps the existence of a superordinate identity (identifying with the nation) makes black South Africans more sensitive to the preferences of their white fellow citizens, and therefore more likely to be influenced by the need of the land owner (see, e.g., Huo et al. 1996 and Gibson 2006). As González and Brown assert (2003, 211), encouraging dual identities may be an effective "strategy for promoting generalization of positive intergroup attitudes where minorities and majorities co-exist." Moreover, perhaps a connection exists between national identities and emphasis on procedural justice as a universalistic norm. The belief that everyone is connected by virtue of being South African imbues all citizens with rights, including the right to be treated with dignity, even while being evicted from an unlawful land grab.[32] It is more difficult to distinguish the justice judgments of racial and ethnic identifiers (but see especially Huo 2003), except to note the general hypothesis that the broader and more inclusive an identity, the more likely are universalistic theories of justice to be embraced.

Table 4.6 reports the OLS results for each of the three types of group identities among black South Africans. Each of the equations includes the three manipulation dichotomies and the three variables measuring the perceptions of the manipulation.[33] Note should be taken of the

---

[31] The battery of identity questions was asked prior to the vignette, so identities were primed or to some degree activated when the respondents were asked to make the justice judgments.

[32] Miller (1999, 101) recognizes dignity as a criterion by which the procedural justice of a situation is judged: "Thus we can say that a fair procedure is one that does not require people to behave in undignified ways or to have things done to them that would normally be thought of as offensive or degrading." All of these are elements of respect: "It is disrespectful of people not to give equal attention to their claims, not to attempt to gain an accurate picture of their circumstances, not to explain the reasons for decisions, and to use methods that violate their dignity" (1999, 102).

[33] Because the need of the land owner has virtually no influence on justice judgments, I continue to exclude it from the equations. And obviously, with an analysis limited to black South Africans, no interaction variables are necessary for race.

TABLE 4.6. *The Interactive Effect of Group Identity and Justice Judgments, Black South Africans, 2004*

	National			General group (racial)			Specific group (ethnic)		
Predictor	b	s.e.	β	b	s.e.	β	b	s.e.	β
Squatter need	−.04	.04	−.07	.02	.02	.03	.03	.02	.05
Squatter deservingness	−.04	.04	−.07	−.05	.02	−.09*	.03	.02	.06
Procedural justice	−.01	.04	−.02	.02	.03	.03	−.05	.03	−.09
Perceived squatter need	−.29	.10	−.24**	−.43	.07	−.28***	−.22	.08	−.14**
Perceived squatter deservingness	−.12	.10	−.10	−.26	.08	−.16***	−.29	.07	−.19***
Perceived procedural justice	.44	.07	.49***	.27	.04	.35***	.21	.04	.28***
Intercept	.51	.09		.79	.08		.61	.09	
Standard deviation – dependent variable	.29			.29			.26		
Standard error of estimate	.23			.24			.24		
R^2			.39***			.31***			.17***
N	136			396			414		

Note: Significance of standardized regression coefficients (β): ***$p < .001$, **$p < .01$, *$p < .05$.

somewhat smaller numbers of cases of black South Africans with a national identity, which makes statistical significance a more demanding standard to achieve. Consequently, as before, I focus in this analysis on the magnitude of both the standardized and unstandardized regression coefficients.

I first observe that the direct effect of the manipulation variables is trivial to small in virtually all instances, which suggests that the causal process works through perceptions of the circumstances portrayed in the vignette. Second, a substantial amount of variance in justice judgments is explained by these variables, although the equation does a considerably poorer job in predicting the justice judgments of blacks with a relatively narrow ethnic identity. This may have something to do with the type of South African who adopts an ethnic identity (perhaps they are more poorly educated, rural, etc. – characteristics that are associated with larger quantities of measurement error).[34]

Perhaps the most important finding from this table concerns the substantially stronger role of procedural justice perceptions among those adopting a South African identity. This stands in contrast, for instance, to the case of those who adopt ethnic identities, for whom procedural justice is considerably less important (.21 vs. .44). Indeed, comparing the procedural justice coefficient among those with a national identity with the coefficients from each of the other two types of identity reveals that the differences are statistically significant.[35] To the extent that the influence of procedural justice in this analysis has to do with the dignity and respect owed all South African citizens, even squatters, this analysis seems to confirm Skitka's hypothesis that "people are influenced more by socio-emotional outcomes like standing, status, and respect as the relative salience of their social identity concerns increases" (Skitka 2003, 290).[36]

---

[34] A cursory examination of the data reveals no strong correlates of the type of identity adopted by the respondent. Some relationship exists with level of education, but it is weak. Perhaps surprisingly, no connection between identity and size of place of residence can be found in these data. Adopting a national identity is equally likely in the large metropolitan areas and the rural countryside.

[35] An alternative, but equivalent, means of analyzing these data is within a single equation incorporating identity dummy variables and the interaction terms between the identity variables and the experimental manipulations and their perceptions. When the twelve interactions terms are added to the basic equation (which now includes two identity dummy variables), the change in R^2 is statistically significant at $p = .001$. By varying which type of identity is scored as the excluded group, each pair of OLS coefficients was tested under the null hypothesis of no statistically significant difference. Comparing the ethnic group coefficients with the others, the interaction term of perceived procedural justice and claiming a national identity is significant at $p = .002$ (although the difference in the coefficients of racial group and ethnic identifiers does not achieve statistical significance). Two other interaction coefficients (racial group identity and both the deservingness manipulation and perceptions of need) are significant at $.05 < p < .01$. When those subscribing to a national identity are treated as the excluded group, significant interactions exist only on the two comparisons of perceived procedural justice.

[36] Skitka, Winquist, and Hutchinson (2003, 333) also argue that when people "have a clear *a priori* moral mandate – i.e., a strong conviction that a given outcome is right or wrong, moral or immoral – that procedural justice becomes a much less salient concern." Perhaps these results, in which justice claims are *not* seen in unambiguous, zero-sum relationship to one another, are influenced by the absence of moral mandates on issues such as squatting. Issues on which all sides can generate readily accepted claims of justice and injustice are not issues on which clear moral mandates exist.

None of the other differences across types of identities in the determinants of fairness judgments are of much note.[37] I do note, however, that the squatter's need influences the fairness judgments of those with each type of group attachment, including those primarily identifying themselves as South African. Thus, holding a national identity is not incompatible with sympathy for the conditions of specific group members (squatter need).[38] At the same time, additional concerns about basic procedural fairness – presumably something due *all* South Africans – heavily structure fairness judgments. Perhaps both need and procedural justice reflect a broader commitment to the rule of law, with need understood within the context of rules and policies indicating who has a right to housing.

I note as well the interconnection between perceived need and perceived deservingness: Among those with a national identity, a very strong correlation exists between these two perceptions ($r = .52$), while the correlations within the other two groups are substantially weaker: .32 and .31. Black South Africans who primarily identify themselves as South Africans differentiate less between need and deservingness than do other blacks, which may be indicative of a more universalistic approach to defining the rights of all South African citizens.

DISCUSSION AND CONCLUDING COMMENTS

If squatting were a straightforward issue of property rights, then few South Africans would support squatters. Indeed, when asked in general terms whether property rights ought to be protected from land grabs, substantial majorities *of every racial group* reply that they should. How is it then that there is any support at all for squatting?

Part of the answer suggested by this analysis is that squatting implicates group concerns and interests. Owing to the twin historical

---

[37] As I noted above, a couple of the other tests of the difference of coefficients reveal statistically significant results. Perhaps the only finding of any substantive interest is that those holding a racial identity are slightly ($p = .045$) more influenced by the perceived need of the squatter than those with an ethnic identity. Since all three types of identities are associated with reliance on need in forming justice judgments, this difference seems to be of little importance.

[38] Both the analysis in Chapter 3 (above) and Gibson (2006) have shown that group and national attachments are positively, not negatively, correlated for virtually all identities in South Africa, a finding confirming the results reported by Gibson and Gouws (2003) from an earlier survey in South Africa. See also Huo 2003.

injustices of colonialism and apartheid, the claims of squatters acquire some degree of legitimacy; therefore, squatters cannot be treated with disrespect when being evicted from land they occupy. Justice calculations seem to be complex. Most oppose squatting. But by their need and deservingness, squatters have a legitimate claim to a place to live. Therefore, it is unfair to evict them. However, since most people disapprove of land grabs, squatters must be evicted. Procedural justice can compensate for the unfairness of dislodging the squatters, among all South Africans, but especially among black South Africans identifying with the country as whole. Thus, South Africans traverse the territory from opposing squatting to supporting the squatter to accepting the eviction of the squatter through a relatively complex blend of theories of distributive and procedural justice. Justice thinking therefore appears to be multidimensional, mixing alternative and even conflicting theories of fairness.

Among black South Africans, identities seem to be activated by issues of historical land injustices, and they therefore have something to do with how the different aspects of justice are assigned priority. For instance, concern over procedural justice is exacerbated among those adopting the most inclusive group identity. Perhaps one consequence of adopting a national identity is the emphasis on a more general sense of inclusiveness and universalism when it comes to judging fellow citizens. Thus, group identities certainly have a role to play in justice judgments; future research should focus on specifying that role more precisely.

This research clearly demonstrates that judgments of fairness are based on a variety of factors, factors that are pluralistic and that may or may not be in alignment with each other. I have not been able to discover the principles by which justice conflicts are adjudicated; as with prior research, the best I have achieved in this chapter is to show that specific fairness judgments reflect a mix of concerns about justice. Future research would likely profit from a within-subjects design in which the context of the conflict is varied, for example, with some controversies implicating identities but others not, or with some disputes involving all parties with strong justice arguments, but others characterized by justice asymmetries. Understanding how citizens make judgments within the context of conflicting justice imperatives is a crucial step for future research on the role of justice concerns in politics.

Finally, cultural variability in justice judgments must receive much more sustained attention. The racial differences I observe in this chapter – differences largely centered on how the various elements of the squatter vignette are perceived – may well reflect broader intercultural differences in values, such as individualism versus collectivism. It is possible, for instance, that individualism is associated with a universalistic orientation to the rule of law, which in turn gives rise to both national identities and strong emphasis on procedural justice. South Africa continues to be a fecund environment for investigating such cultural differences, given the African, European, and Asian mix of its population.

Land issues, worldwide, have reached new apogees of salience and divisiveness. Such controversies are not just about who gets land and who does not; instead, fairness and justice are central components of land conflicts. Understanding how people apply theories of justice to such disputes would contribute mightily to limiting the destructive potential of such clashes, especially in transitional and historically divided polities.

Perhaps the most important lesson of this analysis is that fairness matters, that issues such as rectifying historical land injustices cannot be understood as encapsulating nothing more than relatively simple dimensions of distributive and redistributive politics. Politics is certainly about who gets what, but it is also about whether what one gets (or does not get) is fair. Perhaps this analysis will contribute to reinvigorated attention to the central role of justice in political disputes, past and present.

APPENDIX TO CHAPTER 4: THE FULL SQUATTER VIGNETTES

Squatter Vignette, Story 1 *(aaaa)*

[1a] Patience and her family are squatters. They are squatting because they want to live in the city, but have no other place to live. [2a] Patience had earlier applied to the government to be given a place to live, but the government told her she must wait in the queue of land seekers, and that it is likely to take several months before the government can provide her some land. [3a] The land where Patience squats is several hectares, and it is not currently being used by the owner of the land. [4a] The owner of the land objects to Patience living on his property, and he hires security people to evict Patience and her family

from his land. Patience asks for some time to sort herself out, but the owner goes ahead and evicts Patience immediately.

Squatter Vignette, Story 2 (aaab)

[1a] Patience and her family are squatters. They are squatting because they want to live in the city, but have no other place to live. [2a] Patience had earlier applied to the government to be given a place to live, but the government told her she must wait in the queue of land seekers, and that it is likely to take several months before the government can provide her some land. [3a] The land where Patience squats is several hectares, and it is not currently being used by the owner of the land. [4b] The owner of the land objects to Patience living on his property, and he goes to court to get an order to evict Patience from his land. Patience is given some time to sort things out, and then the police evicts her from the property.

Squatter Vignette, Story 3 (aaba)

[1a] Patience and her family are squatters. They are squatting because they want to live in the city, but have no other place to live. [2a] Patience had earlier applied to the government to be given a place to live, but the government told her she must wait in the queue of land seekers, and that it is likely to take several months before the government can provide her some land. [3b] The land where Patience squats is several hectares, and it is currently being used by the owner of the land for his own purposes. [4a] The owner of the land objects to Patience living on his property, and he hires security people to evict Patience and her family from his land. Patience asks for some time to sort herself out, but the owner goes ahead and evicts Patience immediately.

Squatter Vignette, Story 4 (aabb)

[1a] Patience and her family are squatters. They are squatting because they want to live in the city, but have no other place to live. [2a] Patience had earlier applied to the government to be given a place to live, but the government told her she must wait in the queue of land seekers, and that it is likely to take several months before the government can provide her some land. [3b] The land where Patience squats is several hectares, and it is currently being used by the owner of the land for his own purposes. [4b] The owner of the land objects to Patience

living on his property, and he goes to court to get an order to evict Patience from his land. Patience is given some time to sort things out, and then the police evicts her from the property.

Squatter Vignette, Story 5 (abaa)

[1a] Patience and her family are squatters. They are squatting because they want to live in the city, but have no other place to live. [2b] Patience had earlier applied to the government to be given a place to live, but the government told her she is not eligible for government assistance because she has not lived in the area long enough. [3a] The land where Patience squats is several hectares, and it is not currently being used by the owner of the land. [4a] The owner of the land objects to Patience living on his property, and he hires security people to evict Patience and her family from his land. Patience asks for some time to sort herself out, but the owner goes ahead and evicts Patience immediately.

Squatter Vignette, Story 6 (abab)

[1a] Patience and her family are squatters. They are squatting because they want to live in the city, but have no other place to live. [2b] Patience had earlier applied to the government to be given a place to live, but the government told her she is not eligible for government assistance because she has not lived in the area long enough. [3a] The land where Patience squats is several hectares, and it is not currently being used by the owner of the land. [4b] The owner of the land objects to Patience living on his property, and he goes to court to get an order to evict Patience from his land. Patience is given some time to sort things out, and then the police evicts her from the property.

Squatter Vignette, Story 7 (abba)

[1a] Patience and her family are squatters. They are squatting because they want to live in the city, but have no other place to live. [2b] Patience had earlier applied to the government to be given a place to live, but the government told her she is not eligible for government assistance because she has not lived in the area long enough. [3b] The land where Patience squats is several hectares, and it is currently being used by the owner of the land for his own purposes. [4a] The owner of the land objects to Patience living on his property, and he hires

security people to evict Patience and her family from his land. Patience asks for some time to sort herself out, but the owner goes ahead and evicts Patience immediately.

Squatter Vignette, Story 8 (abbb)

[1a] Patience and her family are squatters. They are squatting because they want to live in the city, but have no other place to live. [2b] Patience had earlier applied to the government to be given a place to live, but the government told her she is not eligible for government assistance because she has not lived in the area long enough. [3b] The land where Patience squats is several hectares, and it is currently being used by the owner of the land for his own purposes. [4b] The owner of the land objects to Patience living on his property, and he goes to court to get an order to evict Patience from his land. Patience is given some time to sort things out, and then the police evicts her from the property.

Squatter Vignette, Story 9 (baaa)

[1b] Patience and her family are squatters. They are squatting because they think the place where they are currently living is too far away from the place where Patience works. [2a] Patience had earlier applied to the government to be given a place to live, but the government told her she must wait in the queue of land seekers, and that it is likely to take several months before the government can provide her some land. [3a] The land where Patience squats is several hectares, and it is not currently being used by the owner of the land. [4a] The owner of the land objects to Patience living on his property, and he hires security people to evict Patience and her family from his land. Patience asks for some time to sort herself out, but the owner goes ahead and evicts Patience immediately.

Squatter Vignette, Story 10 (baab)

[1b] Patience and her family are squatters. They are squatting because they think the place where they are currently living is too far away from the place where Patience works. [2a] Patience had earlier applied to the government to be given a place to live, but the government told her she must wait in the queue of land seekers, and that it is likely to take several months before the government can provide her some land.

[3a] The land where Patience squats is several hectares, and it is not currently being used by the owner of the land. [4b] The owner of the land objects to Patience living on his property, and he goes to court to get an order to evict Patience from his land. Patience is given some time to sort things out, and then the police evicts her from the property.

Squatter Vignette, Story 11 *(baba)*

[1b] Patience and her family are squatters. They are squatting because they think the place where they are currently living is too far away from the place where Patience works. [2a] Patience had earlier applied to the government to be given a place to live, but the government told her she must wait in the queue of land seekers, and that it is likely to take several months before the government can provide her some land. [3b] The land where Patience squats is several hectares, and it is currently being used by the owner of the land for his own purposes. [4a] The owner of the land objects to Patience living on his property, and he hires security people to evict Patience and her family from his land. Patience asks for some time to sort herself out, but the owner goes ahead and evicts Patience immediately.

Squatter Vignette, Story 12 *(babb)*

[1b] Patience and her family are squatters. They are squatting because they think the place where they are currently living is too far away from the place where Patience works. [2a] Patience had earlier applied to the government to be given a place to live, but the government told her she must wait in the queue of land seekers, and that it is likely to take several months before the government can provide her some land. [3b] The land where Patience squats is several hectares, and it is currently being used by the owner of the land for his own purposes. [4b] The owner of the land objects to Patience living on his property, and he goes to court to get an order to evict Patience from his land. Patience is given some time to sort things out, and then the police evicts her from the property.

Squatter Vignette, Story 13 *(bbaa)*

[1b] Patience and her family are squatters. They are squatting because they think the place where they are currently living is too far away from the place where Patience works. [2b] Patience had earlier applied to the

government to be given a place to live, but the government told her she is not eligible for government assistance because she has not lived in the area long enough. [3a] The land where Patience squats is several hectares, and it is not currently being used by the owner of the land. [4a] The owner of the land objects to Patience living on his property, and he hires security people to evict Patience and her family from his land. Patience asks for some time to sort herself out, but the owner goes ahead and evicts Patience immediately.

Squatter Vignette, Story 14 (bbab)
[1b] Patience and her family are squatters. They are squatting because they think the place where they are currently living is too far away from the place where Patience works. [2b] Patience had earlier applied to the government to be given a place to live, but the government told her she is not eligible for government assistance because she has not lived in the area long enough. [3a] The land where Patience squats is several hectares, and it is not currently being used by the owner of the land. [4b] The owner of the land objects to Patience living on his property, and he goes to court to get an order to evict Patience from his land. Patience is given some time to sort things out, and then the police evicts her from the property.

Squatter Vignette, Story 15 (bbba)
[1b] Patience and her family are squatters. They are squatting because they think the place where they are currently living is too far away from the place where Patience works. [2b] Patience had earlier applied to the government to be given a place to live, but the government told her she is not eligible for government assistance because she has not lived in the area long enough. [3b] The land where Patience squats is several hectares, and it is currently being used by the owner of the land for his own purposes. [4a] The owner of the land objects to Patience living on his property, and he hires security people to evict Patience and her family from his land. Patience asks for some time to sort herself out, but the owner goes ahead and evicts Patience immediately.

Squatter Vignette, Story 16 (bbbb)
[1b] Patience and her family are squatters. They are squatting because they think the place where they are currently living is too far away from the place where Patience works. [2b] Patience had earlier applied to the

government to be given a place to live, but the government told her she is not eligible for government assistance because she has not lived in the area long enough. [3b] The land where Patience squats is several hectares, and it is currently being used by the owner of the land for his own purposes. [4b] The owner of the land objects to Patience living on his property, and he goes to court to get an order to evict Patience from his land. Patience is given some time to sort things out, and then the police evicts her from the property.

5

Judging the Past

Historical versus Contemporary Claims to Land

The vignette reported in Chapter 4 concerned an interracial conflict over land. We saw enormous racial differences in the reactions to the events portrayed in that scenario; nearly everything about the conflict seemed to be defined in terms of race, at least in the minds of most respondents. Consequently, it is perhaps not surprising that group identities seemed to have been activated by the dispute and that they played an important role in how people judged the controversy.

However, with interracial conflict essentially a constant in that vignette, it is not possible to assess how powerful a role race plays. That is, the type of conflict portrayed in the vignette was the same for all respondents; therefore, this constant could not account for variability in the assessments of the vignette (constants cannot explain variables). A more powerful means of estimating the role of race in identity activation would be to vary the nature of the land conflict from interracial to intraracial. That is precisely the nature of the experimental vignette reported in this chapter.

The purpose of this chapter is therefore to investigate the conflict between claims of injustice grounded in the past versus those grounded in the present, while varying the racial context of the dispute. In order to do so, a second experiment was employed. This vignette includes a manipulation of the races of the disputants in a historical land conflict. Because the vignette varies the racial composition of the dispute, the role of race and sociotropic justice concerns in evaluating historical land injustices can be rigorously estimated.

THE EXPERIMENT: THE LAND CONFLICT VIGNETTE

As I have noted, two experimental vignettes were included in the Land Reconciliation Survey, with one-half of the respondents (randomly selected) hearing a vignette about Patience, a squatter (see Chapter 4), and the other half of the respondents hearing a story about a dispute over the ownership of some land (also with random assignment).

The two versions of the land conflict vignette differed with regard to the adversaries. In one version, the conflict was said to be between Fanie and Sifiso, while in the other Thapelo and Zola disagreed about a land ownership issue. The former story was designed as an interracial conflict, while the latter represents an intraracial dispute, with the race of the adversaries being clearly stated or implied within the vignette (on the manipulation-check results, see below). Within the South African context, there is no ambiguity whatsoever about the implied race of the names: Sifiso, Thapelo, and Zola are widely understood to be names of black people, whereas Fanie is without doubt a white person (an Afrikaner, which is also consistent with being a farmer). Thus, one of the experimental manipulations for this vignette is the racial structure of the conflict over land, and the hypothesis is that how one judges claims of historical injustice varies by the racial makeup of the disputants.

In both versions of the vignette, a conflict is depicted between someone currently occupying the land and another who makes a claim to the property based on a historical injustice: a forced removal during the 1980s. The premise of the interracial conflict vignette is the following.

A dispute about who is the true owner of some property arises between Fanie and Sifiso. Fanie is a white farmer who currently occupies the land and claims it as his own. Sifiso, a black farmer, says that he is the true owner of the land, since he and his family owned the property before being forcibly removed from the land in the 1980s.

For the intraracial conflict version, the vignette began as follows.

A dispute about who is the true owner of some property arises between two farmers, Thapelo and Zola. Both are members of the same "tribe," but Thapelo currently occupies the land and claims it as his own. Zola says that he is the true owner of the land, since he and his family owned the property before Thapelo was put on the land as a result of being forcibly removed from his own place in the 1980s.

This premise sets the stage as either an interracial or intraracial dispute, and allows the strength of the claims of the two adversaries to be manipulated within the other elements of the story.

The first such manipulation has to do with the rule of law and the legitimacy of the claim. The manipulation is a trichotomy indicating the relative strength of each disputant's legal claim to the land. One-third of the respondents were told that the first party rejects the legal claim of the other; one-third heard that the second party rejects the claim of the first; and one-third were told that "each side in the dispute recognizes the validity of the claim of the other side." Thus, in theoretical terms, the manipulation ascribes superior legality to either the present (the current land owner), the past (the claimant), or neither. This manipulation applies to both the interracial and intraracial set of vignettes. For example, for the interracial conflict version of the vignette, the three elements are as follows (note the italicized portion).

Both parties are able to produce some legal documents supporting their claim of ownership of the land. However, though Fanie accepts that Sifiso has a legal right to the property, *Sifiso completely rejects Fanie's claim*, asserting that Fanie's legal documents do not provide adequate proof of his ownership of the property.

Both parties are able to produce some legal documents supporting their claim of ownership of the land. However, though Sifiso accepts that Fanie has a legal right to the property, *Fanie completely rejects Sifiso's claim*, asserting that Sifiso's legal documents do not provide adequate proof of his ownership of the property.

Both parties are able to produce legal documents supporting their claim of ownership. *Each side in the dispute recognizes the validity of the claim of the other side.*

Thus, the vignette varies the strength of the claims from the past and the present. How one weights the past versus the present is hypothesized to depend on the nature of one's group attachments and identities.

The second manipulation has to do with the need of the claimant. In one-third of the stories, the current land occupant has superior need; in one-third he has need inferior to that of the historical claimant; and in one-third the need of the parties is equal (and high). For example, the versions of the intraracial vignette are:

Without this land, Zola has nowhere else to live since he is old and has no family or children to help him, and he and his wife will have to move to the city where they will most likely live in poverty. Thapelo, on the other hand, has other land on which to live, since he is mainly trying to expand his farm in order to make more money.

Without this land, Thapelo has nowhere else to live since he is old and has no family or children to help him, and he and his wife will have to move to the city where they will most likely live in poverty. Zola, on the other hand, has other land on which to live, since he is mainly trying to expand his farm in order to make more money.

Without this land, neither Zola nor Thapelo has anywhere else to live since they are both old and have no family or children to help them. Whoever doesn't get the land will have to move to the city, where they will most likely live in poverty.

I hypothesize that greater perceived need will be associated with perceptions of fairness.

Finally, the outcome of the dispute was varied according to who gets the land, as follows.

The dispute goes to the Constitutional Court of South Africa, which decides that Sifiso has total rights of ownership to the land and that Fanie has no rights whatsoever. Sifiso gets the land.

The dispute goes to the Constitutional Court of South Africa, which decides that Fanie has total rights of ownership to the land and that Sifiso has no rights whatsoever. Fanie gets the land.

In the analysis that follows, all variables are coded in terms of the conflict between the historical claimant (Sifiso or Zola) and the contemporary claimant (Fanie or Thapelo).

As with the first vignette, this is a $2 \times 3 \times 3 \times 2$ fully crossed factorial design. Each respondent heard only a single version of the vignette, with random assignment of individuals to vignette. As with the vignette reported in Chapter 4, this research design has the significant advantages of both internal and external validity: high confidence in causal inferences and generalizability. The full text of the 36 versions of the vignettes is reported in the Appendix to this chapter.

The Races of the Disputants

Given the centrality of the racial composition of the conflict to the primary theoretical purposes of this vignette, I deemed it prudent to check that the respondents correctly perceived the races of the various actors in the stories. In fact, the disputants' races were quite readily discerned, with the percentages of all respondents correctly identifying the race being 98.2% for Sifiso, 96.3% for Fanie, 86.8% for Thapelo, and 87.7% for Zola. Practically no differences exist across the *race of the respondent* in the ability to identify the *race of the participants* in the vignette. Only one of the three chi-square tests is statistically significant ($p = .03$), and on that test, it is those of Asian origin who are best able to identify Thapelo's race, not blacks. Across all respondents and both vignettes, fully 89.4% of the respondents correctly recognized the race of the historical and contemporary claimants. In general, the racial manipulation was highly successful. In the analysis that follows, I do not typically control for the accuracy of the respondent's perception of the racial content of the vignette since that "variable" is very nearly a constant.

The Strength of the Legal Claim to the Land

Recall that, according to the vignette, either both disputants had equally valid land claims or one of the two parties had an uncontested claim to superiority. This manipulation was checked with a question asking which disputant, if any, had a "stronger legal right to the land." One option provided to the respondents was that "both had an equal legal right to the land." Table 5.1 reports the results of the manipulation check.

The figures in Table 5.1 represent the percentages of respondents in the treatment condition who accurately perceived the experimental state. Consider the results for black South Africans. When the vignette portrayed interracial conflict, the black respondents were extremely

TABLE 5.1. *Accuracy in the Perceptions of the Strength of the Legal Claim Manipulation*

	Manipulation: strength of claim		
	Contemporary superior	Equal	Historical superior
Interracial conflict (Fanie v. Sifiso)			
Black	9.2	28.6	65.9
White	30.6	53.4	14.1
Coloured	20.8	46.6	32.7
Asian origin	28.9	51.6	30.6
Intraracial conflict (Thapelo v. Zola)			
Black	23.0	40.6	31.4
White	25.0	57.4	31.1
Coloured	25.7	47.9	27.4
Asian origin	13.2	65.8	27.3

Note: The entries are the percentages of respondents in the treatment condition who accurately perceived the stimulus. Thus, 9.2% of the black respondents told that Fanie had a superior legal claim responded to the manipulation check question that Fanie's claim was superior to that of Sifiso. The contemporary claimants are Fanie and Thapelo; the historical claimants are Sifiso and Zola.

reluctant to accept the claim that Fanie's legal position is stronger (the contemporary claimant), even though Sifiso (the historical claimant) was said to accept Fanie's claim: Only 9.2% of the respondents who heard the story in which Fanie's claim is recognized as legitimate rated Fanie's claim as superior. Nor is the percentage much larger in the instance of intraracial conflict. For instance, no more than one-fourth of the respondents judged the contemporary claimant's legal position superior even when they were told it was acknowledged as such. Indeed, in no instance is there a statistically significant difference in the perceived strength of the claim across the versions of the vignette (data not shown). Generally, in the interracial conflict vignette, the respondents tended to rate Sifiso's claim as superior, while in the instance of intraracial conflict, there was a tendency to rate each claim roughly equally.

The logic of this manipulation is that a concession by one of the disputants could legitimize the claim of the other party. Thus, when we said that Sifiso accepts Fanie's right to the property, we expected the respondents to also accept Fanie's right. In general, that did not happen; the respondents instead asserted that Sifiso had a superior claim.

This finding may be evidence of strong sociotropic justice factors at work. Sifiso *by himself* cannot legitimate the claim of the white land owner. Instead, the claim is grounded in group-based injustices that work to deny the legitimacy of Fanie's claim. To some considerable extent, it seems that the respondents are not reacting to Sifiso the claimant, but to Sifiso's group in general. In the intraracial vignette, there is more evidence of individuation, although there is still a considerable tendency to rate the claims of each party as equal.

Despite the fact that the manipulation itself failed to produce differences in perceptions, racial differences in how the vignette was received are substantial. Consider the condition in which Fanie's position is said to be superior. Only a tiny fraction of blacks accepted that view, while 30.6% of the whites accepted Fanie's claim as superior. That the figure for whites is less than a majority is indicative of the overall failure of the manipulation to alter the preconceptions of the respondents. Nonetheless, white people were far more likely than blacks to accept the claim made in the vignette. Those of Asian origin reacted similarly to whites, while Coloured people were between the two extremes.

Similar biases can be seen throughout the first part of this table. When white people were told that Sifiso's claim was superior, only a small fraction accepted that (14.1%), but a substantial majority of blacks did (65.9%). In general, in the interracial conflict vignette, whites, Coloured people, and those of Asian origin were biased toward the perception of equal rights to the two claimants, and this lack of favoritism for one race or the other is even more pronounced in the intraracial circumstance. Note should also be taken of the strong differences in the way blacks react to the two vignettes. In the interracial vignette, a strong bias toward the black claimant exists; in the intraracial context, such a bias does not (and cannot) exist. Without race as a cue, most respondents tend to rate the claims as equal.

Indeed, as Table 5.2 further shows, in nearly all instances, the modal response was for the respondents to judge the claims of the two parties in the conflict to be equal. The only exception to this generalization is among blacks, who favored the historical claimant in four out of six instances. Black South Africans are distinctive in the degree to which they are willing to recognize the legitimacy of claims to land based on the historical injustices perpetrated by whites.

TABLE 5.2. *Accuracy in the Perceptions of the Strength of the Legal Claim Manipulation – Modal Responses*

| | Strength of claim | | |
	Contemporary superior	Equal	Historical superior
Interracial conflict			
Black	Historical: 54.2%	Historical: 61.6%	Historical: 65.9%
White	Equal: 59.5%	Equal: 53.4%	Equal: 52.5%
Coloured	Equal: 56.3%	Equal: 6.6%	Equal: 46.9%
Asian origin	Equal: 50.0%	Equal: 51.6%	Equal: 61.2%
Intraracial conflict			
Black	Historical: 40.2%	Equal: 40.6%	Equal: 46.7%
White	Equal: 48.0%	Equal: 57.4%	Equal: 52.5%
Coloured	Equal: 44.3%	Equal: 47.9%	Equal: 66.1%
Asian origin	Equal: 60.5%	Equal: 65.8%	Equal: 54.5%

Note: The entries are modal responses within each of the treatment conditions, as well as the percentages of respondents giving that response. For instance, when black South Africans were told in the interracial conflict vignette that the contemporary party had a superior legal claim to the land, the most common response to the manipulation check question was that the historical party had the stronger claim. That response was given by 54.2% of the respondents.

In retrospect, it appears that this manipulation may have been too complicated to accomplish its purpose. Conversely, a simple but strong bias in favor of equality may have colored the responses, rendering the manipulation impotent. Moreover, South Africans of all races may be skeptical about the veracity and utility of legal documents recording land rights. When respondents are uncertain about how to answer a question like this, the most appropriate response is most likely one asserting equal legal positions. While blacks tended to emphasize race in their reactions to the manipulations, most respondents perceived the legal claims of the disputants as equal. Thus, I hypothesize that this aspect of the dispute will have little impact on the perceived fairness of the outcome.

The Need Manipulation

One of the most important contemporary justifications for giving land to a claimant is the need of the person. Need is an element of deservingness, and consequently need usually contributes to justice under some theory of desert. Thus, the vignette portrayed three conditions: The land owner's need is greater than that of the landless; the landless person's need is greater; and both parties are of equal need. This manipulation was checked by questions asking the respondent to rate each party's need for the land on a ten-point scale. From these responses, I created a "difference of need" indicator. The relationship of this variable to the manipulations is shown in Tables 5.3 (interracial conflict) and 5.4 (intraracial conflict).

Highly significant differences in need perceptions exist across the manipulation trichotomy, within each set of vignettes. In the interracial conflict vignette (Table 5.3), differences in the need assessments of blacks vary substantially depending on the story ($r = .39$), as do the need assessments in the intraracial vignettes ($r = .46$; see Table 5.4). Thus, in general, the manipulation had the desired effect, across all four racial groups.

TABLE 5.3. *Manipulation Check: Claimant's Need, Interracial Vignette*

Difference of need: historical vs. contemporary interracial conflict	Which claimant has superior need?		
	Contemporary	Equal	Historical
Black			
Mean	.05	.25	.51
Std. dev.	.51	.39	.43
N	128	123	123
White			
Mean	−.45	−.03	.10
Std. dev.	.51	.30	.46
N	110	104	111
Coloured			
Mean	.24	.13	.49
Std. dev.	.62	.35	.55
N	62	57	59
Asian origin			
Mean	−.26	.10	.39
Std. dev.	.56	.32	.49
N	35	35	50

Note: Cross-treatment difference of means tests: black: $r = .39, p < .001$; white: $r = .48$, $p < .001$; Coloured: $r = .50, p < .001$; Asian origin: $r = .51, p < .001$.

However, two qualifications to the conclusion that the manipulation succeeded must be acknowledged. First, across all of the vignettes, the difference in need perceptions between the stories depicting equal need and the stories depicting superior need for the landless claimant is significant but still skewed toward the high end of need. For instance, when Sifiso (the claimant) is described as needy, 98.4% of the black respondents judged him needy. But when both parties were said to be equally needy, 95.1% of the black respondents judged Sifiso needy by virtue of being landless. This inability to accept the scenario in which both parties are said to be equally needy seems to be a function of who currently has the land. When need is equal, the landless party still is judged to be more needy. Thus, this represents a partial failure of the manipulation – as well as partial success (as indicated by the strong

TABLE 5.4. *Manipulation Check: Claimant's Need, Intraracial Vignette*

Difference of need: historical vs. contemporary intraracial conflict	Which claimant has superior need?		
	Contemporary	Equal	Historical
Black			
Mean	−.35	.03	.26
Std. dev.	.51	.34	.58
N	135	129	132
White			
Mean	−.32	−.03	.19
Std. dev.	.29	.56	.55
N	111	90	132
Coloured			
Mean	−.39	−.00	.39
Std. dev.	.65	.27	.57
N	60	58	68
Asian origin			
Mean	−.23	.01	.25
Std. dev.	.52	.34	.59
N	36	38	37

Note: Cross-treatment difference of means tests: black: $r = .46, p < .001$; white: $r = .40$, $p < .001$; Coloured: $r = .52, p < .001$; Asian origin: $r = .37, p < .001$.

correlations) – and may require that the trichotomous manipulation be collapsed in the analysis below.

A second qualification has to do with the level of need of the party *not* described as needy. When Fanie is described as needy, and Sifiso not, 76.6% of the black respondents nonetheless viewed Sifiso as needy. This likely reflects in part the fact that Sifiso does not own the land; therefore, he is in need of land, even if he has another place to stay. The effect of Fanie's need among blacks was not nearly so great: 36.3% viewed Fanie as to some degree needy even when he is not described as needy, with the comparable figures for Thapelo being 52.6% and for Zola 51.1%. In this sense, then, the experiment was not entirely successful in convincing the respondents that one party had high need and the other little if any need. Instead, the experiment was successful in creating differences of perceptions of relative need, which is of course its purpose.

Summary

Thus, the results of the manipulation checks vary widely. At one extreme, practically everyone correctly perceived the races of the disputants, and consequently the interracial versus intraracial conflict variable is quite valid and reliable. At the other extreme, the legal position of the claimants was not at all well perceived; instead, most respondents under most conditions judged the claims of each party to the dispute to be equivalent. In the middle lies the need manipulation, which the data strongly validate, but not as strongly as the race manipulation. Because the outcome manipulation was so obvious, and because it immediately preceded the questions about the fairness of the outcome, no manipulation check was deemed necessary.

FAIRNESS JUDGMENTS: THE DEPENDENT VARIABLE

The dependent variable throughout this analysis is a judgment of the fairness of awarding the land to one party or the other. Rather than assuming that fairness judgments are locked in zero-sum relationship, I asked independent questions about fairness to the winner and to the loser in the land dispute. As it turns out, fairly strong *positive* correlations exist for all fairness judgments. For instance, the correlation between judgments of how fairly Sifiso was treated when he won the conflict are correlated at .54 with judgments of how fairly Fanie was treated in losing the land dispute. The correlations differ somewhat across the racial context of the vignette (interracial vs intraracial, .54 vs .39). Thus, few South Africans view this conflict in zero-sum terms. Those who see the outcome as fair to the winner tend also to judge the outcome as fair to the loser. Using a dichotomized version of the ten-point scale (and with a "don't know" category), from 68.5% to 74.2% of the respondents judge the outcome as either fair to both parties or unfair to both parties, even if most see the outcome as unfair to both parties. South Africans who assert that the outcome is fair to one party and unfair to the other are a fairly small minority.

Because the analytical issue under consideration here has to do with contemporary versus historical claims to justice, the dependent variable throughout this analysis is whether the outcome is thought to be fair to the party making a contemporary justice claim. In particular, the dependent variable is coded as the perceived fairness of the dispute from the perspective of the historical land claimants (Sifiso and Zola), and the contemporary land claimants (Fanie and Thapelo). Across all versions of the vignettes, 37.4% of the respondents judged the outcome to be fair to the historical claimant, while 39.7% thought the contemporary claimant was treated fairly.[1] Thus, generally speaking, the respondents were considerably more likely to judge the outcome of the vignette as unfair than fair. Across all versions of the vignette, the vignette version can account for 17.3% of the variance in judgments of fairness to the past, but only 9.1% of the variance in assessments of fairness to the present (both of these are highly statistically significant). Judgments of fairness to the historical claimant vary from 6.1% to 71.7%, which is of course a quite considerable range. Perceived fairness to the contemporary claimant also varies widely, from 9.8% to 73.2%. On balance, 36.0% of the respondents assigned the same fairness score to both

---

[1] Fairness judgments were measured on a continuous scale, which has been rescored to vary between 0 and 1. For illustrative purposes (only), I occasionally report on a categorized version of this scale. Scores greater than .5 are said to be judgments of fairness, with scores lower than that midpoint referred to as unfairness. I also utilize a five-category scoring of the variable for some purposes. This variable varies from "very unfair" (0 to .2) to "very fair" (.8 to 1.0). These categorical variables are never used for analytical purposes.

parties in the dispute; 34.1% thought the contemporary claimant got more fairness than the historical party; and 29.8% judged the historical party to have been treated more fairly than the contemporary party. I assume that similar fairness scores represent the belief that each got what he deserved, and that mixed fairness scores reflect the view that the justice subdimensions of the outcome were mixed, with fairness also producing unfairness. Whether this variability is systematic is not yet determined, but certainly the different scenarios presented in the vignette stimulated different assessments of the outcome.

Across all versions of the vignette, assessments of fairness are *not* dependent on the respondent's race. Indeed, the differences across race in judgments of fairness to the historical claimant do not even achieve statistical significance, and the ratings of fairness to the contemporary claimant vary significantly but trivially. These are, however, the simple and direct effects of race and they do not preclude finding that race has significant indirect effects on the judgments of fairness.

ANALYSIS

I begin the analysis by considering the simplest, distributive justice hypothesis: The outcome will be judged to be most fair to the winner of the dispute.

The data reveal surprising variability across the three racial groups. For blacks and Coloured people, the relationship is precisely as expected. When the historical claimant is awarded the land, the outcome is judged to be considerably more fair to that claimant. The correlations between the outcome dichotomy and judgments of fairness are .36 and .26, for blacks and Coloured people, respectively. For those of Asian origin, the relationship is similar but considerably weak ($r = .12$). Whites, however, are an important exception. When the historical claimant loses, the average fairness score is .45; when the claimant wins, the fairness mean is also .45. White South Africans seem to be impervious to who wins the dispute in forming their judgments of fairness. Some other aspects of the conflict must be driving fairness judgments.

However, an important aspect of these findings has to do with the hypothesized effect of the racial composition of the conflict. For white South Africans, there is a strong interaction between the racial composition of the conflict and the importance of winning. In the instance of interracial conflict, winning is associated with perceived fairness (β = .18), but in the intraracial vignette, a victory for the historical claimant is associated with perceived unfairness (β = −.20). Both coefficients are statistically significant at $p < .001$. This finding suggests that whites are reacting primarily to the race of the claimant in the intraracial vignette.

Among blacks, an interactive effect can also be found. In the same-race vignette, winning is moderately associated with perceived fairness (β = .21), but in the interracial vignette, the relationship is much stronger (β = .51). Among Coloured people, a similar difference of coefficients is observed (β = .13 vs .40). Among the Asian respondents, the two coefficients are .23 and .02, indicating that the outcome has nothing to do with fairness in the instance of interracial conflict. For all racial groups, but especially for blacks and whites, the racial makeup of the disputes matters significantly for how the outcome is judged.

In light of this initial confirmation of the hypothesis that the racial composition of the conflict matters for assessing the outcome of the vignette, it is essential that all additional analysis take this variability into account. Indeed, following the analytical format of Chapter 4, the remaining analysis posits (1) direct effects of race, (2) interactive effects between race and perceptions of the manipulations, (3) the manipulations themselves, (4) direct effects of racial composition of the conflict manipulation, and (5) interactions between the racial composition variable and other variables in the equation.

Consequently, Table 5.5 reports the various effects of the racial and distributive justice (outcome) manipulations. The equation includes the experimental manipulations, the perceptions of the manipulations, the race of the respondent (with Africans constituting the excluded category), the interactions among race and the manipulations and perceptual variables, and the interaction between winning and the racial composition of the dispute. A considerable amount of information is included in this table.[2]

---

[2] This analysis combines both versions of the vignette (interracial and intraracial) within a single equation. The nature of the conflict is then represented by a dummy variable, which is also used to create interaction terms.

TABLE 5.5. *Predicting Justice Judgments, Interracial versus Intraracial Conflict*

	r	b	s.e.	β
Respondent race				
White	.03	.03	.07	.05
Coloured	−.03	.13	.09	.15
Asian origin	−.02	.10	.11	.10
Perception of the manipulation:				
disputants' races	−.04	−.02	.03	−.02
Race/perception of disputants' race interactions				
White	.02	.01	.04	.03
Coloured	−.04	−.06	.04	−.14
Asian origin	−.03	−.06	.05	−.10
Experimental manipulation: whether interracial	.01	−.10	.03	−.14**
Experimental manipulation: historical claimant wins	.22	.17	.03	.24***
Manipulation interaction: whether interracial: historical claimant wins	.15	.25	.05	.30***
Race/manipulation interaction: whether interracial				
White	.00	.18	.05	.19***
Coloured	−.02	.03	.06	.03
Asian origin	−.00	.18	.07	.12**
Race/manipulation interactions: historical claimant wins				
White	.02	−.06	.05	−.06
Coloured	.07	−.08	.06	−.06
Asian origin	.02	−.03	.07	−.02
Race/manipulation interaction: whether interracial: historical claimant wins				
White	−.05	−.47	.07	−.36***
Coloured	.08	−.07	.08	−.04
Asian origin	.00	−.36	.10	−.17***
Equation statistics				
Intercept		.38	.06	

(*continued*)

TABLE 5.5 (*continued*)

	r	b	s.e.	β
Standard deviation – dependent variable		.35		
Standard error of estimate		.33		
R²				.11***
N		1,987		

Note: Significance of standardized regression coefficients (β): ***p < .001, **p < .01, *p < .05.

I first note that in this multivariate equation, the tests of the difference of the intercepts between Africans and the other races reveal no statistically significant differences. This is seen in the trivial and nonsignificant coefficients for the dummy variables representing whites, Coloured people, and those of Asian origin. Once all the control variables are included, no significant differences in fairness judgments remain across the various racial groups.

I also note that the perceptions of the *races of the disputants* have no effect on fairness judgments, either directly or in interaction with the respondents' races. As I noted above, little variance exists in these perceptual variables, and I therefore consider this finding entirely unremarkable.

The two manipulations analyzed in this table themselves produce statistically significant differences in justice judgments. Not surprisingly, when the historical claimants win possession of the land, the outcome is judged to be substantially more fair (b = 17). When the conflict is intraracial, the outcome is also seen as less fair (b = −.10). Both of these coefficients are statistically significant. Moreover, as suggested by the bivariate results reported above, a highly significant interaction exists between the outcome and the racial makeup of the conflict. When the dispute is interracial and the historical claimant wins, the outcome is judged to be extremely fair (b = (.25 + .17) = .42), in contrast to the intraracial case (β = (−.10 + .25) = .15). Thus, the effect of winning is quite different across the types of racial conflict: When intraracial, the benefit of winning is relatively small (.15); when the dispute is interracial, the coefficient balloons to .42. Conversely, when the historical claimant loses, interracial conflict is seen as less fair (b = −.10); when the claimant wins, the effect of interracial conflict is boosted to +.15. Thus, it seems that winning contributes to perceived fairness via two mechanisms: (1) getting the land, and (2) taking away the land from a racial opponent, one who most likely acquired the land via the unfair system of apartheid. To reiterate, the influence of getting the land differs depending on whom the land is being taken from; this conflict thus seems to be about more than who gets to keep the land. Distributive justice concerns are being supplemented by retributive or restorative justice concerns.

These relationships are made more complicated still by the existence of substantial interactions between race and the racial makeup of the dispute. The justice judgments of whites are particularly influenced by whether the conflict is intra- or interracial. To a lesser degree, those of Asian origin are also influenced by the racial makeup of the controversy.

No simple interactions are found between the respondent's race and whether the historical claimant wins − none of the interactions terms even approach statistical significance. But the coefficients defined by the interaction among race, interracial conflict, and whether the historical claimant wins are highly significant for whites and those of Asian origin, although not even marginally significant for Coloured South Africans. The coefficients for white are interesting. The interaction among whites for the interracial conflict with the historical claimant winning produces a coefficient of −.47, which indicates a substantial decline in perceived fairness when the historical claimant wins in the interracial disputes. When a black South African succeeds in pressing a claim grounded in the past, whites view the outcome as substantially unfair. To a lesser degree, the same finding characterizes South Africans of Asian origin. Coloured South Africans are unaffected by whether the conflict is interracial or by whether the land claim is grounded in a claim of historical injustices.

Finally, I note that the need of the various parties to the dispute, even relative need, has practically no impact on perceptions of fairness. It appears to me that South Africans are judging this dispute in sociotropic terms and that the characteristics of the specific individuals involved in the dispute are of little consequence.

The Impact of Group Identities on Fairness
Judgments: Black South Africans

The foregoing analysis focused on differences in how blacks, whites, Coloured people, and South Africans of Asian origin reacted to the vignette. The primary finding from that analysis is that the race of the claimant matters greatly, and that whites are especially unwilling to attribute much legitimacy to demands for justice that are grounded in the past.

It remains to consider, however, whether differences among black South Africans can be explained using social identity theory. Following the analytical strategy employed in Chapter 4, I begin this analysis by investigating the consequences of the type of group identity held by the respondents for their views of the land dispossession vignette. Because regression analysis of the vignette judgments reveals that need and the strength of the claim have little influence on fairness judgments (either as manipulations or as perceptions of manipulations), I have excluded these variables from further analysis. The variables of primary interest are therefore whether the conflict is interracial or intraracial, and whether the historical claimant wins or loses. The results of the fairness assessments are shown in Figure 5.1.

The data reported in this figure are the average fairness judgments (ranging from 0 to 1) according to the racial makeup of the conflict, who won, and the respondent's type of group identity.

So for instance, among those adopting a South African national identity, fairness judgments range from a low of .21 when the historical claimant loses in an interracial dispute to a high of .80 when the historical claimant wins in an interracial dispute. The data in this figure support a variety of conclusions.

Consider first those adopting a national identity. For those presented with a vignette involving the intraracial dispute, it matters not at all whether the historical claimant wins (means fairness scores of .41 and .45). The dispute therefore does not seem to be one in which historical injustices are implicated.

However, in the interracial context, winning and losing matter enormously (.21 vs. .80). That the white land owner wins drives the fairness judgment down (.21 vs. .41 in the intraracial dispute), and a black claimant winning against a white dramatically increases perceptions

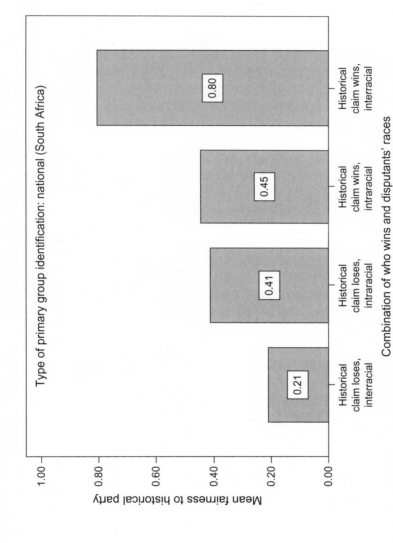

FIGURE 5.1. The influence of group identities on perceptions of fairness – the historical land dis-possession vignette, black South Africans.

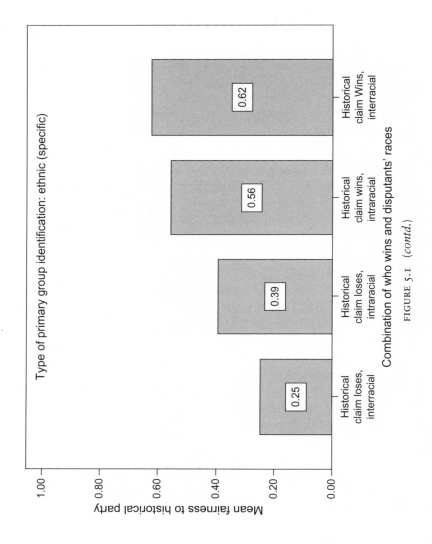

Type of primary group identification: ethnic (specific)

FIGURE 5.1 (contd.)

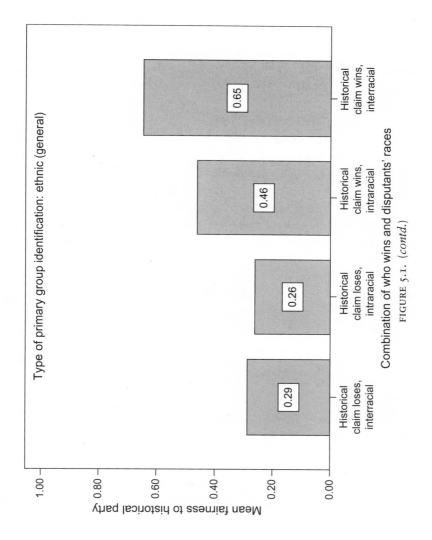

Type of primary group identification: ethnic (general)

FIGURE 5.1. (*contd.*)

of justice (.80 vs. .45). For blacks with a national identity, land conflicts are more about race than history.

For those adopting a general ethnic identity, the findings are not nearly as extreme. For instance, when the historical claimant loses, it matters little whether a black or white land owner wins (.29 vs. .26). On the other hand, winning against a white land owner does increase perceptions of fairness (.65 vs. .46), presumably because the black claimant got the land fairly and the white land owner lost the land fairly. Still, those with a national identity are considerably more influenced by the scenario in which land is taken from a white land owner and given to a black claimant (.80 vs. .65).

Among those adopting a narrow ethnic identity, the findings parallel those with a general ethnic attachment. Both winning and race matter, but not to the extent they do among those with a national identity.

At the most general level, the effects of types of group identity are seen in (1) the strong influence among those with a national identity of a historical claimant taking possession of land from a white land owner, and (2) the indifference of those with a general ethnic group identity to a black losing against a black instead of a white. Thus, the data indicate that those with a national identity are most strongly influenced by interracial land conflicts, that those with ethnic identities (general and specific) are less concerned that the white land owner be stripped of his land, but that for all respondents, the most fair outcome occurs when a black historical claimant is awarded the land of a white land owner.[3]

If we juxtapose these findings with those from Chapter 4, a couple of speculations seem reasonable. First, black South Africans with a national identity seem to subscribe to a theory of justice somewhat different from those adopting ethnic identities. They care about universal proceduralism, and they seem to be concerned with both the unfairness of some not having land in contemporary South Africa and the unfairness of others having land. For these respondents, land conflicts seem to take on more of a zero-sum character. Fairness means giving land to those who were unfairly denied land in the past and taking land

---

[3] Note that the eta coefficients for the differences of means reported in Figure 5.1 differ significantly according to the type of identity selected by the respondent. Among those with general and specific ethnic identities, the etas are .40 and .38, respectively. Among those with a national identity, eta rises to .53.

away from those who may have profited from unjust enrichment under apartheid and colonialism. In this sense, national identities may be associated with a more global and balanced sense of justice, with justice defined in sociotropic terms, in terms of what groups get and what they are denied.

Ethnic identities may be more focused on who wins than on who loses. Among these black South Africans, it is more important that black people be given land than that land be taken from whites. Thus, land conflicts are to a greater degree potentially positive sum in the sense that fairness does not require that whites necessarily be punished. It is possible that ethnic identifiers are most interested in getting land for members of their group and little more. In this sense, their concept of land justice is perhaps more parochial and ultimately more negotiable.

DISCUSSION AND CONCLUDING COMMENTS

It is certainly true that this vignette has produced considerably more clouded results than the vignette reported in Chapter 4. This is in part owing to the complicated structure of this vignette, and in part to the simple fact that land conflicts in South Africa are multifaceted and people therefore have complex and often contradictory views of what is fair. Moreover, perceptions of land disputes have been heavily shaped by larger attitudes toward intergroup politics in South Africa. Attitudes toward land restitution and redistribution reflect less the needs of the individual claimants and more the historical conflicts among racial groups in South Africa.

Nonetheless, a number of important conclusions emerge from this analysis. First, and most obvious, the politics of land restitution and redistribution are heavily shaped by race. As shown in earlier chapters, black and white South Africans hold nearly opposite views about land conflicts grounded in the past. At the simplest level, blacks want to take the past into consideration; whites do not. White attitudes, however, are not shaped just by the past; it is specifically the past as it applies to interracial conflict today that influences white attitudes. Although the data are not capable of fully supporting this conclusion, my strong impression is that whites are concerned about how their group will prevail in future land conflicts associated with historical injustices.

For whites, and to a lesser degree those of Asian origin, land is a socio-tropic political issue.

At the same time, blacks seem unwilling to accept the legitimacy of white claims to contemporary land justice. Even when the vignette reported in this chapter describes the white land claim as legitimate, and as accepted as legitimate by the black land claimant, these respondents are loathe to recognize contemporary land rights. To many blacks – and especially those adopting a national identity – the issue of land today is an issue of historical dispossessions by whites of blacks in the past. These historical injustices remain salient to the African majority and render the negotiation of land claims even more problematic than they might otherwise be. Blacks and whites define the polar extremes on willingness and unwillingness to take the past into consideration in dealing with land problems in the present, with Coloured people and those of Asian origin in the middle. But perhaps the most politically significant conclusion of this chapter, and ultimately of this entire analysis, is that blacks care about the past and think it should be relevant in land restitution and redistribution today; whites do not.

APPENDIX TO CHAPTER 5: FULL VIGNETTES – HISTORICAL LAND CONFLICTS

Interracial Land Dispute

Story 1 (aaa)

A dispute about who is the true owner of some property arises between Fanie and Sifiso. Fanie is a white farmer who currently occupies the land and claims it as his own. Sifiso, a black farmer, says that he is the true owner of the land, since he and his family owned the property before being forcibly removed from the land in the 1980s. [2a] Both parties are able to produce some legal documents supporting their claim of ownership of the land. However, though Fanie accepts that Sifiso has a legal right to the property, Sifiso completely rejects Fanie's claim, asserting that Fanie's legal documents do not provide adequate proof of his ownership of the property. [3a] Without this land, Fanie has nowhere else to live since he is old and has no family or children to help him, and he and his wife will have to move to the city where they will most likely live in poverty. Sifiso, on the other hand, has other land on which to live, since he is mainly trying to expand his farm in order to make more money. [4a] The dispute goes to the Constitutional Court of South Africa, which decides that Sifiso has total rights of ownership to the land and that Fanie has no rights whatsoever. Sifiso gets the land.

Story 2 *(aab)*

A dispute about who is the true owner of some property arises between Fanie and Sifiso. Fanie is a white farmer who currently occupies the land and claims it as his own. Sifiso, a black farmer, says that he is the true owner of the land, since he and his family owned the property before being forcibly removed from the land in the 1980s. [2a] Both parties are able to produce some legal documents supporting their claim of ownership of the land. However, though Fanie accepts that Sifiso has a legal right to the property, Sifiso completely rejects Fanie's claim, asserting that Fanie's legal documents do not provide adequate proof of his ownership of the property. [3a] Without this land, Fanie has nowhere else to live since he is old and has no family or children to help him, and he and his wife will have to move to the city where they will most likely live in poverty. Sifiso, on the other hand, has other land on which to live, since he is mainly trying to expand his farm in order to make more money. [4b] The dispute goes to the Constitutional Court of South Africa, which decides that Fanie has total rights of ownership to the land and that Sifiso has no rights whatsoever. Fanie gets the land.

Story 3 *(aba)*

A dispute about who is the true owner of some property arises between Fanie and Sifiso. Fanie is a white farmer who currently occupies the land and claims it as his own. Sifiso, a black farmer, says that he is the true owner of the land, since he and his family owned the property before being forcibly removed from the land in the 1980s. [2a] Both parties are able to produce some legal documents supporting their claim of ownership of the land. However, though Fanie accepts that Sifiso has a legal right to the property, Sifiso completely rejects Fanie's claim, asserting that Fanie's legal documents do not provide adequate proof of his ownership of the property. [3b] Without this land, Sifiso has nowhere else to live since he is old and has no family or children to help him, and he and his wife will have to move to the city where they will most likely live in poverty. Fanie, on the other hand, has other land on which to live, since he is mainly trying to expand his farm in order to make more money. [4a] The dispute goes to the Constitutional Court of South Africa, which decides that Sifiso has total rights of ownership to the land and that Fanie has no rights whatsoever. Sifiso gets the land.

Story 4 *(abb)*

A dispute about who is the true owner of some property arises between Fanie and Sifiso. Fanie is a white farmer who currently occupies the land and claims it as his own. Sifiso, a black farmer, says that he is the true owner of the land, since he and his family owned the property before being forcibly removed from the land in the 1980s. [2a] Both parties are able to produce some legal documents supporting their claim of ownership of the land. However, though Fanie accepts that Sifiso has a legal right to the property, Sifiso completely rejects Fanie's claim, asserting that Fanie's legal documents do not provide adequate proof of his ownership of the property. [3b] Without this land, Sifiso has nowhere else to live since he is old and has no family or children to help him, and he and his wife will have to move to the city where they will most likely live in poverty. Fanie, on the other hand, has other land on which to live, since he is mainly trying to expand his farm in order to make more money. [4b] The dispute goes to the Constitutional Court of South Africa, which decides that Fanie has total rights of ownership to the land and that Sifiso has no rights whatsoever. Fanie gets the land.

Story 5 *(aca)*

A dispute about who is the true owner of some property arises between Fanie and Sifiso. Fanie is a white farmer who currently occupies the land and claims it as his own. Sifiso, a black farmer, says that he is the true owner of the land, since he and his family owned the property before being forcibly removed from the land in the 1980s. [2a] Both parties are able to produce some legal documents supporting their claim of ownership of the land. However, though Fanie accepts that Sifiso has a legal right to the property, Sifiso completely rejects Fanie's claim, asserting that Fanie's legal documents do not provide adequate proof of his ownership of the property. [3c] Without this land, neither Fanie nor Sifiso has anywhere else to live since they are both old and have no family or children to help them. Whoever doesn't get the land will have to move to the city, where they will most likely live in poverty.

[4a] The dispute goes to the Constitutional Court of South Africa, which decides that Sifiso has total rights of ownership to the land and that Fanie has no rights whatsoever. Sifiso gets the land.

Story 6 (acb)

A dispute about who is the true owner of some property arises between Fanie and Sifiso. Fanie is a white farmer who currently occupies the land and claims it as his own. Sifiso, a black farmer, says that he is the true owner of the land, since he and his family owned the property before being forcibly removed from the land in the 1980s. [2a] Both parties are able to produce some legal documents supporting their claim of ownership of the land. However, though Fanie accepts that Sifiso has a legal right to the property, Sifiso completely rejects Fanie's claim, asserting that Fanie's legal documents do not provide adequate proof of his ownership of the property. [3c] Without this land, neither Fanie nor Sifiso has anywhere else to live since they are both old and have no family or children to help them. Whoever doesn't get the land will have to move to the city, where they will most likely live in poverty. [4b] The dispute goes to the Constitutional Court of South Africa, which decides that Fanie has total rights of ownership to the land and that Sifiso has no rights whatsoever. Fanie gets the land.

Story 7 (baa)

A dispute about who is the true owner of some property arises between Fanie and Sifiso. Fanie is a white farmer who currently occupies the land and claims it as his own. Sifiso, a black farmer, says that he is the true owner of the land, since he and his family owned the property before being forcibly removed from the land in the 1980s. [2b] Both parties are able to produce some legal documents supporting their claim of ownership of the land. However, though Sifiso accepts that Fanie has a legal right to the property, Fanie completely rejects Sifiso's claim, asserting that Sifiso's legal documents do not provide adequate proof of his ownership of the property. [3a] Without this land, Fanie has nowhere else to live since he is old and has no family or children to help him, and he and his wife will have to move to the city where they will most likely live in poverty. Sifiso, on the other hand, has other land on which to live, since he is mainly trying to expand his farm in order to make more money. [4a] The dispute goes to the Constitutional Court of

South Africa, which decides that Sifiso has total rights of ownership to the land and that Fanie has no rights whatsoever. Sifiso gets the land.

Story 8 *(bab)*

A dispute about who is the true owner of some property arises between Fanie and Sifiso. Fanie is a white farmer who currently occupies the land and claims it as his own. Sifiso, a black farmer, says that he is the true owner of the land, since he and his family owned the property before being forcibly removed from the land in the 1980s. [2b] Both parties are able to produce some legal documents supporting their claim of ownership of the land. However, though Sifiso accepts that Fanie has a legal right to the property, Fanie completely rejects Sifiso's claim, asserting that Sifiso's legal documents do not provide adequate proof of his ownership of the property. [3a] Without this land, Fanie has nowhere else to live since he is old and has no family or children to help him, and he and his wife will have to move to the city where they will most likely live in poverty. Sifiso, on the other hand, has other land on which to live, since he is mainly trying to expand his farm in order to make more money. [4b] The dispute goes to the Constitutional Court of South Africa, which decides that Fanie has total rights of ownership to the land and that Sifiso has no rights whatsoever. Fanie gets the land.

Story 9 *(bba)*

A dispute about who is the true owner of some property arises between Fanie and Sifiso. Fanie is a white farmer who currently occupies the land and claims it as his own. Sifiso, a black farmer, says that he is the true owner of the land, since he and his family owned the property before being forcibly removed from the land in the 1980s. [2b] Both parties are able to produce some legal documents supporting their claim of ownership of the land. However, though Sifiso accepts that Fanie has a legal right to the property, Fanie completely rejects Sifiso's claim, asserting that Sifiso's legal documents do not provide adequate proof of his ownership of the property. [3b] Without this land, Sifiso has nowhere else to live since he is old and has no family or children to help him, and he and his wife will have to move to the city where they will most likely live in poverty. Fanie, on the other hand, has other land on which to live, since he is mainly trying to expand his farm in order to make more money. [4a] The dispute goes to the Constitutional Court of

South Africa, which decides that Sifiso has total rights of ownership to the land and that Fanie has no rights whatsoever. Sifiso gets the land.

Story 10 *(bbb)*

A dispute about who is the true owner of some property arises between Fanie and Sifiso. Fanie is a white farmer who currently occupies the land and claims it as his own. Sifiso, a black farmer, says that he is the true owner of the land, since he and his family owned the property before being forcibly removed from the land in the 1980s. [2b] Both parties are able to produce some legal documents supporting their claim of ownership of the land. However, though Sifiso accepts that Fanie has a legal right to the property, Fanie completely rejects Sifiso's claim, asserting that Sifiso's legal documents do not provide adequate proof of his ownership of the property. [3b] Without this land, Sifiso has nowhere else to live since he is old and has no family or children to help him, and he and his wife will have to move to the city where they will most likely live in poverty. Fanie, on the other hand, has other land on which to live, since he is mainly trying to expand his farm in order to make more money. [4b] The dispute goes to the Constitutional Court of South Africa, which decides that Fanie has total rights of ownership to the land and that Sifiso has no rights whatsoever. Fanie gets the land.

Story 11 *(bca)*

A dispute about who is the true owner of some property arises between Fanie and Sifiso. Fanie is a white farmer who currently occupies the land and claims it as his own. Sifiso, a black farmer, says that he is the true owner of the land, since he and his family owned the property before being forcibly removed from the land in the 1980s. [2b] Both parties are able to produce some legal documents supporting their claim of ownership of the land. However, though Sifiso accepts that Fanie has a legal right to the property, Fanie completely rejects Sifiso's claim, asserting that Sifiso's legal documents do not provide adequate proof of his ownership of the property. [3c] Without this land, neither Fanie nor Sifiso has anywhere else to live since they are both old and have no family or children to help them. Whoever doesn't get the land will have to move to the city, where they will most likely live in poverty. [4a] The dispute goes to the Constitutional Court of South Africa, which decides that Sifiso has total rights of ownership to the land and that Fanie has no rights whatsoever. Sifiso gets the land.

Story 12 (bcb)

A dispute about who is the true owner of some property arises between Fanie and Sifiso. Fanie is a white farmer who currently occupies the land and claims it as his own. Sifiso, a black farmer, says that he is the true owner of the land, since he and his family owned the property before being forcibly removed from the land in the 1980s. [2b] Both parties are able to produce some legal documents supporting their claim of ownership of the land. However, though Sifiso accepts that Fanie has a legal right to the property, Fanie completely rejects Sifiso's claim, asserting that Sifiso's legal documents do not provide adequate proof of his ownership of the property. [3c] Without this land, neither Fanie nor Sifiso has anywhere else to live since they are both old and have no family or children to help them. Whoever doesn't get the land will have to move to the city, where they will most likely live in poverty. [4b] The dispute goes to the Constitutional Court of South Africa, which decides that Fanie has total rights of ownership to the land and that Sifiso has no rights whatsoever. Fanie gets the land.

Story 13 (caa)

A dispute about who is the true owner of some property arises between Fanie and Sifiso. Fanie is a white farmer who currently occupies the land and claims it as his own. Sifiso, a black farmer, says that he is the true owner of the land, since he and his family owned the property before being forcibly removed from the land in the 1980s. [2c] Both parties are able to produce legal documents supporting their claim of ownership. Each side in the dispute recognizes the validity of the claim of the other side. [3a] Without this land, Fanie has nowhere else to live since he is old and has no family or children to help him, and he and his wife will have to move to the city where they will most likely live in poverty. Sifiso, on the other hand, has other land on which to live, since he is mainly trying to expand his farm in order to make more money. [4a] The dispute goes to the Constitutional Court of South Africa, which decides that Sifiso has total rights of ownership to the land and that Fanie has no rights whatsoever. Sifiso gets the land.

Story 14 (cab)

A dispute about who is the true owner of some property arises between Fanie and Sifiso. Fanie is a white farmer who currently occupies the land and claims it as his own. Sifiso, a black farmer, says that he is the true owner of the land, since he and his family owned the property before being forcibly removed from the land in the 1980s. [2c] Both parties are able to produce legal documents supporting their claim of ownership. Each side in the dispute recognizes the validity of the claim of the other side. [3a] Without this land, Fanie has nowhere else to live since he is old and has no family or children to help him, and he and his wife will have to move to the city where they will most likely live in poverty. Sifiso, on the other hand, has other land on which to live, since he is mainly trying to expand his farm in order to make more money. [4b] The dispute goes to the Constitutional Court of South Africa, which decides that Fanie has total rights of ownership to the land and that Sifiso has no rights whatsoever. Fanie gets the land.

Story 15 (cba)

A dispute about who is the true owner of some property arises between Fanie and Sifiso. Fanie is a white farmer who currently occupies the land and claims it as his own. Sifiso, a black farmer, says that he is the true owner of the land, since he and his family owned the property before being forcibly removed from the land in the 1980s. [2c] Both parties are able to produce legal documents supporting their claim of ownership. Each side in the dispute recognizes the validity of the claim of the other side. [3b] Without this land, Sifiso has nowhere else to live since he is old and has no family or children to help him, and he and his wife will have to move to the city where they will most likely live in poverty. Fanie, on the other hand, has other land on which to live, since he is mainly trying to expand his farm in order to make more money. [4a] The dispute goes to the Constitutional Court of South Africa, which decides that Sifiso has total rights of ownership to the land and that Fanie has no rights whatsoever. Sifiso gets the land.

Story 16 (cbb)

A dispute about who is the true owner of some property arises between Fanie and Sifiso. Fanie is a white farmer who currently occupies the land and claims it as his own. Sifiso, a black farmer, says that he is the true owner of the land, since he and his family owned the property before being forcibly removed from the land in the 1980s. [2c] Both parties are able to produce legal documents supporting their claim of ownership. Each side in the dispute recognizes the validity of the claim of the other side. [3b] Without this land, Sifiso has nowhere else to live since he is old and has no family or children to help him, and he and his wife will have to move to the city where they will most likely live in poverty. Fanie, on the other hand, has other land on which to live, since he is mainly trying to expand his farm in order to make more money. [4b] The dispute goes to the Constitutional Court of South Africa, which decides that Fanie has total rights of ownership to the land and that Sifiso has no rights whatsoever. Fanie gets the land.

Story 17 (cca)

A dispute about who is the true owner of some property arises between Fanie and Sifiso. Fanie is a white farmer who currently occupies the land and claims it as his own. Sifiso, a black farmer, says that he is the true owner of the land, since he and his family owned the property before being forcibly removed from the land in the 1980s. [2c] Both parties are able to produce legal documents supporting their claim of ownership. Each side in the dispute recognizes the validity of the claim of the other side. [3c] Without this land, neither Fanie nor Sifiso has anywhere else to live since they are both old and have no family or children to help them. Whoever doesn't get the land will have to move to the city, where they will most likely live in poverty. [4a] The dispute goes to the Constitutional Court of South Africa, which decides that Sifiso has total rights of ownership to the land and that Fanie has no rights whatsoever. Sifiso gets the land.

Story 18 (ccb)

A dispute about who is the true owner of some property arises between Fanie and Sifiso. Fanie is a white farmer who currently occupies the land and claims it as his own. Sifiso, a black farmer, says that he is the true owner of the land, since he and his family owned the property before being forcibly removed from the land in the 1980s. [2c] Both parties are able to produce legal documents supporting their claim of ownership. Each side in the dispute recognizes the validity of the claim of the other side. [3c] Without this land, neither Fanie nor Sifiso has anywhere else to live since they are both old and have no family or children to help them. Whoever doesn't get the land will have to move to the city, where they will most likely live in poverty. [4b] The dispute goes to the Constitutional Court of South Africa, which decides that Fanie has total rights of ownership to the land and that Sifiso has no rights whatsoever. Fanie gets the land.

Intraracial Land Dispute

Story 1 (aaa)

A dispute about who is the true owner of some property arises between two farmers, Thapelo and Zola. Both are members of the same "tribe," but Thapelo currently occupies the land and claims it as his own. Zola says that he is the true owner of the land, since he and his family owned the property before Thapelo was put on the land as a result of being forcibly removed from his own place in the 1980s. [2a] Both parties are able to produce some legal documents supporting their claim of ownership of the land. However, though Zola accepts that Thapelo has a legal right to the property, Thapelo completely rejects Zola's claim, asserting that Zola's legal documents do not provide adequate proof of his ownership of the property. [3a] Without this land, Zola has nowhere else to live since he is old and has no family or children to help him, and he and his wife will have to move to the city where they will most likely live in poverty. Thapelo, on the other hand, has other land on which to live, since he is mainly trying to expand his farm in order to make more money. [4a] The dispute goes to the Constitutional Court of South Africa, which decides that Thapelo has total rights of ownership to the land and that Zola has no rights whatsoever. Thapelo gets the land.

Story 2 (aab)

A dispute about who is the true owner of some property arises between two farmers, Thapelo and Zola. Both are members of the same "tribe," but Thapelo currently occupies the land and claims it as his own. Zola says that he is the true owner of the land, since he and his family owned the property before Thapelo was put on the land as a result of being forcibly removed from his own place in the 1980s. [2a] Both parties are able to produce some legal documents supporting their claim of ownership of the land. However, though Zola accepts that Thapelo has a legal right to the property, Thapelo completely rejects Zola's claim, asserting that Zola's legal documents do not provide adequate proof of his ownership of the property. [3a] Without this land, Zola has nowhere else to live since he is old and has no family or children to help him, and he and his wife will have to move to the city where they will most likely live in poverty. Thapelo, on the other hand, has other land on which to live, since he is mainly trying to expand his farm in order to make more money. [4b] The dispute goes to the Constitutional Court of South Africa, which decides that Zola has total rights of ownership to the land and that Thapelo has no rights whatsoever. Zola gets the land.

Story 3 *(aba)*

A dispute about who is the true owner of some property arises between two farmers, Thapelo and Zola. Both are members of the same "tribe," but Thapelo currently occupies the land and claims it as his own. Zola says that he is the true owner of the land, since he and his family owned the property before Thapelo was put on the land as a result of being forcibly removed from his own place in the 1980s. [2a] Both parties are able to produce some legal documents supporting their claim of ownership of the land. However, though Zola accepts that Thapelo has a legal right to the property, Thapelo completely rejects Zola's claim, asserting that Zola's legal documents do not provide adequate proof of his ownership of the property. [3b] Without this land, Thapelo has nowhere else to live since he is old and has no family or children to help him, and he and his wife will have to move to the city where they will most likely live in poverty. Zola, on the other hand, has other land on which to live, since he is mainly trying to expand his farm in order to make more money. [4a] The dispute goes to the Constitutional Court of South Africa, which decides that Thapelo has total rights of ownership to the land and that Zola has no rights whatsoever. Thapelo gets the land.

Story 4 *(abb)*

A dispute about who is the true owner of some property arises between two farmers, Thapelo and Zola. Both are members of the same "tribe," but Thapelo currently occupies the land and claims it as his own. Zola says that he is the true owner of the land, since he and his family owned the property before Thapelo was put on the land as a result of being forcibly removed from his own place in the 1980s. [2a] Both parties are able to produce some legal documents supporting their claim of owner-ship of the land. However, though Zola accepts that Thapelo has a legal right to the property, Thapelo completely rejects Zola's claim, asserting that Zola's legal documents do not provide adequate proof of his own-ership of the property. [3b] Without this land, Thapelo has nowhere else to live since he is old and has no family or children to help him, and he and his wife will have to move to the city where they will most likely live in poverty. Zola, on the other hand, has other land on which to live, since he is mainly trying to expand his farm in order to make more money. [4b] The dispute goes to the Constitutional Court of South Africa, which decides that Zola has total rights of ownership to the land and that Thapelo has no rights whatsoever. Zola gets the land.

Story 5 (aca)

A dispute about who is the true owner of some property arises between two farmers, Thapelo and Zola. Both are members of the same "tribe," but Thapelo currently occupies the land and claims it as his own. Zola says that he is the true owner of the land, since he and his family owned the property before Thapelo was put on the land as a result of being forcibly removed from his own place in the 1980s. [2a] Both parties are able to produce some legal documents supporting their claim of owner-ship of the land. However, though Zola accepts that Thapelo has a legal right to the property, Thapelo completely rejects Zola's claim, asserting that Zola's legal documents do not provide adequate proof of his own-ership of the property. [3c] Without this land, neither Zola nor Thapelo has anywhere else to live since they are both old and have no family or children to help them. Whoever doesn't get the land will have to move to the city, where they will most likely live in poverty. [4a] The dispute goes to the Constitutional Court of South Africa, which decides that Thapelo has total rights of ownership to the land and that Zola has no rights whatsoever. Thapelo gets the land.

Story 6 (acb)

A dispute about who is the true owner of some property arises between two farmers, Thapelo and Zola. Both are members of the same "tribe," but Thapelo currently occupies the land and claims it as his own. Zola says that he is the true owner of the land, since he and his family owned the property before Thapelo was put on the land as a result of being forcibly removed from his own place in the 1980s. [2a] Both parties are able to produce some legal documents supporting their claim of ownership of the land. However, though Zola accepts that Thapelo has a legal right to the property, Thapelo completely rejects Zola's claim, asserting that Zola's legal documents do not provide adequate proof of his ownership of the property. [3c] Without this land, neither Zola nor Thapelo has anywhere else to live since they are both old and have no family or children to help them. Whoever doesn't get the land will have to move to the city, where they will most likely live in poverty. [4b] The dispute goes to the Constitutional Court of South Africa, which decides that Zola has total rights of ownership to the land and that Thapelo has no rights whatsoever. Zola gets the land.

Story 7 (baa)

A dispute about who is the true owner of some property arises between two farmers, Thapelo and Zola. Both are members of the same "tribe," but Thapelo currently occupies the land and claims it as his own. Zola says that he is the true owner of the land, since he and his family owned the property before Thapelo was put on the land as a result of being forcibly removed from his own place in the 1980s. [2b] Both parties are able to produce some legal documents supporting their claim of ownership of the land. However, though Thapelo accepts that Zola has a legal right to the property, Zola completely rejects Thapelo's claim, asserting that Thapelo's legal documents do not provide adequate proof of his ownership of the property. [3a] Without this land, Zola has nowhere else to live since he is old and has no family or children to help him, and he and his wife will have to move to the city where they will most likely live in poverty. Thapelo, on the other hand, has other land on which to live, since he is mainly trying to expand his farm in order to make more money. [4a] The dispute goes to the Constitutional Court of South Africa, which decides that Thapelo has total rights of ownership to the land and that Zola has no rights whatsoever. Thapelo gets the land.

Story 8 (bab)

A dispute about who is the true owner of some property arises between two farmers, Thapelo and Zola. Both are members of the same "tribe," but Thapelo currently occupies the land and claims it as his own. Zola says that he is the true owner of the land, since he and his family owned the property before Thapelo was put on the land as a result of being forcibly removed from his own place in the 1980s. [2b] Both parties are able to produce some legal documents supporting their claim of ownership of the land. However, though Thapelo accepts that Zola has a legal right to the property, Zola completely rejects Thapelo's claim, asserting that Thapelo's legal documents do not provide adequate proof of his ownership of the property. [3a] Without this land, Zola has nowhere else to live since he is old and has no family or children to help him, and he and his wife will have to move to the city where they will most likely live in poverty. Thapelo, on the other hand, has other land on which to live, since he is mainly trying to expand his farm in order to make more money. [4b] The dispute goes to the Constitutional Court of South Africa, which decides that Zola has total rights of ownership to the land and that Thapelo has no rights whatsoever. Zola gets the land.

Story 9 (bba)

A dispute about who is the true owner of some property arises between two farmers, Thapelo and Zola. Both are members of the same "tribe," but Thapelo currently occupies the land and claims it as his own. Zola says that he is the true owner of the land, since he and his family owned the property before Thapelo was put on the land as a result of being forcibly removed from his own place in the 1980s. [2b] Both parties are able to produce some legal documents supporting their claim of ownership of the land. However, though Thapelo accepts that Zola has a legal right to the property, Zola completely rejects Thapelo's claim, asserting that Thapelo's legal documents do not provide adequate proof of his ownership of the property. [3b] Without this land, Thapelo has nowhere else to live since he is old and has no family or children to help him, and he and his wife will have to move to the city where they will most likely live in poverty. Zola, on the other hand, has other land on which to live, since he is mainly trying to expand his farm in order to make more money. [4a] The dispute goes to the Constitutional Court of South Africa, which decides that Thapelo has total rights of ownership to the land and that Zola has no rights whatsoever. Thapelo gets the land.

Story 10 (bbb)

A dispute about who is the true owner of some property arises between two farmers, Thapelo and Zola. Both are members of the same "tribe," but Thapelo currently occupies the land and claims it as his own. Zola says that he is the true owner of the land, since he and his family owned the property before Thapelo was put on the land as a result of being forcibly removed from his own place in the 1980s. [2b] Both parties are able to produce some legal documents supporting their claim of ownership of the land. However, though Thapelo accepts that Zola has a legal right to the property, Zola completely rejects Thapelo's claim, asserting that Thapelo's legal documents do not provide adequate proof of his ownership of the property. [3b] Without this land, Thapelo has nowhere else to live since he is old and has no family or children to help him, and he and his wife will have to move to the city where they will most likely live in poverty. Zola, on the other hand, has other land on which to live, since he is mainly trying to expand his farm in order to make more money. [4b] The dispute goes to the Constitutional Court of South Africa, which decides that Zola has total rights of ownership to the land and that Thapelo has no rights whatsoever. Zola gets the land.

Story 11 (bca)

A dispute about who is the true owner of some property arises between two farmers, Thapelo and Zola. Both are members of the same "tribe," but Thapelo currently occupies the land and claims it as his own. Zola says that he is the true owner of the land, since he and his family owned the property before Thapelo was put on the land as a result of being forcibly removed from his own place in the 1980s. [2b] Both parties are able to produce some legal documents supporting their claim of ownership of the land. However, though Thapelo accepts that Zola has a legal right to the property, Zola completely rejects Thapelo's claim, asserting that Thapelo's legal documents do not provide adequate proof of his ownership of the property. [3c] Without this land, neither Zola nor Thapelo has anywhere else to live since they are both old and have no family or children to help them. Whoever doesn't get the land will have to move to the city, where they will most likely live in poverty. [4a] The dispute goes to the Constitutional Court of South Africa, which decides that Thapelo has total rights of ownership to the land and that Zola has no rights whatsoever. Thapelo gets the land.

Story 12 (bcb)

A dispute about who is the true owner of some property arises between two farmers, Thapelo and Zola. Both are members of the same "tribe," but Thapelo currently occupies the land and claims it as his own. Zola says that he is the true owner of the land, since he and his family owned the property before Thapelo was put on the land as a result of being forcibly removed from his own place in the 1980s. [2b] Both parties are able to produce some legal documents supporting their claim of ownership of the land. However, though Thapelo accepts that Zola has a legal right to the property, Zola completely rejects Thapelo's claim, asserting that Thapelo's legal documents do not provide adequate proof of his ownership of the property. [3c] Without this land, neither Zola nor Thapelo has anywhere else to live since they are both old and have no family or children to help them. Whoever doesn't get the land will have to move to the city, where they will most likely live in poverty. [4b] The dispute goes to the Constitutional Court of South Africa, which decides that Zola has total rights of ownership to the land and that Thapelo has no rights whatsoever. Zola gets the land.

Story 13 (caa)

A dispute about who is the true owner of some property arises between two farmers, Thapelo and Zola. Both are members of the same "tribe," but Thapelo currently occupies the land and claims it as his own. Zola says that he is the true owner of the land, since he and his family owned the property before Thapelo was put on the land as a result of being forcibly removed from his own place in the 1980s. [2c] Both parties are able to produce legal documents supporting their claim of ownership. Each side in the dispute recognizes the validity of the claim of the other side. [3a] Without this land, Zola has nowhere else to live since he is old and has no family or children to help him, and he and his wife will have to move to the city where they will most likely live in poverty. Thapelo, on the other hand, has other land on which to live, since he is mainly trying to expand his farm in order to make more money. [4a] The dispute goes to the Constitutional Court of South Africa, which decides that Thapelo has total rights of ownership to the land and that Zola has no rights whatsoever. Thapelo gets the land.

Story 14 *(cab)*

A dispute about who is the true owner of some property arises between two farmers, Thapelo and Zola. Both are members of the same "tribe," but Thapelo currently occupies the land and claims it as his own. Zola says that he is the true owner of the land, since he and his family owned the property before Thapelo was put on the land as a result of being forcibly removed from his own place in the 1980s. [2c] Both parties are able to produce legal documents supporting their claim of ownership. Each side in the dispute recognizes the validity of the claim of the other side. [3a] Without this land, Zola has nowhere else to live since he is old and has no family or children to help him, and he and his wife will have to move to the city where they will most likely live in poverty. Thapelo, on the other hand, has other land on which to live, since he is mainly trying to expand his farm in order to make more money. [4b] The dispute goes to the Constitutional Court of South Africa, which decides that Zola has total rights of ownership to the land and that Thapelo has no rights whatsoever. Zola gets the land.

Story 15 *(cba)*

A dispute about who is the true owner of some property arises between two farmers, Thapelo and Zola. Both are members of the same "tribe," but Thapelo currently occupies the land and claims it as his own. Zola says that he is the true owner of the land, since he and his family owned the property before Thapelo was put on the land as a result of being forcibly removed from his own place in the 1980s. [2c] Both parties are able to produce legal documents supporting their claim of ownership. Each side in the dispute recognizes the validity of the claim of the other side. [3b] Without this land, Thapelo has nowhere else to live since he is old and has no family or children to help him, and he and his wife will have to move to the city where they will most likely live in poverty. Zola, on the other hand, has other land on which to live, since he is mainly trying to expand his farm in order to make more money. [4a] The dispute goes to the Constitutional Court of South Africa, which decides that Thapelo has total rights of ownership to the land and that Zola has no rights whatsoever. Thapelo gets the land.

Story 16 (cbb)

A dispute about who is the true owner of some property arises between two farmers, Thapelo and Zola. Both are members of the same "tribe," but Thapelo currently occupies the land and claims it as his own. Zola says that he is the true owner of the land, since he and his family owned the property before Thapelo was put on the land as a result of being forcibly removed from his own place in the 1980s. [2c] Both parties are able to produce legal documents supporting their claim of ownership. Each side in the dispute recognizes the validity of the claim of the other side. [3b] Without this land, Thapelo has nowhere else to live since he is old and has no family or children to help him, and he and his wife will have to move to the city where they will most likely live in poverty. Zola, on the other hand, has other land on which to live, since he is mainly trying to expand his farm in order to make more money. [4b] The dispute goes to the Constitutional Court of South Africa, which decides that Zola has total rights of ownership to the land and that Thapelo has no rights whatsoever. Zola gets the land.

Story 17 (cca)

A dispute about who is the true owner of some property arises between two farmers, Thapelo and Zola. Both are members of the same "tribe," but Thapelo currently occupies the land and claims it as his own. Zola says that he is the true owner of the land, since he and his family owned the property before Thapelo was put on the land as a result of being forcibly removed from his own place in the 1980s. [2c] Both parties are able to produce legal documents supporting their claim of ownership. Each side in the dispute recognizes the validity of the claim of the other side. [3c] Without this land, neither Zola nor Thapelo has anywhere else to live since they are both old and have no family or children to help them. Whoever doesn't get the land will have to move to the city, where they will most likely live in poverty. [4a] The dispute goes to the Constitutional Court of South Africa, which decides that Thapelo has total rights of ownership to the land and that Zola has no rights whatsoever. Thapelo gets the land.

Story 18 (ccb)

A dispute about who is the true owner of some property arises between two farmers, Thapelo and Zola. Both are members of the same "tribe," but Thapelo currently occupies the land and claims it as his own. Zola says that he is the true owner of the land, since he and his family owned the property before Thapelo was put on the land as a result of being forcibly removed from his own place in the 1980s. [2c] Both parties are able to produce legal documents supporting their claim of ownership. Each side in the dispute recognizes the validity of the claim of the other side. [3c] Without this land, neither Zola nor Thapelo has anywhere else to live since they are both old and have no family or children to help them. Whoever doesn't get the land will have to move to the city, where they will most likely live in poverty. [4b] The dispute goes to the Constitutional Court of South Africa, which decides that Zola has total rights of ownership to the land and that Thapelo has no rights whatsoever. Zola gets the land.

6

Land Reconciliation and Theories of Justice

The purposes of this book have been twofold. First, I have sought to contribute to understanding the politics of land in contemporary South Africa. Second, and equally as important, I have used the policy context of land to test theories of group identity and sociotropic justice. All of this analysis is grounded in the broader context of theories of transitional justice and societal reconciliation.

Myriad conclusions – some big and some small – emerge from the analysis reported here. First, many ordinary South Africans, and large portions of the black majority, are indeed concerned about issues of historical injustices, and large proportions of the population view land as an unsettled issue from the country's apartheid and colonial past. I do not contend that the various aspects of the land issue are seen by South Africans as being as urgent as the big three: poverty and unemployment, crime, and HIV/AIDs. But addressing the historical injustices of land dispossessions is nevertheless an issue of considerable concern for a majority of South Africans.

I have argued in other contexts that, in comparison to their highly conflictual past, South Africans are remarkably well reconciled (Gibson 2004a). However, the second important conclusion of this research is that land reconciliation cannot be said to be very widespread in South African society today. On nearly every issue connected to land, South Africans of different races are not reconciled; instead, they are deeply and perhaps irrevocably divided. Indeed, it is difficult to imagine how opinion could be any more polarized than it is on issues of historical land injustices. President Mbeki sometimes complains of "two nations" in South Africa (e.g., in 1998), one black, the other white. On various land issues, this charge could not be more apposite.

Third, justice seems to matter to a very large portion of the South African population. But justice is a multidimensional concept. For black South Africans, justice implicates both the past and the present. For whites, the past is of much less concern.

Moreover, various justice domains are relevant to the land issue. For instance, when it comes to squatters, most South Africans – of all races – would deny redistributive justice – that is, they would not allow squatters to grab land. But at the same time, procedural justice considerations are activated, meaning that squatters deserve some measure of dignity and due process even while being evicted. My survey did not ask about crime and criminals, but my strong suspicion is that most South Africans (of all races) would be quite content to deny due process protections to "known" criminals. Something about the squatter's "crime" renders it far less despicable and far more worthy of some measure of fairness. Land issues stretch across multiple domains of justice, and these domains often conflict with each other. Because squatters are needy and deserving, they ought to be extended procedural justice even if distributive justice cannot be provided. Justice, it seems, is a multidimensional construct in the minds of most South Africans.

Sociotropic justice is also important to many South Africans. For instance, preferences on policies governing land restitution and redistribution do not simply reflect egocentric instrumentalism but instead represent both concerns for historical injustices perpetrated against groups, by groups, as well as symbolic attitudes (such as the symbolic attachment to land). One need not be personally aggrieved in order to care about the issue of historical land injustices; it is one's group that matters.

One goal of this research has been to investigate how different domains of justice get adjudicated when political problems are multidimensional, with conflict across fairness domains. Some progress on this score has been reported. An important source of ordering among justice considerations is group identities, and especially the degree to which the identities are parochial or cosmopolitan. Narrow group identities tie people more closely to the past; broader identities tend to be associated with greater concern over contemporary aspects of injustice, including procedural justice (which is only indirectly dependent on the past). In some senses, identities transform issues; they provide a frame for how people perceive and evaluate issues like land injustices. For many South Africans, group identities provide a bridge to the past.

Identities also tend to result in defining issues in more symbolic terms. In the South African case, this is particularly problematic since a vast gulf exists in the basic values of ordinary people. Whites, for instance, tend to value private property rights highly, but express little symbolic attachment to land. Blacks, on the other hand, seem much more organically attached to land, and value private property considerably less. Similar (but somewhat smaller) differences exist with regard to support for the rule of law. These differences in basic value orientations constitute a deep and deeply significant chasm dividing South Africa's various racial groups.

The rule of law is a particularly important value for the politics of land in South Africa. As I have just noted, blacks and whites differ in their abstract commitments to the rule of law. But when it comes to land policies, South Africans of all races seem to prefer that the rule of law prevail. An interesting tension therefore exists here, even while much of the data analysis suggests that lawless land grabs would not be tolerated by the South African people.

On another hand, it may surprise many to learn that South Africans do not unequivocally condemn the land redistribution process in Zimbabwe. It is important to note that my survey data come from 2004, not 2008 (as Zimbabwe seems to be totally imploding), but at least in 2004, many South Africans saw Zimbabwe's experiences in a fairly positive light. For instance, we asked our respondents whether the Zimbabwe experiment with land represents a role model for what should happen in South Africa: Is Zimbabwe an exemplar? The answer depends on one's race. Among Africans, 54.8% agreed that the land experience in Zimbabwe "shows how the land issue should be handled in South Africa." Another 22.4% were uncertain. Coloured people and those of Asian origin were less likely to accept that Zimbabwe offers a positive model on land, with 39.1% and 34.9% agreeing, respectively. It is perhaps somewhat surprising that 23.0% of the white respondents viewed the Zimbabwean experience positively, with another 13.5% being uncertain.[1] In general, the data reveal no widespread condemnation by ordinary South Africans of the Zimbabwe "land reform" program.

Perhaps one implication of these seemingly contradictory findings is that the South African people can be influenced by their leaders. At present, South African political elites seem firmly committed to land reform through the rule of law. Even when discussions of expropriations surface – or thoughts of abandoning the willing seller/willing buyer principle are voiced – the debate among South Africa's leaders never seems to stray far from the rule of law. Whatever their motives (sincere or strategic), South African elites have not succumbed to the rabble-rousing, demagogish appeals of a Robert Mugabe.

But this is not to say that such appeals are inevitably doomed to failure. South Africans care deeply about historical injustices even when they have no direct stake in the outcome of any given land dispute, and these feelings are rooted in their group identities and symbolic attitudes. Were an elite faction to appeal to the mass public, attempting to mobilize this enduring sense of the unfairness of the past, the chance of success would not be negligible. Land is a volatile issue in South African politics and it has considerable political potential, especially were it to be exploited by popular (and populist) political leaders.

And of course, South Africa is headed (as of 2008) into what is most likely a period of considerable political uncertainty and even instability. The hegemony of the African National Congress (ANC) is unlikely to be broken in the short term, but serious fracturing of the ANC seems likely even in the very near term. The succession fight between Jacob Zuma and the ANC establishment could have serious consequences for South African politics. Might Zuma attempt to mobilize the land issue?

---

[1] Uncertainty is fairly high on the Zimbabwe questions, but perhaps this uncertainty is better understood as ambivalence. For instance, when asked whether Zimbabwe shows "how the land issue should not be handled," majorities of each racial group agree. That is, while 54.8% of blacks agree that Zimbabwe shows how the issue should be handled, 55.5% agree that Zimbabwe shows how the land issue should not be handled. Thus, it appears that South Africans are drawing mixed conclusions about the lessons of the Zimbabwe experience. It is clear from the data, however, that unequivocal condemnation of Zimbabwe's land policy is not widespread in South Africa. Indeed, perhaps the most telling evidence concerns the statement that Zimbabwe "shows just how dangerous it is not to deal with the land expectations of people," a statement with which large majorities of each racial group agree (albeit perhaps for different reasons).

At this point, I cannot say. But should he attempt to do so, I can confidently predict that the issue will resonate with many South Africans. And, of course, Zuma cannot lose support among South African whites (since zero minus zero is still zero). Zuma has demonstrated remarkable tenacity and ingenuity, and he is a very skillful politician currently backed by several powerful organizations and institutions. A campaign to "return the land to those who had it wrongfully expropriated from them under colonialism and apartheid" is the sort of effort that many can imagine Zuma mounting. Whatever the outcome, the possibility that Zuma (or another desperate elite) will attempt to mobilize the land issue adds worrying uncertainty to contemporary South African politics.

EXPANDING RESEARCH ON PUBLIC OPINION AND LAND ISSUES

Despite my focus on the land of apartheid, the conclusions of this analysis are not limited to South Africa. Instead, land issues are ubiquitous throughout the world today, and dealing with historical injustices is a problem that is broader still. From the South African case, we learn several specific lessons:

- To understand the complexities of land issues, it is necessary to attempt to understand how ordinary people conceive of and think about such issues.
- Land issues may be enshrouded in other symbolic values and concerns.
- Land issues are not relevant only to the landless, or to the aggrieved. Instead, land may become an issue of sociotropic justice, broadly important to large segments of society.
- Land issues are frequently multidimensional, activating a variety of symbolic values and domains of justice.
- To the extent that land evokes symbolic concerns, it may implicate group identities. If so, the issue changes its character.
- Land issues may become associated with the valuation of the rule of law, and it is perhaps valuable to frame the issues on this dimension.
- In turn, the rule of law may mobilize concerns about procedural justice. Because the landless have a measure of justice on their side, their claims cannot be summarily dismissed.

- Cosmopolitan group identities have beneficial effects and should therefore be promoted.

Those who seek to manage and mollify perceived historical injustices would do well to heed these lessons.

DIRECTIONS FOR RESEARCH ON GROUP IDENTITIES

Finally, perhaps the most important contention of this analysis is that identities connect people to their group's past and especially to its experiences of historical injustices. But many unanswered questions about identities also emerge from this research.

My analysis of the group identities of South Africans exhibits both the strengths and weaknesses of extant theory. I have succeeded to some degree in demonstrating that identities can link individuals to their groups and, in the context of transitional justice, to the historical injustices perpetrated against the groups. Identities frame how people think about political issues like land, causing some to emphasize the injustices of the past, others to focus on contemporary criteria. This, I submit, is a contribution to the study of political psychology and to theories of commonsense justice.

But there is still much about group identities that is not understood. In particular, the interface between identities and exogenous events is poorly mapped. Identities are not obdurate – at least not in their degree to salience, but probably in their other attributes as well – and their connections to contemporary political events wax and wane over time. Several processes are involved, including those related to the activation of group identities, and the connection of identities to issues via framing processes. Identities are not always relevant, but certain political issues seem to mobilize group attachments and concerns. More about these processes must be analyzed and dissected.

At present, these processes are not well understood. Elites often proffer gambits based on symbolic and identity-arousing issues. For instance, Gibson and Howard (2007) have shown that even though some elites have sought to scapegoat Russia's Jews with the problems of the political, social, and economic transitions in that country, they have been remarkably unsuccessful in their efforts. Little theory exists to explain why some efforts at mobilization succeed, while others do not.

Perhaps one explanation of why elite appeals to the mass public fail so often is that framing based on identities is a reasonably contextual process. As Druckman (2004) has shown, framing effects depend considerably on context, and as a consequence "framing effects appear to be neither robust nor particularly pervasive" (2004, 683). He notes, for instance, that competition among elites can neutralize frames, leading to the hypothesis that social identities are only readily mobilized under the condition of elite consensus. Much more research needs to be done to understand precisely which elements of context are important, and how they become activated.

At least a few of these elements can, however, now be specified: Identities must be strongly subscribed to, and people must see politics as a zero-sum, intergroup struggle. In South Africa, the land issue provides the zero-sum condition, at least from the viewpoint of public opinion. Here, I find some evidence that group identities connect or disconnect people to the past. The crucial unanswered questions, however, are: What accounts for variability in the salience of group identities? And what conditions lead people to view politics in group-relevant terms? These are difficult questions to answer – requiring as they do a longitudinal research design – but future research on the consequences of identities must focus on these crucial conditional processes. Only by further research on real-world sites where salient policy issues implicate identities can these complex processes be unraveled and understood.

Methodological problems abound in the study of group identities, and future research must address some of these. Perhaps one of the most pressing shortcomings in research on group identities has to do with measurement. Frankly, the measurement of identities is typically either invalid or so unreliable that substantive findings cannot be cumulated. For instance, Ferree (2006) draws strong conclusions about the limited importance of identities, but the conclusions are based on extraordinarily weak measures of group attachments. As my research has shown, identities are complex, not simple. People vary in the benefits they derive from their identities, just as they vary in the beliefs they associate with their groups (e.g., the need for group solidarity). The notion that group attachments can be measured in any meaningful way with just a simple query or two should now be completely discredited. The psychometrics of identity indicators need much further and more extensive investigation.

CONCLUDING COMMENTS

In Chapter 1 I noted that du Bois (2008, 116) defines historical injustice as follows:

I use the term "historical injustice" to refer to injustices committed in a setting that has become historical by virtue of some fundamental and lasting change in the socio political structure such as the end of slavery, colonial rule, or non-representative government. Because of the break in continuity all these situations raise the question of how political institutions should deal with injustices that are not of their own making.

This definition could not fit the South African case better. Senses of historical land injustices are common in South Africa – in Chapter 2, I estimated that 11,844,000 black adults believe they hold a historical land grievance – and as the land restitution/redistribution processes has unfolded, the proportion of grievers has increased, not decreased. Public perceptions and judgments of the various land problems in South Africa make the land issue highly volatile. Thus, the tinderbox of historical land injustice may, with the right spark, ignite in a critical political conflagration engulfing the entire country. Political fires fueled by deeply felt senses of injustice are difficult indeed to extinguish. In the end, perhaps nothing is more important in politics than unrequited feelings of unfairness and injustice.

Appendix A

A Note on Race in South Africa

It is common in South Africa to divide the total population into four racial categories for the purposes of research or the explanation of demographic realities and/or socio-economic conditions in the country, and I follow this practice throughout the analysis reported in this book.[1] As James and Lever (2000, 44) note: "The use of these categories is unavoidable given the fixity that they have come to acquire both in popular consciousness and official business." The use of these racial terminologies, however, differs from the way racial categorization may be understood in other societies. It is therefore important to understand the historical development of these categories, especially the legal boundaries imposed on racial groups by the apartheid government.[2]

The four racial groups are African, white, Coloured, and South Africans of Asian origin (Indian). These groups are also often referred to as population groups, ethnic groups (although this term usually refers to African subcategories such as Xhosa or Zulu), or national groups. The African majority has been known by European settlers

---

[1] For a most useful review of racial categorization under apartheid, see Posel 2001.

[2] The editor of a special issue of *Daedalus* focused on South Africa had this to say about the use of racial terms in the articles in the journal: "Many of the authors in this issue observe the South African convention of dividing the country's population into four racial categories: white (of European descent), colored (of mixed ancestry), Indian (forebears from the Indian subcontinent), and African. The official nomenclature for 'Africans' has itself varied over the years, changing from 'native' to 'Bantu' in the middle of the apartheid era, and then changing again to 'black' or, today, 'African/black.' All of these terms appear in the essays that follow." See Graubard 2001, viii.

by different names over time, such as "native," "Bantu," or "Black," and some of these terminologies were later formalized by apartheid legislation. The Africans were the original inhabitants of the area now called South Africa and were descendants of Iron Age farmers speaking different variants of Bantu languages, spoken in sub-Saharan Africa, east of Cameroon (James and Lever 2000, 44). Generally, I refer to these people as Africans or blacks.

The white inhabitants of South Africa (also formerly called Europeans) are descendants of Dutch, German, French (Huguenots who fled France due to religious persecution), English, and other European and Jewish settlers. Though South Africa was colonized by the Dutch and the British in different historical periods, the British colonization entrenched English as the most commonly spoken language.

"Coloured" is considered a mixed race category, although as James and Lever (2000, 44) argue, it is actually a residual category of people with quite divergent descents. Coloured refers to the children of inter-marriages between whites, Khoikhoi (often referred to as "Hottentots") and the San (commonly referred to as "Bushmen"), plus slaves from Madagascar and Southeast Asia and the Indonesian archipelago, and Africans (Thompson and Prior 1982, 34).

The Indian population came to South Africa largely as indentured laborers to work in the sugar plantations in Natal in the late nineteenth and early twentieth century. Yet they came from different regions in the Indian Subcontinent, adhered to different religions, and spoke different languages, so that they, like Coloured people, are not a homogeneous group. I refer to these people as South Africans of Asian origin, despite the fact that some Coloured people also are technically of Asian origin.

Earlier research has documented enormous differences across South Africa's groups in terms of a wide variety of political attitudes (e.g., Gibson and Gouws 2003, Gibson 2004a). Consequently, it is essential that race be incorporated into the analyses in this book. To ignore race would be to fail to recognize that South African politics today contin-ues to be shaped by its racist and colonial history. To incorporate race into this analysis is not to accept anything about apartheid, but is in-stead merely to acknowledge that apartheid shaped – and continues to shape – political reality in the country.

Appendix B

The Survey Methodology

The survey blends probability and quota methods of respondent selection, and therefore requires discussion of the two portions of the research design separately. The samples, however, do begin from a common sampling frame.

The survey firm Markinor first stratified each South African location according to province, community size, individual city, town or rural areas, suburb (within the large cities), and the predominant race of the residents of the area. Strong residential segregation makes the latter variable much less ambiguous than might otherwise be the case. Within each stratum, sampling points were randomly selected. Within each sampling point, either four or six interviews were conducted.

For the black subsample, area probability methods were then used. Households were enumerated and one was randomly selected. Within the chosen household, an adult individual was also chosen randomly. Up to four attempts were made to interview the designated individual. No respondent substitution was allowed. Gender stratification was imposed, however, to ensure against over-representation of females. This means that within each household, the gender of the respondent was predetermined. Thus, the African subsample was drawn via standard area probability methods.

Out of the 1,778 designated individual Africans,[1] interviews were completed with 1,549, for a raw response rate of 87.1%. Of the 229 households in which no interview was conducted, this was due to the designated respondent being sick, deaf, or blind in 21 instances, and to a language barrier in another three cases. The respondent was not available in 76 households (33.2% of the 229 incomplete interviews) and 129 respondents (56.3%) refused to be interviewed (or refused to complete the interview). With such a high response rate, there can be little doubt about the representativeness of the black subsample.

Quite different methods were used to select individual white, Coloured, and Indian respondents. Rather than randomly selecting all households, a mixture of probability and quota methods was employed.[2] The quota was defined in terms of gender, age, and the working status of the individual to be interviewed. Consequently, no response rate for these three subsamples can be calculated, and, as a result, no response rate for the overall sample can be computed. Sampling error for the three subsamples and the entire sample also cannot be estimated.

In addition, Markinor fielded a supplementary (and subsequent) probability sample of whites, Coloured people, and Asian South Africans. Among the white probability sample, the response rate was 32.1%, with clear evidence of unrepresentativeness in the sample (e.g., the over-representation of Afrikaans speakers). The

---

[1] I have excluded from this number the following: 130 households in which a male was designated to be interviewed, but in which no males resided; 63 households in which a female was designed to be interviewed, but in which no females resided; and three households in which we expected to find black residents, but in fact found residents of another race.

[2] It is easy to see why Markinor uses probability methods for the black subsample, since probability samples have a wide range of known useful attributes. In addition, however, Markinor believes that probability methods are called for by the relatively high mobility of the black population (thereby rendering current population statistics less reliable), and by the frequency with which multiple households are found to occupy a single location or house. Justifying the use of quota sample is a more demanding task. According to Markinor, the driving factor is very high noncompletion rates among whites, Coloured people, and Indians. Noncompletion is due to lack of access to individual homes as well as outright refusals. Markinor believes that substitution rates are so high with probability samples that the theoretical basis of such samples is entirely undone.

response rate for the Coloured probability sample was 65.1%, with no obvious evidence of under- or over-representation of any particular group. Among South Africans of Asian origin, the probability sample yielded a response rate of 63.5%, also with little obvious evidence of misrepresentation.[3]

Several tests suggest that it is possible to combine the probability and quota samples among Coloured and Asian South Africans. For instance, differences in home language are trivial – 76.6% of the Coloured respondents in the quota sample speak Afrikaans as their home language; the comparable figure in the probability sample is 78.5%. (Since virtually all South Africans of Asian origin speak English as their home language, no differences exist across the two subsamples on this variable.) Other key variables support a similar conclusion that these two subsamples can be merged. Consequently, for Coloured and Asian South Africans, the two subsamples were joined into a single sample. That sample was subjected to poststratification to further ensure representativeness. This poststratification weighting does not change the number of observations. In the weighted data, 79.3% of the Coloured respondents speak Afrikaans as their home language. A total of 98.0% of the 459 weighted Asian respondents speak English as their home language. Thus, when I report data on the Coloured people and South Africans of Asian origin, I use the weighted, combined data set.

The white samples raise more difficult methodological challenges. First, the response rate in the probability sample was low, and evidence of misrepresentation exists. Similarly, the quota sample seems to lack representativeness. Obviously, these data can be (and have been) combined and poststratified so that 57% of the respondents speak Afrikaans as their home language and 42% speak English. The unanswered question is whether poststratification is appropriate under these circumstances.

---

[3] An overall response rate cannot be calculated for the survey since calculating such figures is impossible for the quota samples. As I have noted, the response rates for the four probability samples are: blacks, 87.1%, whites, 32.1%, Coloured people, 65.1%, and South Africans of Asian origin, 63.5%. Thus, for the purely probability portions of this survey, the overall response rate is on the order of 76.9%. This figure of course reflects the facts that (1) the response rate among black South Africans was very high, and (2) black South Africans constitute a very large proportion of the total South African population.

With all of these various caveats, a reasonable set of conclusions to be drawn about the results derived from these samples is that: (1) substantial confidence can be vested in the findings about black South Africans, (2) moderate confidence attaches to the conclusions about Coloured and Asian South Africans, and (3) relatively low confidence can be claimed for my conclusions about whites.

The interviews were conducted face-to-face by trained interviewers. The median length of interview was 85 minutes (mean = 89.7 minutes, standard deviation = 90.0 minutes).[4] The interview length varied substantially by language, with the longest interviews in Tsonga and Xhosa and the shortest interviews in Afrikaans, English, and Zulu.

Generally, nearly all respondents (96%) were interviewed by same-race interviewers. The largest exception to this rule is among Coloured respondents, 5% of whom were interviewed by black interviewers and 8% of whom were interviewed by white interviewers.

The questionnaire was first prepared in English and then translated into Afrikaans, Zulu, Xhosa, North Sotho, South Sotho, Tswana, and Tsonga. The methodology of creating a multilingual questionnaire follows closely that recommended by Brislin (1970). After producing an English-language version of the questionnaire, trained translators (employed by the survey firm) translated the questionnaire, and then another translator translated the translated questionnaire back to English. The "input" and the "output" English were then reconciled in a large and lengthy meeting involving all of the translators, back-translators, and survey firm staff (and me). At these meetings, a version of the questionnaire was prepared for the pretesting.

A formal pretest of the questionnaire was conducted. On the basis of statistical analysis of the pretest data the questionnaire was further revised. Virtually all revisions involved deleting items from the pretest instrument.

Respondents were interviewed in their language of choice. In 55% of the interviews, the interview was conducted in a single language, while 27% of the interviews occasionally mixed languages, and 18% often switched from one language to another.[5] Fully 34% of the

---

[4] For the purposes of describing the characteristics of the sample, no weighting is employed.

[5] Of course, we never allowed the interviewers to engage in simultaneous translation. The questionnaires are themselves multilingual: Each question in the questionnaire is printed in both English and the language of choice of the respondent.

interviews were conducted in English, followed by 23% in Afrikaans, 15% in Zulu, and 10% in Xhosa.

Most of the respondents (74%) were judged by their interviewer to hold a "friendly" attitude toward the interview, with another 18% being "cooperative but not particularly interested."

Appendix C

The Questionnaire

ORIGINAL HOUSEHOLD		CALL DATE/TIME BEST CALL-BACK-TIME/DAY
NAME:	C1	1.
FLAT/STREET:	C2	
SUBURB:	C3	2.
TOWN:	C4	
POSTAL CODE:	C5	3.
PHONE: (H)	C6	
(W)		SUB
CELL NO:		
AREA CODE:		

SAMPLE POINT NO:
C7

9- 10- 11- 12- 13- 14- 15- 16- 17-

INTERVIEWER NO:

18- 19- 20- 21-

DATE:

2004

22- 23- 24- 25- 26- 27-
DAY MONTH

INTERVIEWER STARTED: TIME
ON THIS INTERVIEW (24-HOUR CLOCK)

28- 29- 30- 31-

EVEN 32-1

ODD -2

INTERVIEWER: I hereby certify that this interview has been carried out by me according to the instructions I received from Markinor and has been checked.

NAME: .... SIGNED: ....

		VISIT 1		VISIT 2		VISIT 3		VISIT 4	
Date	/	/04	33-	/ /04	42-	/ /04	51-	/ /04	60-
Time	H		37-	H	46-	H	55-	H	64-
Result	Code:		41-	Code:	50-	Code:	59-	Code:	68-

Results codes:

1. Completed
2. Respondent not available
3. Refused
4. Partially completed
5. Respondent sick, deaf, blind
6. Language barrier
7. No. males
8. No. females

FINAL OUTCOME OF
INTERVIEW - SEE RESULTS
CODE AND RECORD

69-

CHECKING TO FIELD/ INTERVIEWER		EDIT TO CHECKING		BACKCHECK:	Personal	72-1
70-1	Yes	71-5	Yes		Telephone	73-2
-2	No	-6	No	OFFICE USE ONLY	Neither	74-3

1.	How many different families who arrange their own food live in this household or in the back yard?	HOUSEHOLD:	FAMILY NAME	DESCRIPTION	H/HOLD SELEC-TED
		No.1 Main household			77-1
	NO: .... 75- IF MORE THAN ONE: WRITE IN HOUSEHOLD IDENTIFICATION OPPOSITE. LIST HOUSEHOLDS ACCORDING TO DISTANCE FROM MAIN HOUSEHOLD.	No.2 (Closest to No.1) (Can be inside of main household)			-2
		No.3 (Second closest)			-3
		No.4 (Third closest)			-4
		No.5 (Furthest away from No.1)			-5

SELECTION OF MALE RESPONDENT							
	ORIGINAL HOUSEHOLD						
NO. OF MALES 16+	AGES				WORKING		RING ORIGINAL QUALIFYING RESPONDENT
WRITE IN:	16-24	25-34	35-49	50+	YES	NO	
YOUNGEST	39-1	-2	-3	-4	45-1	-2	51-1
2ND YOUNGEST	40-1	-2	-3	-4	46-1	-2	-2
3RD YOUNGEST	41-1	-2	-3	-4	47-1	-2	-3
4TH YOUNGEST	42-1	-2	-3	-4	48-1	-2	-4
5TH YOUNGEST	43-1	-2	-3	-4	49-1	-2	-5
IF SUBSTITUTION RING AGE AND WORKING STATUS	44-1	-2	-3	-4	50-1	-2	

SELECTION PROCEDURE

IF NONE: TERMINATE

IF ONE: INTERVIEW THIS ONE

IF TWO: INTERVIEW YOUNGEST IF Q.NO. ENDS IN 0, 2, 4, 6, 8. INTERVIEW OLDEST IF Q.NO. ENDS IN 1, 3, 5, 7, 9

IF THREE: INTERVIEW YOUNGEST IF Q.NO. ENDS IN 1, 2, 3. INTERVIEW MIDDLE ONE IF Q.NO. ENDS IN 4, 5, 6

INTERVIEW OLDEST IF Q.NO. ENDS IN 7, 8, 9

IF Q.NO. ENDS IN 0, APPLY THIS PROCEDURE TO SECOND OR THIRD LAST DIGIT OF Q.NO.

IF FOUR: INTERVIEW YOUNGEST IF Q.NO. ENDS IN 1, 2. INTERVIEW SECOND YOUNGEST IF Q.NO. ENDS IN 3, 4

INTERVIEW SECOND OLDEST IF Q.NO. ENDS IN 5, 6. INTERVIEW OLDEST IF Q.NO. ENDS IN 7, 8

IF Q.NO. ENDS IN 9 OR 0, APPLY THIS PROCEDURE TO SECOND OR THIRD LAST DIGIT OF Q.NO.

IF FIVE: INTERVIEW YOUNGEST IF Q.NO. ENDS IN 1, 2. INTERVIEW SECOND YOUNGEST IF Q.NO. ENDS IN 3, 4

INTERVIEW MIDDLE ONE IF Q.NO. ENDS IN 5, 6

INTERVIEW SECOND OLDEST IF Q.NO. ENDS IN 7, 8. INTERVIEW OLDEST IF Q.NO. ENDS IN 9, 0

TERMINATE ONLY IF ORIGINAL SELECTED PERSON CANNOT BE CONTACTED EVEN AFTER 4 CALLS, INCLUDING EVENING CALLS. ESTABLISH AGE AND WORKING STATUS OF ORIGINAL SELECTED PERSON (FROM NEIGHBOUR IF NECESSARY).

CARD 9

SELECTION OF FEMALE RESPONDENT

NO. OF FEMALES 16+ WRITE IN:	ORIGINAL HOUSEHOLD						RING ORIGINAL QUALIFYING RESPONDENT
	AGES				WORKING		
	16-24	25-34	35-49	50+	YES	NO	
YOUNGEST	39-1	-2	-3	-4	45-1	-2	51-1
2ND YOUNGEST	40-1	-2	-3	-4	46-1	-2	-2
3RD YOUNGEST	41-1	-2	-3	-4	47-1	-2	-3
4TH YOUNGEST	42-1	-2	-3	-4	48-1	-2	-4
5TH YOUNGEST	43-1	-2	-3	-4	49-1	-2	-5
IF SUBSTITUTION RING AGE AND WORKING STATUS	44-1	-2	-3	-4	50-1	-2	

SELECTION PROCEDURE

IF NONE: TERMINATE

IF ONE: INTERVIEW THIS ONE

IF TWO: INTERVIEW YOUNGEST IF Q.NO. ENDS IN 0, 2, 4, 6, 8. INTERVIEW OLDEST IF Q.NO. ENDS IN 1, 3, 5, 7, 9

IF THREE: INTERVIEW YOUNGEST IF Q.NO. ENDS IN 1, 2, 3. INTERVIEW MIDDLE ONE IF Q.NO. ENDS IN 4, 5, 6

INTERVIEW OLDEST IF Q.NO. ENDS IN 7, 8, 9

IF Q.NO. ENDS IN 0, APPLY THIS PROCEDURE TO SECOND OR THIRD LAST DIGIT OF Q.NO.

IF FOUR: INTERVIEW YOUNGEST IF Q.NO. ENDS IN 1, 2. INTERVIEW SECOND YOUNGEST IF Q.NO. ENDS IN 3, 4

INTERVIEW SECOND OLDEST IF Q.NO. ENDS IN 5, 6. INTERVIEW OLDEST IF Q.NO. ENDS IN 7, 8

IF Q.NO. ENDS IN 9 OR 0, APPLY THIS PROCEDURE TO SECOND OR THIRD LAST DIGIT OF Q.NO.

IF FIVE: INTERVIEW YOUNGEST IF Q.NO. ENDS IN 1, 2. INTERVIEW SECOND YOUNGEST IF Q.NO. ENDS IN 3, 4

INTERVIEW MIDDLE ONE IF Q.NO. ENDS IN 5, 6

INTERVIEW SECOND OLDEST IF Q.NO. ENDS IN 7, 8. INTERVIEW OLDEST IF Q.NO. ENDS IN 9, 0

TERMINATE ONLY IF ORIGINAL SELECTED PERSON CANNOT BE CONTACTED EVEN AFTER 4 CALLS, INCLUDING EVENING CALLS.

ESTABLISH AGE AND WORKING STATUS OF ORIGINAL SELECTED PERSON (FROM NEIGHBOUR IF NECESSARY).

INSTRUCTIONS FOR SELECTING STORY VERSIONS

Step 1:

> ➤ If the questionnaire number ends on an EVEN number – the respondent completes Q. 33 – the squatter story

> ➤ If the questionnaire number ends on an ODD number – the respondent completes Q. 75a OR Q.75b – the conflict over land story

Step 2:

> ➤ If the respondent was selected to complete either Q.75a or Q.75b proceed as follows:

> > o If the number printed on this page ends on an EVEN NUMBER the respondent completes Q.75a (Fanie and Sifiso).

> > o If the number printed on this page ends on an ODD NUMBER, the respondent completes Q.75b (Zola and Thapelo)

> > o <u>IMPORTANT INSTRUCTION</u>: CHECK AGAINST NUMBER PRINTED ON THIS PAGE – PAGE 4

Q.33	Q.75a AND Q.75b	
ABOUT SQUATTERS	**ABOUT A CONFLICT OVER LAND**	
Version should be selected sequentially. Repeating the 16 version sequence. E.g. Quex #1 should have version 1 Quex #2 should have version 2 Quest #17 should have version 1	Version should be selected sequentially, repeating the 18 version sequence. E.g. Quex #1 should have version 1 Quex #2 should have version 2 Quex #19 should have version 1	
	Version 2A – Q.75a – Q.81a **Fanie & Sifiso**	**Version 2B – Q.75b – Q.81b** **Zola & Thapelo**
.................................5-01	7-01	9-01
.................................-02	.................................-02	.................................-02
.................................-03	.................................-03	.................................-03
.................................-04	.................................-04	.................................-04
.................................-05	.................................-05	.................................-05
.................................-06	.................................-06	.................................-06
.................................-07	.................................-07	.................................-07
.................................-08	.................................-08	.................................-08
.................................-09	.................................-09	.................................-09
.................................-10	.................................-10	.................................-10
.................................-11	.................................-11	.................................-11
.................................-12	.................................-12	.................................-12
.................................-13	.................................-13	.................................-13
.................................-14	.................................-14	.................................-14
.................................-15	.................................-15	.................................-15
.................................-16	.................................-16	.................................-16
	.................................-17	.................................-17
	.................................-18	.................................-18

			GO TO:
	ONE MENTION ONLY.		
1.1 How often do you watch or listen to news programmes on television or on the radio?	1. Never	11-1	
	2. Less than once a week	-2	
	3. Once a week	-3	
	4. Several times a week	-4	
	5. Every day	-5	
	7. No answer – **(DO NOT READ OUT)**	-7	
	8. Refused – **(DO NOT READ OUT)**	-8	
	9. Don't know – **(DO NOT READ OUT)**	-9	
1.2 And what about newspapers? How often do you read them?	**ONE MENTION ONLY.**		
	1. Never	12-1	Q.1.3
	2. Less than once a week	-2	
	3. Once a week	-3	
	4. Several times a week	-4	
	5. Every day	-5	
	7. No answer – **(DO NOT READ OUT)**	-7	
	8. Refused – **(DO NOT READ OUT)**	-8	
	9. Don't know – **(DO NOT READ OUT)**	-9	
1.3 **IF THE ANSWER IS NEVER CODE -1, ASK:** Is there a newspaper in your language available locally?	1. Yes	13-1	
	2. No	-2	
	7. No answer – **(DO NOT READ OUT)**	-7	
	8. Refused – **(DO NOT READ OUT)**	-8	
	9. Don't know – **(DO NOT READ OUT)**	-9	
2. When you get together with your friends, would you say you discuss political matters frequently, occasionally or never?	**ONE MENTION ONLY.**		
	1. Frequently	14-1	
	2. Occasionally	-2	
	3. Never	-3	
	7. No answer – **(DO NOT READ OUT)**	-7	
	8. Refused – **(DO NOT READ OUT)**	-8	
	9. Don't know – **(DO NOT READ OUT)**	-9	
3. **SHOW CARD:** How do you think the general economic situation in South Africa has changed over the last 12 months? Would you say it has…?	**READ OUT. ONE MENTION ONLY.**		
	1. Got a lot worse	15-1	
	2. Got a little worse	-2	
	3. Stayed the same	-3	
	4. Got a little better	-4	
	5. Got a lot better	-5	
	7. No answer – **(DO NOT READ OUT)**	-7	
	8. Refused – **(DO NOT READ OUT)**	-8	
	9. Don't know – **(DO NOT READ OUT)**	-9	

CARD 10

4.	**SHOW CARD:** How do you think the economic situation in South Africa will change in the next 12 months? Will it…?	**READ OUT. ONE MENTION ONLY.**	
		1. Get a lot worse	16-1
		2. Get a little worse	-2
		3. Stay the same	-3
		4. Get a little better	-4
		5. Get a lot better	-5
		7. No answer – **(DO NOT READ OUT)**	-7
		8. Refused – **(DO NOT READ OUT)**	-8
		9. Don't know – **(DO NOT READ OUT)**	-9
5.	**SHOW CARD:** Compared with 12 months ago, would you say your family's living standards are…?	**READ OUT. ONE MENTION ONLY.**	
		1. A lot worse	17-1
		2. A little worse	-2
		3. Stayed the same	-3
		4. A little better	-4
		5. A lot better	-5
		7. No answer – **(DO NOT READ OUT)**	-7
		8. Refused – **(DO NOT READ OUT)**	-8
		9. Don't know – **(DO NOT READ OUT)**	-9
6.	**SHOW CARD:** And what about the next 12 months? How do you think your family's living standard will be **compared to now**? Would you say you and your family's living standard will…?	**READ OUT. ONE MENTION ONLY.**	
		1. Get a lot worse	18-1
		2. Get a little worse	-2
		3. Nothing will change	-3
		4. Get a little better	-4
		5. Get a lot better	-5
		7. No answer – **(DO NOT READ OUT)**	-7
		8. Refused – **(DO NOT READ OUT)**	-8
		9. Don't know – **(DO NOT READ OUT)**	-9

CARD 10

7. **SHOW CARD:** How much do you agree or disagree with the following statements? Would you say you agree strongly, agree, are uncertain, disagree or disagree strongly? ONE MENTION ONLY PER STATEMENT.

		AGREE STRONGLY	AGREE	UNCERTAIN	DISAGREE	DISAGREE STRONGLY	NO ANSWER (DNRO)	REFUSED (DNRO)	DON'T KNOW (DNRO)
5.	In order to fight crime, police should be granted greater power, even if it means searching houses without permission	23-1	-2	-3	-4	-5	-7	-8	-9
7.	Sometimes it might be better to ignore the law and solve problems immediately rather than wait for a legal solution	25-1	-2	-3	-4	-5	-7	-8	-9
1.	There are better ways to choose our political leaders than elections amongst candidates from several political parties	30-1	-2	-3	-4	-5	-7	-8	-9
2.	If the leaders we elect cannot improve the situation in the country, then it is better not to have competitive elections in the future	31-1	-2	-3	-4	-5	-7	-8	-9
3.	Those supporting multi-party elections are doing harm to the country	32-1	-2	-3	-4	-5	-7	-8	-9
4.	It's alright to get around the law as long as you don't actually break it	33-1	-2	-3	-4	-5	-7	-8	-9
5.	In times of emergency, the government ought to be able to suspend law in order to solve pressing social problems	34-1	-2	-3	-4	-5	-7	-8	-9

(Row-side labels: 9. / 9. / 9. / 9. / 9.)

8. **SHOW CARD:** Please tell me how well each of the following statements describes you. Would you say it describes you extremely well, pretty well, but not completely, doesn't describe you very well or doesn't describe you at all? ONE MENTION ONLY PER STATEMENT.

		EXTREMELY WELL	PRETTY WELL, BUT NOT COM-PLETELY	DOESN'T DESCRIBE ME VERY WELL	DOESN'T DESCRIBE ME AT ALL	NO ANSWER (DNRO)	REFUSED (DNRO)	DON'T KNOW (DNRO)
1.	It is usually easy for me to like people who have different values from me	26-1	-2	-3	-4	-7	-8	-9
2.	Listening to opposing viewpoints is usually a waste of time	27-1	-2	-3	-4	-7	-8	-9
3.	I generally don't like people who have different ideas from me	28-1	-2	-3	-4	-7	-8	-9

COL 19-22 BLANK

COL 24 BLANK

COL 29 BLANK

CARD 10

9. **SHOW CARD**: How much do you agree or disagree with the following statements? Would you say you agree strongly, agree, are uncertain, disagree or disagree strongly? ONE MENTION ONLY PER STATEMENT.

	AGREE STRONGLY	AGREE	UNCERTAIN	DISAGREE	DISAGREE STRONGLY	NO ANSWER (DNRO)	REFUSED (DNRO)	DON'T KNOW (DNRO)
6. People shouldn't accept everything the authorities say without questioning it	35-1	-2	-3	-4	-5	-7	-8	-9
7. All this country really needs is a single political party to rule the country	36-1	-2	-3	-4	-5	-7	-8	-9
8. People should not try to change how society works but just accept the way it is	37-1	-2	-3	-4	-5	-7	-8	-9
9. Even if the laws are not always fair, it is more important that government actions follow the law than that they be fair	38-1	-2	-3	-4	-5	-7	-8	-9
10. A country made up of many ethnic groups should be ruled by only one political party to prevent too much ethnic conflict from occurring	39-1	-2	-3	-4	-5	-7	-8	-9
11. Democracy in South Africa is too fragile to allow many political parties to compete with each other	40-1	-2	-3	-4	-5	-7	-8	-9
12. The party that gets the support of the majority ought not to have to share political power with the political minority	41-1	-2	-3	-4	-5	-7	-8	-9
13. It is not necessary to obey the laws of a government that I did not vote for	42-1	-2	-3	-4	-5	-7	-8	-9
14. Owners of a piece of property should have the right to do whatever they want with the property, even if that means not using the property	43-1	-2	-3	-4	-5	-7	-8	-9
17. If the majority of the people want something, the constitution should not be used to keep them from getting what they want	46-1	-2	-3	-4	-5	-7	-8	-9

10. **SHOW CARD:** Next I will read through a list of rights and freedoms. Please tell me how important these rights are **to you personally** on a scale from 1 = not very important to 5 = very important. ONE MENTION ONLY PER STATEMENT.

READ OUT.	NOT VERY IMPORTANT	SLIGHTLY IMPORTANT	SOMEWHAT IMPORTANT	IMPORTANT	VERY IMPORTANT	NO ANSWER (DNRO)	REFUSED (DNRO)	DON'T KNOW (DNRO)
1. The freedom to express your political views	47-1	-2	-3	-4	-5	-7	-8	-9
2. The freedom to join and take part in social and political groups and unions	48-1	-2	-3	-4	-5	-7	-8	-9
3. The right to be treated equally under the law	49-1	-2	-3	-4	-5	-7	-8	-9
5. The right to own land	51-1	-2	-3	-4	-5	-7	-8	-9
6. The right to a clean and safe environment, free from pollution	52-1	-2	-3	-4	-5	-7	-8	-9
7. The right to education in my own language	53-1	-2	-3	-4	-5	-7	-8	-9
9. The right to adequate housing	55-1	-2	-3	-4	-5	-7	-8	-9

COL 44-45 BLANK

COL 50 BLANK

COL 54 BLANK

11. **SHOW CARD:** How much do you agree or disagree with the following statements? Would you say you agree strongly, agree, are uncertain, disagree or disagree strongly? ONE MENTION ONLY PER STATEMENT.

	AGREE STRONGLY	AGREE	UNCERTAIN	DISAGREE	DISAGREE STRONGLY	NO ANSWER (DNRO)	REFUSED (DNRO)	DON'T KNOW (DNRO)
1. People should go along with whatever is best for the group, even when they disagree	57-1	-2	-3	-4	-5	-7	-8	-9
4. The most important thing in my life is to make myself happy	60-1	-2	-3	-4	-5	-7	-8	-9
5. Individuals have to look after themselves; the community shouldn't be responsible for the actions of each person	61-1	-2	-3	-4	-5	-7	-8	-9
6. It is great that people today have greater freedom to protest against everything they do not like	62-1	-2	-3	-4	-5	-7	-8	-9
7. I must make decisions about my life on my own, and not just do what my family says I should do	63-1	-2	-3	-4	-5	-7	-8	-9
8. It is better for people to do their own thing by themselves than to always try to please their family	64-1	-2	-3	-4	-5	-7	-8	-9

COL 58-59 BLANK

12.1 SHOW CARD: People see themselves in many different ways. Using this list, which **ONE** of these best describes you? Please take a moment to look at all of the terms on the list. **READ OUT WHOLE LIST. PROBE VERY STRONGLY TO GET AN ANSWER. IF NO ANSWER IS GIVEN i.e. NO ANSWER, REFUSED OR DON'T KNOW, SKIP TO Q.13**

ONE MENTION ONLY.

1.	African	65-01	18.	Siswati/ Swazi	-18
2.	Afrikaner	-02	19.	South Sotho/ Sesotho	-19
3.	Asian	-03	20.	South African	-20
4.	Black	-04	21.	Tsonga/ Shangaan	-21
5.	Boer	-05	22.	Tswana	-22
6.	Brown	-06	23.	Venda	-23
7.	Christian	-07	24.	White	-24
8.	Coloured	-08	25.	Xhosa	-25
9.	English	-09	26.	Zulu	-26
10.	European	-10	27.	Ndebele	-27
11.	Hindu	-11	28.	Other (PLEASE SPECIFY): (Volunteered) **DNRO**	
12.	Indian	-12		....	-28
13.	Jewish	-13		....	
14.	Malaysian	-14	97.	No answer **(DNRO)**	-97
15.	Muslim	-15	98.	Refused **(DNRO)**	-98
16.	North Sotho/ Sepedi	-16	99.	Don't know **(DNRO)**	-99
17.	North Sotho	-17			

12.2 How important is this identity to you? Would you say it is very important, somewhat important, not very important or not important at all for you to think of yourself as ... **(READ ANSWER GIVEN IN Q.12.1)**

ONE MENTION ONLY.

1.	Very important	67-1
2.	Somewhat important	-2
3.	Not very important	-3
4.	Not important at all	-4
5.	Not applicable – no identity selected **(DNRO)**	-5
7.	No answer **(DNRO)**	-7
8.	Refused **(DNRO)**	-8
9.	Don't know **(DNRO)**	-9

13.	**SHOW CARD:** Still looking at the card, do you think of yourself in any of the other terms as well? (WRITE IN). **READ OUT LIST IF NECCESARY. CANNOT BE THE SAME AS Q12.1**	**ONE MENTION ONLY.**	
		1. African	68-01
		2. Afrikaner	-02
		3. Asian	-03
		4. Black	-04
		5. Boer	-05
		6. Brown	-06
		7. Christian	-07
		8. Coloured	-08
		9. English	-09
		10. European	-10
		11. Hindu	-11
		12. Indian	-12
		13. Jewish	-13
		14. Malaysian	-14
		15. Muslim	-15
		16. North Sotho/ Sepedi	-16
		17. Siswati/ Swazi	-17
		18. South Sotho/ Sesotho	-18
		19. South African	-19
		20. Tsonga/ Shangaan	-20
		21. Tswana	-21
		22. Venda	-22
		23. White	-23
		24. Xhosa	-24
		25. Zulu	-25
		26. Ndebele	-26
		27. All the others, the rest	-27
		28. No, none	-28
		29. Other (Specify) Volunteerd **(DNRO)**	-29
		....	
		97. No answer **(DNRO)**	-97
		98. Refused **(DNRO)**	-98
		99. Don't know **(DNRO)**	-99

14.	**SHOW CARD**: Still looking at the card, which would you say most strongly does **NOT** describe you? (WRITE IN). Should respondent have difficulty because he/she would like to select more than one: ASK: But, which ONE would you say *most strongly* does **NOT** describe you? **IMPORTANT: PROBE FULLY, IT IS IMPORTANT TO OBTAIN AN ANSWER. IF NO ANSWER IS GIVEN i.e. NO ANSWER, REFUSED OR DON'T KNOW, SKIP TO Q.16**	**ONE MENTION ONLY.**	
		1. African	70-01
		2. Afrikaner	-02
		3. Asian	-03
		4. Black	-04
		5. Boer	-05
		6. Brown	-06
		7. Christian	-07
		8. Coloured	-08
		9. English	-09
		10. European	-10
		11. Hindu	-11
		12. Indian	-12
		13. Jewish	-13
		14. Malaysian	-14
		15. Muslim	-15
		16. North Sotho/ Sepedi	-16
		17. Siswati/ Swazi	-17
		18. South Sotho/ Sesotho	-18
		19. South African	-19
		20. Tsonga/ Shangaan	-20
		21. Tswana	-21
		22. Venda	-22
		23. White	-23
		24. Xhosa	-24
		25. Zulu	-25
		26. Ndebele	-26
		27. All the others, the rest	-27
		28. No, none	-28
		29. Other (Specify) (Volunteered) **(DNRO)**	-29
		....	
		97. No answer **(DNRO)**	-97
		98. Refused **(DNRO)**	-98
		99. Don't know **(DNRO)**	-99

15.	**INTRODUCTION**: People have different sorts of feelings as a result of being a member of a group. Which of the following characteristics describes how you feel about being a ..... **(READ ANSWER GIVEN IN Q.12.1)?**		
		ONE MENTION ONLY.	
15.1	It makes me feel (READ OUT SCALE) ... (ANSWER IN Q.12.1)	1. Very secure	72-1
		2. Fairly secure	-2
		3. How secure I feel does NOT depend on being a ...	-3
		4. Not applicable **(DNRO)**	-4
		7. No answer **(DNRO)**	-7
		8. Refused **(DNRO)**	-8
		9. Don't know **(DNRO)**	-9
15.2	It makes me feel (READ OUT SCALE) ... (ANSWER IN Q.12.1)	1. Very important	73-1
		2. Fairly important	-2
		3. How important I feel does NOT depend on being a ...	-3
		4. Not applicable **(DNRO)**	-4
		7. No answer **(DNRO)**	-7
		8. Refused **(DNRO)**	-8
		9. Don't know **(DNRO)**	-9
15.3	It makes me think (READ OUT SCALE) ... (ANSWER IN Q.12.1)	1. Much better of myself	74-1
		2. A little better of myself	-2
		3. How I think about myself does NOT depend on being a ...	-3
		4. Not applicable **(DNRO)**	-4
		7. No answer **(DNRO)**	-7
		8. Refused **(DNRO)**	-8
		9. Don't know **(DNRO)**	-9

16.	**SHOW CARD:** How much do you agree or disagree with the following statements? Would you say you agree strongly, agree, are uncertain, disagree or disagree strongly? ONE MENTION ONLY PER STATEMENT.								
		AGREE STRONGLY	**AGREE**	**UNCERTAIN**	**DISAGREE**	**DISAGREE STRONGLY**	**NO ANSWER (DNRO)**	**REFUSED (DNRO)**	**DON'T KNOW (DNRO)**
1.	The way South Africa is right now, if one group gets more power it is usually because another group is getting less power	75-1	-2	-3	-4	-5	-7	-8	-9
2.	The trouble with politics in South Africa is that it is always based on what group you are a member of	76-1	-2	-3	-4	-5	-7	-8	-9
3.	If people don't realise we are all South Africans and stop thinking of themselves as Xhosa or Afrikaans or Zulu or whatever, South Africa will have a very difficult political future	77-1	-2	-3	-4	-5	-7	-8	-9

CARD 11

17. **SHOW CARD:** Now I would like to ask you a few more questions about how you feel about being a ... **(READ ANSWER GIVEN IN Q.12.1).** Would you say you agree strongly, agree, are uncertain, disagree or disagree strongly? ONE MENTION ONLY PER STATEMENT.

.... = (GROUP IN Q.12.1)	AGREE STRONGLY	AGREE	UNCERTAIN	DISAGREE	DISAGREE STRONGLY	NOT APPLICABLE (DNRO)	NO ANSWER (DNRO)	REFUSED (DNRO)	DON'T KNOW (DNRO)
1. Of all the groups in South Africa ... are the best	5-1	-2	-3	-4	-5	-6	-7	-8	-9
2. Even though I might sometimes disagree with the viewpoint taken by other ..., it is extremely important to support the ... point-of-view	6-1	-2	-3	-4	-5	-6	-7	-8	-9
3. What happens to ... in South Africa will affect my life a great deal	7-1	-2	-3	-4	-5	-6	-7	-8	-9
4. When it comes to politics, it is important for all ... to stand together	8-1	-2	-3	-4	-5	-6	-7	-8	-9
5. Unless you are a member of a group like ... it is very difficult to get much out of South African politics	9-1	-2	-3	-4	-5	-6	-7	-8	-9
6. The well-being of ... has more to do with politics than it does with our own hard work	10-1	-2	-3	-4	-5	-6	-7	-8	-9

18. **SHOW CARD:** How much do you agree or disagree with these statements? Would you say you agree strongly, agree, are uncertain, disagree or disagree strongly? ONE MENTION ONLY PER STATEMENT.

	AGREE STRONGLY	AGREE	UNCERTAIN	DISAGREE	DISAGREE STRONGLY	NO ANSWER (DNRO)	REFUSED (DNRO)	DON'T KNOW (DNRO)
1. In a country with so much poverty, the property rights of the wealthy must be reduced	11-1	-2	-3	-4	-5	-7	-8	-9
2. People should have the right to set up their own communities, and not allow those of a different race to live in their communities	12-1	-2	-3	-4	-5	-7	-8	-9
3. When it comes to land, the rights of the community are more important than the rights of individual land owners	13-1	-2	-3	-4	-5	-7	-8	-9
4. Newspapers, radio and television should communicate the views of all political parties, not just the party they support	14-1	-2	-3	-4	-5	-7	-8	-9
5. Newspapers, radio and television should be responsible for presenting all points of view, even those that some people could consider racist	15-1	-2	-3	-4	-5	-7	-8	-9
6. Voting in South African elections should be restricted to those who own property	16-1	-2	-3	-4	-5	-7	-8	-9
7. Newspapers, radio and television should be protected by law from control by the government more than they are now	17-1	-2	-3	-4	-5	-7	-8	-9
8. It is better to live in an orderly society than to allow people so much freedom that they can become disorderly	18-1	-2	-3	-4	-5	-7	-8	-9

19.	Are you very interested, interested, not very interested or not at all interested in politics?	**ONE MENTION ONLY.**	
		1. Very interested	19-1
		2. Interested	-2
		3. Not very interested	-3
		4. Not at all interested	-4
		7. No answer **(DNRO)**	-7
		8. Refused **(DNRO)**	-8
		9. Don't know **(DNRO)**	-9

➢　**NOW WE WOULD LIKE TO ASK YOU SOME QUESTIONS ABOUT SOUTH AFRICA'S HISTORY.**

20.1	**SHOW CARD:** In which decade did the Nationalist Party government first introduce apartheid as the official policy of South Africa?	**READ OUT. ONE MENTION ONLY**	
		1. 1910s	20-01
		2. 1920s	-02
		3. 1930s	-03
		4. 1940s	-04
		5. 1950s	-05
		6. 1960s	-06
		7. 1970s	-07
		8. 1980s	-08
		9. 1990s	-09
		97. No answer **(DNRO)**	-97
		98. Refused **(DNRO)**	-98
		99. Don't know **(DNRO)**	-99
20.2	**SHOW CARD:** Which of the following best defines the term "black spot?" **Should you be asked what a 'black spot' is – respond by saying you do not know.**	**ONE MENTION ONLY.**	
		1. "black spot" refers to land of a very high quality that was reserved for white farmers under apartheid	22-1
		2. "black spot" refers to pockets of strong black opposition to the apartheid system	-2
		3. "black spot" refers to a non-white community living within an area designated for white people by the apartheid government	-3
		7. No answer **(DNRO)**	-7
		8. Refused **(DNRO)**	-8
		9. Don't know **(DNRO)**	-9

CARD 11

				GO TO:
		ONE MENTION ONLY.		
20.3	**SHOW CARD:** Which of the following best defines the term "Bantustan?"	1. A Bantustan is a form of tribal leadership found in some rural areas of South Africa	23-1	
		2. A Bantustan is an area where black people were expected to live under apartheid	-2	
		3. A Bantustan is a farm owned and managed exclusively by black people	-3	
		7. No answer – **(DO NOT READ OUT)**	-7	
		8. Refused – **(DO NOT READ OUT)**	-8	
		9 Don't know – **(DO NOT READ OUT)**	-9	
20.3.1	**INTERVIEWER INSTRUCTION: You DO NOT READ OUT this question: Listen to the answer provided in Q20.3 and should the respondent spontaneously mention any of the following areas while answering in Q20.3, circle the Bantustan mentioned here. THERE COULD BE MULTIPLE RESPONSES.**	**MULTIMENTIONS POSSIBLE. DNRO**		
		1. Ciskei	24-1	
		2. Venda	25-2	
		3. Transkei	26-3	
		4. Lebowa	27-4	
		5. Qwa-Qwa	28-5	
		6. Gazankulu	29-6	
		7. Kangwane	30-7	
		8. KwaZulu	31-8	
		9. Bophuthatswana	32-9	
		10. KwaNdebele	33-0	
		11. No area was mentioned spontaneously	34-0	
20.4	**ASK ALL: SHOW CARD:** Under apartheid, many people were forced to leave their living places and move to other areas of the country. Do you know approximately how many people were forced to move under apartheid? ➤ **RECORD ANSWER THAT CLOSEST REFLECTS RESPONDENT'S ANSWER.**	**READ OUT. ONE MENTION ONLY**		
		1. None	35-01	
		2. Less than 100, 000 people	-02	
		3. Up to ½ million people	-03	
		4. Up to 1 million people	-04	
		5. About 1-2 million people	-05	
		6. About 2-3 million people	-06	
		7. 3 million people or more	-07	
		8. No forced removals took place in SA **(DNRO)**	-08	
		9. No answer – **(DO NOT READ OUT)**	-97	
		10. Refused – **(DO NOT READ OUT)**	-98	
		11. Don't know – **(DO NOT READ OUT)**	-99	

CARD 11

20.5	**ASK ALL: SHOW CARD:** Do you know approximately when the last racially motivated forced removal took place in South Africa?	**READ OUT. ONE MENTION ONLY.**	
		1. 1910s	37-01
		2. 1920s	-02
		3. 1930s	-03
		4. 1940s	-04
		5. 1950s	-05
		6. 1960s	-06
		7. 1970s	-07
		8. 1980s	-08
		9. 1990s	-09
		96. No forced removals took place in SA (Volunteer) – **(DO NOT READ OUT)**	-96
		97. No answer – **(DO NOT READ OUT)**	-97
		98. Refused – **(DO NOT READ OUT)**	-98
		99. Don't know – **(DO NOT READ OUT)**	-99

Q20.6 OMITTED

COL 39 ON CARD 11 BLANK

CARD 11

20.6.1 **SHOW CARD:** How much do you agree or disagree with these statements? Would you say you agree strongly, agree, are uncertain, disagree or disagree strongly? ONE MENTION ONLY PER STATEMENT.

		AGREE STRONGLY	AGREE	UNCERTAIN	DISAGREE	DISAGREE STRONGLY	NO ANSWER (DNRO)	REFUSED (DNRO)	DON'T KNOW (DNRO)
1.	Free speech is just not worth it if it means that we have to put up with the danger to society of radical political views	40-1	-2	-3	-4	-5	-7	-8	-9
2.	If someone has lived on a piece of property for a long time – say 10 years – then that person must be recognised as having the right of ownership to the property	41-1	-2	-3	-4	-5	-7	-8	-9
3.	Society shouldn't have to put up with political views that are fundamentally different from the views of the majority	42-1	-2	-3	-4	-5	-7	-8	-9
4.	It is better for society to let some guilty people go free than to risk convicting an innocent person	43-1	-2	-3	-4	-5	-7	-8	-9
5.	Because demonstrations frequently become disorderly and disruptive, radical and extremist groups shouldn't be allowed to demonstrate	44-1	-2	-3	-4	-5	-7	-8	-9
6.	If police obtain evidence illegally, it should not be used in court, even if it would help convict a guilty person	45-1	-2	-3	-4	-5	-7	-8	-9

CONTINUED OVERLEAF

CARD 11

	AGREE STRONGLY	AGREE	UNCERTAIN	DISAGREE	DISAGREE STRONGLY	NO ANSWER (DNRO)	REFUSED (DNRO)	DON'T KNOW (DNRO)
7. Farmers must receive fair compensation if their farms are taken away by the government for land reform.	46-1	-2	-3	-4	-5	-7	-8	-9
8. It makes me proud to be called a South African	47-1	-2	-3	-4	-5	-7	-8	-9
9. Being a South African is a very important part of how I see myself	48-1	-2	-3	-4	-5	-7	-8	-9
10. If we start taking away the land rights of property owners, chaos will come to South Africa	49-1	-2	-3	-4	-5	-7	-8	-9
11. All white owned land in South Africa ought to be taken away by the government without any compensation to anyone	50-1	-2	-3	-4	-5	-7	-8	-9
12. All land claims from the past from black people ought to be denied, without any compensation to anyone	51-1	-2	-3	-4	-5	-7	-8	-9

GROUP SELECTION GRID	
➢ **Q.21 – Q.25 INTERVIEWER INSTRUCTION:** RING GROUP ASKED ABOUT.	
- IF RESPONDENT IS BLACK ASK ABOUT WHITES	52-1
- IF RESPONDENT IS WHITE ASK ABOUT BLACKS	-2
- IF RESPONDENT IS INDIAN ASK ABOUT BLACKS	-3
➢ IF RESPONDENT IS COLOURED CHECK QUESTIONNAIRE NUMBER AND IF:	
- QUESTIONNAIRE NUMBER ENDS ON AN EVEN NUMBER ASK ABOUT BLACKS	-4
- QUESTIONNAIRE NUMBER ENDS ON AN ODD NUMBER ASK ABOUT WHITES	-5
RECORD RELEVANT GROUP.	

➢ RACE GROUP ASKED ABOUT IN THE INTER-GROUP RELATIONS QUESTIONS.	1.	Asked about whites	53-1
	2.	Asked about blacks	-2
21. **SHOW CARD:** Now we would like to ask about the type of contacts you have with **(RACE GROUP)**. In your work, on a typical working day, how much contact do you have with … **(RACE GROUP)?**		**ONE MENTION ONLY.**	
	1.	A great deal	54-1
	2.	Some	-2
	3.	Not very much	-3
	4.	Hardly any contact	-4
	5.	No contact at all	-5
	6.	Not applicable – Do not work – **(DO NOT READ OUT)**	-6
	7.	No answer – **(DO NOT READ OUT)**	-7
	8.	Refused – **(DO NOT READ OUT)**	-8
	9.	Don't know – **(DO NOT READ OUT)**	-9

CARD 11

22.	**SHOW CARD**: Outside your work, how much contact do you have with … **(RACE GROUP)**?	**ONE MENTION ONLY.**	
		1. A great deal	55-1
		2. Some	-2
		3. Not very much	-3
		4. Hardly any contact	-4
		5. No contact at all	-5
		7. No answer – **(DO NOT READ OUT)**	-7
		8. Refused – **(DO NOT READ OUT)**	-8
		9. Don't know – **(DO NOT READ OUT)**	-9
23.	**SHOW CARD**: How often have you shared a meal with a **(RACE GROUP)**?	**ONE MENTION ONLY.**	
		1. Quite often	56-1
		2. Not very often	-2
		3. Never	-3
		7. No answer – **(DO NOT READ OUT)**	-7
		8. Refused – **(DO NOT READ OUT)**	-8
		9. Don't know – **(DO NOT READ OUT)**	-9
24.	**SHOW CARD**: How many … **(RACE GROUP)** people would you call "true" friends?	**ONE MENTION ONLY.**	
		1. Quite a number of **(RACE** GROUP) people	57-1
		2. Only a small number of **(RACE** GROUP) people	-2
		3. Hardly any **(RACE GROUP)** people	-3
		4. No **(RACE** GROUP) people	-4
		7. No answer – **(DO NOT READ OUT)**	-7
		8. Refused – **(DO NOT READ OUT)**	-8
		9. Don't know – **(DO NOT READ OUT)**	-9

25. **SHOW CARD**: Now we would like to ask your opinion about **(RACE GROUP, e.g. WHITE SOUTH AFRICANS/WHITES)**. Would you say you agree strongly, agree, are uncertain, disagree or disagree strongly? ONE MENTION ONLY.

		AGREE STRONGLY	AGREE	UNCERTAIN	DISAGREE	DISAGREE STRONGLY	NO ANSWER (DNRO)	REFUSED (DNRO)	DON'T KNOW (DNRO)
1.	I find it difficult to understand the customs and ways of **(RACE GROUP)**	58-1	-2	-3	-4	-5	-7	-8	-9
2.	It is hard to imagine ever being friends with a **(RACE GROUP)**	59-1	-2	-3	-4	-5	-7	-8	-9
3.	More than most groups, **(RACE GROUP)** are likely to engage in crime	60-1	-2	-3	-4	-5	-7	-8	-9
4.	**(RACE GROUP)** are untrustworthy	61-1	-2	-3	-4	-5	-7	-8	-9
5.	**(RACE GROUP)** are selfish, and only look after the interests of their own group	62-1	-2	-3	-4	-5	-7	-8	-9
6.	I feel uncomfortable when I am around a group of **(RACE GROUP)**	63-1	-2	-3	-4	-5	-7	-8	-9

CONTINUED OVERLEAF

CARD 11

		AGREE STRONGLY	AGREE	UNCERTAIN	DISAGREE	DISAGREE STRONGLY	NO ANSWER (DNRO)	REFUSED (DNRO)	DON'T KNOW (DNRO)
7.	Most (RACE GROUP) are **not** racists	64-1	-2	-3	-4	-5	-7	-8	-9
8.	I often **don't** believe what (RACE GROUP) say to me	65-1	-2	-3	-4	-5	-7	-8	-9
9.	South Africa would be a better place if there were no (RACE GROUP) in the country	66-1	-2	-3	-4	-5	-7	-8	-9
10.	I could never imagine being part of a political party made up mainly of (RACE GROUP)	67-1	-2	-3	-4	-5	-7	-8	-9

26.1 **SHOW CARD**: Would you say you agree strongly, agree, are uncertain, disagree or disagree strongly? ONE MENTION ONLY.

		AGREE STRONGLY	AGREE	UNCERTAIN	DISAGREE	DISAGREE STRONGLY	NO ANSWER (DNRO)	REFUSED (DNRO)	DON'T KNOW (DNRO)
2.	Black farmers are only capable of producing enough food to feed their families, and cannot be relied upon to produce enough food to feed the nation	69-1	-2	-3	-4	-5	-7	-8	-9
3.	If given the right resources, black farmers could be as successful at farming as white farmers	70-1	-2	-3	-4	-5	-7	-8	-9
4.	White farmers in South Africa have been better than black farmers at creating jobs for workers	71-1	-2	-3	-4	-5	-7	-8	-9
5.	Giving farm land to blacks in South Africa would be economically disastrous	72-1	-2	-3	-4	-5	-7	-8	-9

Q.26.2 OMITTED

COL 68 BLANK

COL 73-76 BLANK

27. And now I'd like to ask you about your attitudes towards some groups of people. I am going to read you a list of some groups that are currently active in social and political life.

Here is a card showing a scale from "1" to "11". The number "1" indicates that you **dislike** the group very much; the number "11" indicates that you **like** the group very much. The number "6" means that you neither like nor dislike the group. The numbers "2" to "5" reflect varying degree of dislike; and the numbers "7" to "10" reflect varying degree of like towards the group.

SHOW CARD: The first group I'd like to ask you about is … **READ OUT GROUP AT STARTING POINT**. If you have an opinion about … please indicate which figure most closely describes your attitude towards them. If you have no opinion, **please be sure to tell me**. ONE MENTION ONLY PER GROUP. **IF THE RESPONDENT HAS 'NO OPINION', CODE '96'**

What is your opinion of …..?

> ➢ **INTERVIEWER:** USE THE GRID BELOW TO SELECT A STARTING POINT. START WITH THAT GROUP AND ROTATE – ASK FOR ALL GROUPS.

> ➢ Record STARTING POINT i.e. statement number, using leading zero for single digit numbers 46 - ⎯ ⎯

Last digit of questionnaire number	0	1	2	3	4	5	6	7	8	9
Start with attribute number	1	2	4	5	6	7	8	10	11	12

ROTATE ORDER			RATING ON SCALE 1 to 11: Or '96' if 'no opinion'
…………	1.	Afrikaners	48-………………………………
…………	2.	Supporters of the ANC	50-………………………………
…………	3.	Supporters of the AWB	52-………………………………
…………	4.	South African Communist Party	54-………………………………
…………	5.	Supporters of the Pan Africanist Congress	56-………………………………
…………	6.	Supporters of the New National Party	58-………………………………
…………	7.	Supporters of the Democratic Alliance	60-………………………………
…………	8.	Supporters of the Inkatha Freedom Party	62-………………………………
…………	9.	People who say "South Africa should have a 1-party state"	64-………………………………
…………	10.	Supporters of the Mishlenti Society	66-………………………………
…………	11.	Supporters of Trade Unions	68-………………………………
…………	12.	Muslims	70-………………………………

				GO TO:
28.1	**ASK ALL:** Is there any **other** group **[not mentioned in Q.27]** active in the life of our country that you **dislike** enough to rate at a "3" or a "2" or a "1" on this scale?	1. Yes	72-1	**Q.28.2**
		2. No	-2	**Q.29.1**
		7. No answer – **(DO NOT READ OUT)**	-7	
		8. Don't know – **(DO NOT READ OUT)**	-8	
		9. Refused – **(DO NOT READ OUT)**	-9	
28.2	What is the name of the group?			
	……………………………………………………………………………………………………		73-	
	CANNOT BE THE SAME AS Q.27		**BLANK 75-**	

CARD 12/13

28.3	SHOW CARD: Would you rate (THE GROUP NAMED IN Q.28.2) as a "3", "2" or "1" on the scale that's on the card?	RATE: ONE MENTION ONLY:	
		One	76-1
		Two	-2
		Three	-3

29.1 **ASK ALL: SHOW CARD:** This card presents a list of groups we have already spoken about. Which of the following groups do you **dislike the most? READ OUT. ONE MENTION ONLY PER COLUMN**

WRITE IN ANSWER FROM Q.28.2   5- .... CARD 13

		THE GROUP THAT YOU DISLIKE THE MOST	THE NEXT MOST DISLIKED GROUP	THIRD MOST DISLIKED GROUP	FOURTH MOST DISLIKED GROUP	GO TO:
		GROUP A				
1.	Afrikaners C13	8-01	10-01	12-01	14-01	
2.	Supporters of the ANC	-02	-02	-02	-02	
3.	Supporters of the AWB	-03	-03	-03	-03	
4.	South African Communist Party	-04	-04	-04	-04	
5.	Supporters of the Pan Africanist Congress	-05	-05	-05	-05	
6.	Supporters of the New National Party	-06	-06	-06	-06	**Q.30**
7.	Supporters of the Democratic Alliance	-07	-07	-07	-07	
8.	Supporters of the Inkatha Freedom Party	-08	-08	-08	-08	
9.	People who say "South Africa should have a 1-party state"	-09	-09	-09	-09	
10.	Supporters of Trade Unions	-10	-10	-10	-10	
11.	Muslims	-11	-11	-11	-11	
12.	Other (PLEASE SPECIFY): **INCLUDE MENTION FROM Q.28.2**	-12	-12	-12	-12	
13.	No group / None	-13	-13	-13	-13	GO TO Q.29.2

➤ **INTERVIEWER INSTRUCTION:** IF RESPONDENT WOULD NOT NAME DISLIKED GROUPS – GO TO Q.29.2.

IF RESPONDENT IDENTIFIED A GROUP IN Q.29.1 – GO TO Q.30

29.2 Do you dislike either of the following groups of people? ONE MENTION ONLY PER STATEMENT.

		YES	NO	NO ANSWER (DNRO)	REFUSED (DNRO)	DON'T KNOW (DNRO)
1.	Those who would re-impose apartheid laws in the country	18-1	-2	-7	-8	-9
2.	Those who would force all whites to leave South Africa	19-1	-2	-7	-8	-9

29.3	IF NO TO BOTH Q.29.1 AND Q.29.2, OR IF YES TO BOTH Q.29.1 AND Q.29.2, ASK: Which of the two groups of people do you dislike the most?	1. Those who would reimpose apartheid laws	20-1
		2. Those who would force all whites to leave South Africa	-2
		7. No answer – (DO NOT READ OUT)	-7
		8. Don't know – (DO NOT READ OUT)	-8
		9. Refused – (DO NOT READ OUT)	-9

➤ **INTERVIEWER INSTRUCTION:** DEAL WITH THE GROUP SELECTED IN Q.29.1 and Q29.3 AS <u>GROUP A</u> WHENEVER GROUP A IS MENTIONED FROM HERE ONWARD.

30. **ASK ALL: SHOW CARD:** Now let's consider the ..... **(GROUP IN Q.29.1 OR Q.29.3 i.e. GROUP A)** a bit more. To what extent do you agree strongly, agree, are uncertain, disagree, or disagree strongly with the following statements about .....? ONE MENTION ONLY.

	AGREE STRONGLY	AGREE	UNCERTAIN	DISAGREE	DISAGREE STRONGLY	NO ANSWER (DNRO)	REFUSED (DNRO)	DON'T KNOW (DNRO)
1. Members of the (GROUP A) should be prohibited from standing as a candidate for an elected position	28-1	-2	-3	-4	-5	-7	-8	-9

			GO TO:
30.1.	And about what percentage of the people in South Africa do you think agree with you on this issue?	1. Percent (0% ...... 100%) **(WRITE IN)** 29-	Q.31.1
		997. No answer – **(DO NOT READ OUT)** -997	
		998. Don't know – **(DO NOT READ OUT)** -998	Q.30.2
		999. Refused – **(DO NOT READ OUT)** -999	

➤ **INTERVIEWER:** IF THE RESPONDENT CANNOT GIVE AN ANSWER IN PERCENTAGE TERMS, ASK Q.30.2.

30.2.	**SHOW CARD:** Do you think most South Africans agree with your view or disagree with your view on this issue?	ONE MENTION ONLY.	
		1. Most agree	32-1
		2. Most disagree	-2
		3. Can't say which – **(DO NOT READ OUT)**	-3
		7. No answer – **(DO NOT READ OUT)**	-7
		8. Don't know – **(DO NOT READ OUT)**	-8
		9. Refused – **(DO NOT READ OUT)**	-9
31.1	**SHOW CARD:** Should members of the (GROUP A) be allowed to hold street demonstrations in your community?	ONE MENTION ONLY.	
		1. Agree strongly	33-1
		2. Agree	-2
		3. Uncertain	-3
		4. Disagree	-4
		5. Disagree strongly	-5
		7. No answer – **(DO NOT READ OUT)**	-7
		8. Don't know – **(DO NOT READ OUT)**	-8
		9. Refused – **(DO NOT READ OUT)**	-9

31.2	**SHOW CARD:** Should (GROUP A) be officially banned from your community?	**ONE MENTION ONLY.**	
		1. Agree strongly	34-1
		2. Agree	-2
		3. Uncertain	-3
		4. Disagree	-4
		5. Disagree strongly	-5
		7. No answer – **(DO NOT READ OUT)**	-7
		8. Don't know – **(DO NOT READ OUT)**	-8
		9. Refused – **(DO NOT READ OUT)**	-9

➢   INTERVIEWER: IF Q.30 ANSWERED CODE "1" OR "2" | 35-1 | PLEASE CIRCLE

                AND Q.31.1 ANSWERED CODE "4" OR "5" | -2 |

                AND Q.31.2 ANSWERED CODE "1" OR "2" | -3 |

➢   **ONLY IF ALL 3 BOXES ARE TICKED, ASK Q.31.3**

31.3	Members of (GROUP A) should be made to permanently leave South Africa.	**ONE MENTION ONLY.**	
		1. Agree strongly	36-1
		2. Agree	-2
		3. Uncertain	-3
		4. Disagree	-4
		5. Disagree strongly	-5
		7. No answer – **(DO NOT READ OUT)**	-7
		8. Refused – **(DO NOT READ OUT)**	-8
		9. Don't know – **(DO NOT READ OUT)**	-9

GROUP SELECTION GRID

➢   **Q.32 AND Q.50.1 – Q.50.9 INTERVIEWER INSTRUCTION: PLEASE CIRCLE THE RELEVANT CODE**

     - IF RESPONDENT IS BLACK ASK "WHITE LAND RADICALS"   37 -1

     - IF RESPONDENT IS WHITE ASK "BLACK LAND RADICALS"   -2

     - IF RESPONDENT IS INDIAN ASK "BLACK LAND RADICALS"   -3

➢   **IF RESPONDENT IS COLOURED CHECK QUESTIONNAIRE NUMBER AND IF:**

     - QUESTIONNAIRE NUMBER ENDS ON AN EVEN NUMBER ASK "BLACK LAND RADICALS"   -4

     - QUESTIONNAIRE NUMBER ENDS ON AN ODD NUMBER ASK "WHITE LAND RADICALS"   -5

     RECORD RELEVANT GROUP. IN SHORT WE WILL LABEL THIS GROUP FOR INTERNAL USE AS THE 'LAND GROUP'

> ➢ "White land radicals" are those who advocate denying all land claims from the past from black people, and not providing any compensation to anyone.

> ➢ "Black land radicals" are those who advocate the expropriation of all white-owned land in South Africa, without any compensation at all.

> READ OUT FULL DESCRIPTION TO RESPONDENT WHEN ASKING STATEMENTS IN Q32.

CARD 13

32. SHOW CARD: Now let's consider the (LAND GROUP) a bit more. To what extent do you agree strongly, agree, are uncertain, disagree, or disagree strongly with the following statements about ...? ONE MENTION ONLY PER STATEMENT.

		AGREE STRONGLY	AGREE	UNCERTAIN	DISAGREE	DISAGREE STRONGLY	NO ANSWER (DNRO)	REFUSED (DNRO)	DON'T KNOW (DNRO)
1.	Members of (LAND GROUP) should be prohibited from standing as a candidate for an elected position	38-1	-2	-3	-4	-5	-7	-8	-9
2.	Members of (LAND GROUP) should be allowed to hold street demonstrations in your community	39-1	-2	-3	-4	-5	-7	-8	-9
3.	(LAND GROUP) should be officially banned in your community	40-1	-2	-3	-4	-5	-7	-8	-9

32.1 ASK ALL: SHOW CARD: There are currently many debates in South Africa over the ownership of land. We are interested in your opinions about this matter. Do you agree strongly, agree, disagree, or disagree strongly with the following statements? ONE MENTION ONLY.

		AGREE STRONGLY	AGREE	UNCERTAIN	DISAGREE	DISAGREE STRONGLY	NO ANSWER (DNRO)	REFUSED (DNRO)	DON'T KNOW (DNRO)
1.	Most land in South Africa was taken unfairly by white settlers, and they therefore have no right to the land today	41-1	-2	-3	-4	-5	-7	-8	-9
2.	Since it is impossible to tell who really owns land in South Africa, we should just accept that current owners have the right to keep their land	42-1	-2	-3	-4	-5	-7	-8	-9
3.	Something like amnesty ought to be given to the current owners of land so that it doesn't matter how they acquired their land and so that they can keep their property	43-1	-2	-3	-4	-5	-7	-8	-9
4.	Land must be returned to blacks in South Africa, no matter what the consequences are for the current owners and for political stability in the country	44-1	-2	-3	-4	-5	-7	-8	-9

Card 13

> **INTERVIEWER INSTRUCTION:** CHECK ON PAGE 4 WHICH NUMBER YOU ARE REQUIRED TO READ OUT.
> READ THIS STORY TO THE RESPONDENT. RECORD THE STORY NUMBER.

45- [ ][ ]

Now I would like to read you a story and get your opinions on it.

➤ 1. Was re-read | Yes   47-1 | No   -2 | **PLEASE CIRCLE**

33.   And now here are some questions concerning your opinions about what happened in this story.

SHOW CARD: First considering all aspects of the story, how fair do you think is it that Patience and her family were evicted from the property on which they were squatting? If "10" means that you believe the outcome is completely fair to Patience and her family and "1" means the outcome is completely unfair to them, which number from "10 to 1" best describes how you feel?

For example, you might answer with a "4" if you think the outcome is only somewhat unfair, or a "7" if you think the outcome is somewhat fair to Patience and her family. CIRCLE ONCE.

Completely unfair	← →									Completely fair
48-01	-02	-03	-04	-05	-06	-07	-08	-09		10

> **INTERVIEWER:** CIRCLE HERE IF THE RESPONDENT ASKS THAT THE STORY BE RE-READ

1. Was re-read   50 [   ]   -1   97. No answer   -97 **(DNRO)**
2. Not re-read   [   ]   -2   98. Refused   -98 **(DNRO)**
                                        99. Don't know -99 **(DNRO)**

34.   **SHOW CARD:** Using the same scale, how fairly was Patience treated during the eviction? CIRCLE ONE.

Completely unfair	← →									Completely fair
51-01	-02	-03	-04	-05	-06	-07	-08	-09		10

> **INTERVIEWER:** CIRCLE HERE IF THE RESPONDENT ASKS THAT THE STORY BE RE-READ

1. Was re-read   53 [   ]   -1   97. No answer   -97 **(DNRO)**
2. Not re-read   [   ]   -2   98. Refused   -98 **(DNRO)**
                                        99. Don't know -99 **(DNRO)**

35.   **SHOW CARD:** How fair was the outcome to the land owner? CIRCLE ONCE.

Completely unfair	← →									Completely fair
54-01	-02	-03	-04	-05	-06	-07	-08	-09		10

> **INTERVIEWER:** CIRCLE HERE IF THE RESPONDENT ASKS THAT THE STORY BE RE-READ

1. Was re-read   56 [   ]   -1   97. No answer   -97 **(DNRO)**
2. Not re-read   [   ]   -2   98. Refused   -98 **(DNRO)**
                                        99. Don't know -99 **(DNRO)**

36.   **OMITTED   COL 57-59 BLANK**

> **INTERVIEWER:** THE STORY SHOULD NOT BE RE-READ ANYMORE, EVEN IF THE RESPONDENT REQUESTS IT. IF ASKED TO RE-READ THE STORY, SAY "I'M NOT ALLOWED TO RE-READ THE STORY FOR THE NEXT SET OF QUESTIONS".

37.	**SHOW CARD**: Thinking back on the story, how badly do you think that Patience and her family need housing? CIRCLE ONCE.

Needed housing	←								→	Did not need housing
60-01	-02	-03	-04	-05	-06	-07	-08	-09		10

97. No answer	-97 **(DNRO)**
98. Refused	-98 **(DNRO)**
99. Don't know	-99 **(DNRO)**

38.	**SHOW CARD**: Compared to other people needing a place to live, how much do you think Patience and her family deserve to be given a place to stay by the government?	**ONE MENTION ONLY.**	
		1. Deserve a place to live very much	63-1
		2. Somewhat deserve a place to live	-2
		3. Does not deserve a place to live very much	-3
		4. Does not at all deserve a place to live	-4
		7. No answer – **(DO NOT READ OUT)**	-7
		8. Refused – **(DO NOT READ OUT)**	-8
		9. Don't know – **(DO NOT READ OUT)**	-9
39.	When Patience and her family were evicted from the property, do you remember who it was that actually evicted them? **READ OUT. ONE MENTION ONLY**	1. The police	64-1
		2. Private security	-2
		3. Other (PLEASE SPECIFY): (DNRO)	
		....	
		....	-3
		7. No answer – **(DO NOT READ OUT)**	-7
		8. Refused – **(DO NOT READ OUT)**	-8
		9. Don't know – **(DO NOT READ OUT)**	-9
39a.	**SHOW CARD**: How certain are you of this?	**ONE MENTION ONLY.**	
		1. Very certain	66-1
		2. Somewhat certain	-2
		3. Not very certain	-3
		4. Not certain at all	-4
		7. No answer – **(DO NOT READ OUT)**	-7
		8. Refused – **(DO NOT READ OUT)**	-8
		9. Don't know – **(DO NOT READ OUT)**	-9

40.	SHOW CARD: How certain are you that the land on which Patience and her family squatted was currently being used by the owner of the land?			
			ONE MENTION ONLY.	
		1.	Certain it was	67-1
		2.	Probably it was	-2
		3.	Probably it was not	-3
		4.	Certain it was not	-4
		7.	No answer – (DO NOT READ OUT)	-7
		8.	Refused – (DO NOT READ OUT)	-8
		9.	Don't know – (DO NOT READ OUT)	-9
41.	SHOW CARD: When Patience and her family were evicted from the property, do you think they were given sufficient time to get sorted out before being forced off the land?			
			ONE MENTION ONLY.	
		1.	Certain they were given sufficient time	68-1
		2.	Probably were given sufficient time	-2
		3.	Probably were not given sufficient time	-3
		4.	Definitely were not given sufficient time	-4
		7.	No answer – (DO NOT READ OUT)	-7
		8.	Refused – (DO NOT READ OUT)	-8
		9.	Don't know – (DO NOT READ OUT)	-9
42.	Do you think that the government must immediately give Patience and her family a place to stay? ONE MENTION ONLY.	1.	Yes	69-1
		2.	No	-2
		7.	No answer – (DO NOT READ OUT)	-7
		8.	Refused – (DO NOT READ OUT)	-8
		9.	Don't know – (DO NOT READ OUT)	-9
42.1	ASK ALL: SHOW CARD: How strongly do you feel about this?			
			ONE MENTION ONLY.	
		1.	Very strongly	70-1
		2.	Somewhat strongly	-2
		3.	Not very strongly	-3
		4.	Not strongly at all	-4
		7.	No answer – (DO NOT READ OUT)	-7
		8.	Refused – (DO NOT READ OUT)	-8
		9.	Don't know – (DO NOT READ OUT)	-9

	➤ Q.43A THROUGH TO Q.44E OMITTED			
	COLUMNS 71-75 ON CARD 13 AND COL 5-9 ON CARD 14 IS BLANK			
45.	ASK ALL: SHOW CARD: Is it important to you, one way or another, whether Patience and her family get a place to stay?			C14
			ONE MENTION ONLY.	
		1.	Very important	10-1
		2.	Somewhat important	-2
		3.	Not very important	-3
		4.	Not at all important	-4
		7.	No answer – (DO NOT READ OUT)	-7
		8.	Refused – (DO NOT READ OUT)	-8
		9.	Don't know – (DO NOT READ OUT)	-9

46. **SHOW CARD:** How much do you agree or disagree with the following statements? Would you say you agree strongly, agree, are uncertain, disagree, or disagree strongly? ONE MENTION ONLY PER STATEMENT.

	AGREE STRONGLY	AGREE	UNCERTAIN	DISAGREE	DISAGREE STRONGLY	NO ANSWER (DNRO)	REFUSED (DNRO)	DON'T KNOW (DNRO)
1. There are two kinds of people in this world: those who are for the truth and those who are against it	11-1	-2	-3	-4	-5	-7	-8	-9
3. Without having a piece of land, one is really not a complete person	13-1	-2	-3	-4	-5	-7	-8	-9
4. Land is a symbol of all that has been taken away from Africans	14-1	-2	-3	-4	-5	-7	-8	-9
5. I feel a special attachment to the place where my ancestors are buried	15-1	-2	-3	-4	-5	-7	-8	-9
6. When times are tough, one can always survive if one owns some land	16-1	-2	-3	-4	-5	-7	-8	-9
7. Land is special: having land is more important than having money	17-1	-2	-3	-4	-5	-7	-8	-9
8. If I had my choice, I would live on a piece of land that I could farm	18-1	-2	-3	-4	-5	-7	-8	-9
10. A group which tolerates too many differences of opinion among its own members cannot exist for long	20-1	-2	-3	-4	-5	-7	-8	-9
11. To compromise with our political opponents is dangerous because it usually leads to the betrayal of our own side	21-1	-2	-3	-4	-5	-7	-8	-9

COL 12 BLANK

COL 19 BLANK

> CHECK BACK TO Q.29.1 AND CIRCLE THE GROUP SELECTED ON THE LIST BELOW – i.e. 'GROUP A' AS IDENTIFIED IN Q.29.1. REPLACE ALL REFERENCES TO GROUP IN QUESTIONS TO FOLLOW WITH THE GROUP CIRCLED.

1.	Afrikaners	22-01
2.	Supporters of the ANC	-02
3.	Supporters of the AWB	-03
4.	South African Communist Party	-04
5.	Supporters of the Pan Africanist Congress	-05
6.	Supporters of the New National Party	-06
7.	Supporters of the Democratic Alliance	-07
8.	Supporters of the Inkatha Freedom Party	-08
9.	People who say "South Africa should have a 1-party state"	-09
10.	Supporters of Trade Unions	-10
11.	Muslims	-11
12.	Group recorded in Q.28.2 - write in group .... - 12	
13.	Group identified in Q.29.3 as 'most disliked': <u>Those who would reimpose apartheid laws</u> (check Q.29.3) - 13	
14.	Group identified in Q.29.3 as 'most disliked': <u>Those who would force all whites to leave South Africa</u> (check Q.29.3) -14	

47a.	**SHOW CARD**: Here is a list of words that can be used to describe various political groups. Taking them one at a time, please tell me how you feel about **GROUP A**. The first pair of words is "not dangerous to society" versus "dangerous to society".	**ONE MENTION ONLY.**
		0. Not dangerous to society 24-0
		1. -1
		2. -2
		3. -3
		4. -4
		5. -5
		6. Dangerous to society -6
		7. No answer – **(DO NOT READ OUT)** -7
		8. Refused – **(DO NOT READ OUT)** -8
		9. Don't know – **(DO NOT READ OUT)** -9
47b.	**SHOW CARD**: To what degree do you think **GROUP A** is…?	**READ OUT. ONE MENTION ONLY.**
		0. Predictable 25-0
		1. -1
		2. -2
		3. -3
		4. -4
		5. -5
		6. Unpredictable -6
		7. No answer – **(DO NOT READ OUT)** -7
		8. Refused – **(DO NOT READ OUT)** -8
		9. Don't know – **(DO NOT READ OUT)** -9
47c.	**SHOW CARD**: To what degree do you think **GROUP A** presents…?	**READ OUT. ONE MENTION ONLY.**
		0. Danger to the normal lives of people 26-0
		1. -1
		2. -2
		3. -3
		4. -4
		5. -5
		6. No danger to the normal lives of people -6
		7. No answer – **(DO NOT READ OUT)** -7
		8. Refused – **(DO NOT READ OUT)** -8
		9. Don't know – **(DO NOT READ OUT)** -9
47d.	**SHOW CARD**: To what degree do you think **GROUP A** is likely to…?	**READ OUT. ONE MENTION ONLY.**
		0. Become very powerful in South Africa 27-0
		1. -1
		2. -2
		3. -3
		4. -4
		5. -5
		6. Unlikely to become very powerful in South Africa -6
		7. No answer – **(DO NOT READ OUT)** -7
		8. Refused – **(DO NOT READ OUT)** -8
		9. Don't know – **(DO NOT READ OUT)** -9

47e.	**SHOW CARD**: To what degree do you think **GROUP A** is…?	**READ OUT. ONE MENTION ONLY.**	
		0. Likely to affect how well my family and I live	28-0
		1.	-1
		2.	-2
		3.	-3
		4.	-4
		5.	-5
		6. Unlikely to affect how well my family and I live	-6
		7. No answer – **(DO NOT READ OUT)**	-7
		8. Refused – **(DO NOT READ OUT)**	-8
		9. Don't know – **(DO NOT READ OUT)**	-9
47f.	**SHOW CARD**: To what degree do you feel…?	**READ OUT. ONE MENTION ONLY.**	
		0. Anger towards **GROUP A**	29-0
		1.	-1
		2.	-2
		3.	-3
		4.	-4
		5.	-5
		6. Indifference towards **GROUP A**	-6
		7. No answer – **(DO NOT READ OUT)**	-7
		8. Refused – **(DO NOT READ OUT)**	-8
		9. Don't know – **(DO NOT READ OUT)**	-9
47g.	**SHOW CARD**: To what degree do you think **GROUP A** is…?	**READ OUT. ONE MENTION ONLY.**	
		0. Willing to follow the rules of democracy	30-0
		1.	-1
		2.	-2
		3.	-3
		4.	-4
		5.	-5
		6. Not willing to follow the rules of democracy	-6
		7. No answer – **(DO NOT READ OUT)**	-7
		8. Refused – **(DO NOT READ OUT)**	-8
		9. Don't know – **(DO NOT READ OUT)**	-9
47h.	**SHOW CARD**: To what degree do you think **GROUP A** is…?	**READ OUT. ONE MENTION ONLY.**	
		0. Powerful	31-0
		1.	-1
		2.	-2
		3.	-3
		4.	-4
		5.	-5
		6. Not powerful	-6
		7. No answer – **(DO NOT READ OUT)**	-7
		8. Refused – **(DO NOT READ OUT)**	-8
		9. Don't know – **(DO NOT READ OUT)**	-9

47i.	**SHOW CARD**: And to what degree do you feel hatred versus indifference towards **GROUP A**...?	**READ OUT. ONE MENTION ONLY.**
		0. Hatred — 32-0
		1. — -1
		2. — -2
		3. — -3
		4. — -4
		5. — -5
		6. Indifference — -6
		7. No answer – **(DO NOT READ OUT)** — -7
		8. Refused – **(DO NOT READ OUT)** — -8
		9. Don't know – **(DO NOT READ OUT)** — -9
47j.	**SHOW CARD**: And to what degree do you think **GROUP A** is trustworthy versus untrustworthy?	**ONE MENTION ONLY.**
		0. Trustworthy — 33-0
		1. — -1
		2. — -2
		3. — -3
		4. — -4
		5. — -5
		6. Untrustworthy — -6
		7. No answer – **(DO NOT READ OUT)** — -7
		8. Refused – **(DO NOT READ OUT)** — -8
		9. Don't know – **(DO NOT READ OUT)** — -9
48a.	**SHOW CARD**: Let's suppose, for a minute, that the **(GROUP A)** came to power in South Africa. Using the scale where "0" means that nothing would change, and "6" means that everything would change completely, please estimate how much you think the political situation in the country would change.	**ONE MENTION ONLY.**
		0. Nothing would change — 34-0
		1. — -1
		2. — -2
		3. — -3
		4. — -4
		5. — -5
		6. Everything would change completely — -6
		7. No answer – **(DO NOT READ OUT)** — -7
		8. Refused – **(DO NOT READ OUT)** — -8
		9. Don't know – **(DO NOT READ OUT)** — -9
48b.	**SHOW CARD**: Considering your own political freedom, to what extent would **(GROUP A)**, if it came to power, affect your personal political freedom?	**ONE MENTION ONLY.**
		0. Would not reduce my personal political freedom at all — 35-0
		1. — -1
		2. — -2
		3. — -3
		4. — -4
		5. — -5
		6. Would greatly reduce my personal political freedom — -6
		7. No answer – **(DO NOT READ OUT)** — -7
		8. Refused – **(DO NOT READ OUT)** — -8
		9. Don't know – **(DO NOT READ OUT)** — -9

CARD 14

<table>
<tr><td>48c.</td><td><u>SHOW CARD</u>: Considering your own personal security, to what extent would the (GROUP A), if it came to power, affect your personal security?</td><td colspan="2">ONE MENTION ONLY.</td><td></td></tr>
<tr><td></td><td></td><td>0.</td><td>Would not reduce my personal security at all</td><td>36-0</td></tr>
<tr><td></td><td></td><td>1.</td><td></td><td>-1</td></tr>
<tr><td></td><td></td><td>2.</td><td></td><td>-2</td></tr>
<tr><td></td><td></td><td>3.</td><td></td><td>-3</td></tr>
<tr><td></td><td></td><td>4.</td><td></td><td>-4</td></tr>
<tr><td></td><td></td><td>5.</td><td></td><td>-5</td></tr>
<tr><td></td><td></td><td>6.</td><td>Would greatly reduce my personal security</td><td>-6</td></tr>
<tr><td></td><td></td><td>7.</td><td>No answer – (DO NOT READ OUT)</td><td>-7</td></tr>
<tr><td></td><td></td><td>8.</td><td>Refused – (DO NOT READ OUT)</td><td>-8</td></tr>
<tr><td></td><td></td><td>9.</td><td>Don't know – (DO NOT READ OUT)</td><td>-9</td></tr>
<tr><td>49.</td><td>Do you personally know at least one member of the (GROUP A)?</td><td>1.</td><td>Yes</td><td>37-1</td></tr>
<tr><td></td><td></td><td>2.</td><td>No</td><td>-2</td></tr>
<tr><td></td><td></td><td>7.</td><td>No answer – (DO NOT READ OUT)</td><td>-7</td></tr>
<tr><td></td><td></td><td>8.</td><td>Refused – (DO NOT READ OUT)</td><td>-8</td></tr>
<tr><td></td><td></td><td>9.</td><td>Don't know – (DO NOT READ OUT)</td><td>-9</td></tr>
<tr><td>➤</td><td><u>INTERVIEWER INSTRUCTION</u>: Circle the group selected on GROUP SELECTION GRID for Q.32 in the column on the right.

Read out full description for each relevant group when asking Q50.1 and Q50.2

White land radicals: "Those who advocate denying all claims from the past from black people, and not providing compensation to anyone"

Black land radicals: "Those who advocate the expropriation of all white-owned land in SA, without any compensation at all"</td><td>1.</td><td>Group 1 – White land radicals</td><td>38-1</td></tr>
<tr><td></td><td></td><td>2.</td><td>Group 2 – Black land radicals</td><td>-2</td></tr>
<tr><td></td><td></td><td>3.</td><td>Group 3 – Black land radicals</td><td>-3</td></tr>
<tr><td></td><td></td><td>4.</td><td>Group 4 – Black land radicals</td><td>-4</td></tr>
<tr><td></td><td></td><td>5.</td><td>Group 5 – White land radicals</td><td>-5</td></tr>
<tr><td></td><td></td><td colspan="2">INSERT THE RECORDED GROUP IN (LAND GROUP) WHEN ADMINISTRING Q.50.1 – Q.50.9</td></tr>
<tr><td>50.1</td><td><u>SHOW CARD</u>: And to what degree do you think (LAND GROUP) is…?</td><td colspan="2">READ OUT. ONE MENTION ONLY.</td><td></td></tr>
<tr><td></td><td></td><td>0.</td><td>Not dangerous to society</td><td>39-0</td></tr>
<tr><td></td><td></td><td>1.</td><td></td><td>-1</td></tr>
<tr><td></td><td></td><td>2.</td><td></td><td>-2</td></tr>
<tr><td></td><td></td><td>3.</td><td></td><td>-3</td></tr>
<tr><td></td><td></td><td>4.</td><td></td><td>-4</td></tr>
<tr><td></td><td></td><td>5.</td><td></td><td>-5</td></tr>
<tr><td></td><td></td><td>6.</td><td>Dangerous to society</td><td>-6</td></tr>
<tr><td></td><td></td><td>7.</td><td>No answer – (DO NOT READ OUT)</td><td>-7</td></tr>
<tr><td></td><td></td><td>8.</td><td>Refused – (DO NOT READ OUT)</td><td>-8</td></tr>
<tr><td></td><td></td><td>9.</td><td>Don't know – (DO NOT READ OUT)</td><td>-9</td></tr>
<tr><td>50.2</td><td><u>SHOW CARD</u>: To what degree do you think (LAND GROUP) is…?</td><td colspan="2">READ OUT. ONE MENTION ONLY.</td><td></td></tr>
<tr><td></td><td></td><td>0.</td><td>Predictable</td><td>40-0</td></tr>
<tr><td></td><td></td><td>1.</td><td></td><td>-1</td></tr>
<tr><td></td><td></td><td>2.</td><td></td><td>-2</td></tr>
<tr><td></td><td></td><td>3.</td><td></td><td>-3</td></tr>
<tr><td></td><td></td><td>4.</td><td></td><td>-4</td></tr>
<tr><td></td><td></td><td>5.</td><td></td><td>-5</td></tr>
<tr><td></td><td></td><td>6.</td><td>Unpredictable</td><td>-6</td></tr>
<tr><td></td><td></td><td>7.</td><td>No answer – (DO NOT READ OUT)</td><td>-7</td></tr>
<tr><td></td><td></td><td>8.</td><td>Refused – (DO NOT READ OUT)</td><td>-8</td></tr>
<tr><td></td><td></td><td>9.</td><td>Don't know – (DO NOT READ OUT)</td><td>-9</td></tr>
</table>

CARD 14

➤	INTERVIEWER INSTRUCTION: YOU MAY SIMPLY REFER TO 'WHITE LAND RADICALS' OR 'BLACK LAND RADICALS' FROM HERE ONWARD	

50.3	**SHOW CARD**: To what degree do you think **(LAND GROUP)** presents…?	**READ OUT. ONE MENTION ONLY.**	
		0. Danger to the normal lives of people	41-0
		1.	-1
		2.	-2
		3.	-3
		4.	-4
		5.	-5
		6. No danger to the normal lives of people	-6
		7. No answer – **(DO NOT READ OUT)**	-7
		8. Refused – **(DO NOT READ OUT)**	-8
		9. Don't know – **(DO NOT READ OUT)**	-9
50.4	**SHOW CARD**: To what degree do you think **(LAND GROUP)** is likely to…?	**READ OUT. ONE MENTION ONLY.**	
		0. Gain a lot of power in South Africa	42-0
		1.	-1
		2.	-2
		3.	-3
		4.	-4
		5.	-5
		6. Unlikely to gain a lot of power in South Africa	-6
		7. No answer – **(DO NOT READ OUT)**	-7
		8. Refused – **(DO NOT READ OUT)**	-8
		9. Don't know – **(DO NOT READ OUT)**	-9
50.5	**SHOW CARD**: To what degree do you think **(LAND GROUP)** is…?	**READ OUT. ONE MENTION ONLY.**	
		0. Likely to affect how well my family and I live	43-0
		1.	-1
		2.	-2
		3.	-3
		4.	-4
		5.	-5
		6. Unlikely to affect how well my family and I live	-6
		7. No answer – **(DO NOT READ OUT)**	-7
		8. Refused – **(DO NOT READ OUT)**	-8
		9. Don't know – **(DO NOT READ OUT)**	-9
50.6	**SHOW CARD**: To what degree do you feel…?	**READ OUT. ONE MENTION ONLY.**	
		0. Anger towards the **LAND** GROUP	44-0
		1.	-1
		2.	-2
		3.	-3
		4.	-4
		5.	-5
		6. Indifference towards the **LAND** GROUP	-6
		7. No answer – **(DO NOT READ OUT)**	-7
		8. Refused – **(DO NOT READ OUT)**	-8
		9. Don't know – **(DO NOT READ OUT)**	-9

CARD 14

50.7	SHOW CARD: To what degree do you think (LAND GROUP) is...?	READ OUT. ONE MENTION ONLY.	
		0. Willing to follow the rules of democracy	45-0
		1.	-1
		2.	-2
		3.	-3
		4.	-4
		5.	-5
		6. Will not be willing to follow the rules of democracy	-6
		7. Refused – (DO NOT READ OUT)	-7
		8. Don't know – (DO NOT READ OUT)	-8
		9. Don't know – (DO NOT READ OUT)	-9
50.8	SHOW CARD: To what degree do you think (LAND GROUP) is...?	READ OUT. ONE MENTION ONLY.	
		0. Powerful	46-0
		1.	-1
		2.	-2
		3.	-3
		4.	-4
		5.	-5
		6. Not powerful	-6
		7. No answer – (DO NOT READ OUT)	-7
		8. Refused – (DO NOT READ OUT)	-8
		9. Don't know – (DO NOT READ OUT)	-9
50.9	SHOW CARD: To what degree do you think (LAND GROUP) is...?	READ OUT. ONE MENTION ONLY.	
		0. Trustworthy	47-0
		1.	-1
		2.	-2
		3.	-3
		4.	-4
		5.	-5
		6. Untrustworthy	-6
		7. No answer – (DO NOT READ OUT)	-7
		8. Refused – (DO NOT READ OUT)	-8
		9. Don't know – (DO NOT READ OUT)	-9
51.	OMITTED		COL 48-52 BLANK

52. SHOW CARD: As a result of the history of our country, many South Africans believe that they have been unfairly deprived of land or land rights that are rightfully theirs. We are interested in whether you or your immediate family is involved in any of these issues. Do any of the following apply to you? ONE MENTION ONLY PER STATEMENT.

		DEFINITELY APPLIES TO ME	PROBABLY APPLIES TO ME	PROBABLY DOES NOT APPLY TO ME	DEFINITELY DOES NOT APPLY TO ME	NO ANSWER (DNRO)	REFUSED (DNRO)	DON'T KNOW (DNRO)
1.	Believe land or land rights were unfairly taken from me or my immediate family in the past	53-1	-2	-3	-4	-7	-8	-9
2.	Was subjected to a forced removal	54-1	-2	-3	-4	-7	-8	-9
3.	Believe I have a right to the land on which I live, even though I do not legally own it	55-1	-2	-3	-4	-7	-8	-9
4.	Deprived of benefits, such as water rights, mineral rights, etc.	56-1	-2	-3	-4	-7	-8	-9
5.	Believe that others might file claim of ownership to my land	57-1	-2	-3	-4	-7	-8	-9

CARD 14/15

53.	SHOW CARD: In South Africa today, a process exists by which people can make claims for land that was taken away from them under the apartheid system. How much would you say you know about this claims process?	ONE MENTION ONLY.	
		1. A great deal	58-1
		2. Some, but not a great deal	-2
		3. Not very much	-3
		4. Nothing at all	-4
		7. No answer – (DO NOT READ OUT)	-7
		8. Refused – (DO NOT READ OUT)	-8
		9. Don't know – (DO NOT READ OUT)	-9

54. SHOW CARD: And do any of the following apply to your circumstances? ONE MENTION ONLY PER STATEMENT.

		DEFINITELY APPLIES TO ME	PROBABLY APPLIES TO ME	PROBABLY DOES NOT APPLY TO ME	DEFINITELY DOES NOT APPLY TO ME	NO ANSWER (DNRO)	REFUSED (DNRO)	DON'T KNOW (DNRO)
1.	Have made a claim before a government agency	59-1	-2	-3	-4	-7	-8	-9
2.	Have made a claim before a non-governmental agency (such as church)	60-1	-2	-3	-4	-7	-8	-9
3.	Have made a claim to the owner of the land	61-1	-2	-3	-4	-7	-8	-9
4.	Have had a dispute with traditional leaders over my rights to some land	62-1	-2	-3	-4	-7	-8	-9

Q.55a – Q59 OMITTED   COL 63-76 ON CARD 14 BLANK AND COL 20-33 ON CARD 15 BLANK

60. SHOW CARD: At the moment, there are many different factors that might influence land policy in South Africa. Would you say that land policy should give high importance, some importance, not very much importance, or no importance to making up for land injustices in the past? ONE MENTION ONLY PER STATEMENT.

		HIGH IMPORT-ANCE	SOME IMPORT-ANCE	NOT VERY MUCH IMPORT-ANCE	NO IMPORT-ANCE	NO ANSWER (DNRO)	REFUSED (DNRO)	DON'T KNOW (DNRO)
1.	Making up for land injustices in the past C15	34-1	-2	-3	-4	-7	-8	-9
3.	Making certain that unequal access to land is reduced	36-1	-2	-3	-4	-7	-8	-9
6.	Making certain that the hardest workers get the greatest amount of land	39-1	-2	-3	-4	-7	-8	-9
7.	Making certain that land reform strictly follows the law	40-1	-2	-3	-4	-7	-8	-9
8.	Making certain that those who suffered most under apartheid get the greatest amount of land	41-1	-2	-3	-4	-7	-8	-9
9.	Making certain that those who acquired land unfairly under apartheid do not get to keep it	42-1	-2	-3	-4	-7	-8	-9

COL 35 BLANK

COL 37-38 BLANK

CARD 16

61.	**SHOW CARD:** We are interested in your views about a number of ways in which land disputes in South Africa might be addressed. Please indicate whether you strongly support, support, are uncertain, oppose, or strongly oppose the following ideas: ONE MENTION ONLY PER STATEMENT.

	STRONGLY SUPPORT	SUPPORT	UNCERTAIN	OPPOSE	STRONGLY OPPOSE	NO ANSWER (DNRO)	REFUSED (DNRO)	DON'T KNOW (DNRO)
1. Returning land to those who had it taken away from them during apartheid	34-1	-2	-3	-4	-5	-7	-8	-9
2. Returning land to those who had it taken away from them by the original white settlers in South Africa	35-1	-2	-3	-4	-5	-7	-8	-9
3. Giving farm workers rights of ownership to the houses in which they are currently living	36-1	-2	-3	-4	-5	-7	-8	-9
4. Preventing squatting by strictly enforcing the law	37-1	-2	-3	-4	-5	-7	-8	-9
6. Forcing large land owners to sell some of their property to the government so that it can be given to landless people	39-1	-2	-3	-4	-5	-7	-8	-9
7. Taxing white property owners at a higher rate than black property owners	40-1	-2	-3	-4	-5	-7	-8	-9
8. Taking land from those who unfairly got property in the past	41-1	-2	-3	-4	-5	-7	-8	-9
9. Giving land only to those who know how to use it productively	42-1	-2	-3	-4	-5	-7	-8	-9
10. Forcing tribal leaders to give each tribal member individual legal ownership of specific plots of land	43-1	-2	-3	-4	-5	-7	-8	-9
11. Requiring that any policy about land and land claims treat men and women equally	44-1	-2	-3	-4	-5	-7	-8	-9
12. Increasing taxes on everyone to pay for distribution of land to the poor	45-1	-2	-3	-4	-5	-7	-8	-9
13. Providing more protection to land owners against squatters	46-1	-2	-3	-4	-5	-7	-8	-9

62.1	**OMITTED COL 38 BLANK / COL 47 BLANK / COL 48-49 BLANK**

62.2	**OMITTED**

62.3	**SHOW CARD:** How much do you agree or disagree with each statement? Would you say you agree strongly, agree, are uncertain, disagree, or disagree strongly with each of these statements? ONE MENTION ONLY PER STATEMENT.

	AGREE STRONGLY	AGREE	UNCERTAIN	DISAGREE	DISAGREE STRONGLY	NO ANSWER (DNRO)	REFUSED (DNRO)	DON'T KNOW (DNRO)
1. Farmers are being murdered in South Africa more because of their race than because of crime itself	50-1	-2	-3	-4	-5	-7	-8	-9
2. The abuse of farm workers is a major cause of the murder of white farmers in South Africa	51-1	-2	-3	-4	-5	-7	-8	-9
3. Crimes against white farmers do not deserve special attention; they must be treated just the same as any other crime	52-1	-2	-3	-4	-5	-7	-8	-9

63.1 **SHOW CARD**: I'm going to read out some different forms of political action that people can take when it comes to land issues, and I'd like you to tell me, for each one, whether you have actually done any of these things, whether you might do any or would never, under any circumstances, do any of these. READ OUT. RECORD BELOW.

63.2 **INTERVIEWER INSTRUCTION: ASK Q63.2 ONLY ABOUT THOSE ACTIONS THAT THE RESPONDENT 'WOULD NEVER DO'. SHOW CARD**: Would you approve or disapprove if others were to do this? READ OUT.

		Q.63.1						Q.63.2						
		HAVE ACTUALLY DONE	MIGHT DO	WOULD NEVER DO	NO ANSWER (DNRO)	RE-FUSED (DNRO)	DON'T KNOW (DNRO)	STRONGLY APPROVE	APPROVE	DIS-APPROVE	STRONGLY DIS-APPROVE	NO ANSWER (DNRO)	RE-FUSED (DNRO)	DON'T KNOW (DNRO)
1.	Illegally occupy the land of another in order to live on the land	53-1	-2	-3	-7	-8	-9	61-1	-2	-3	-4	-7	-8	-9
2.	Join in a protest march over some land issues	54-1	-2	-3	-7	-8	-9	62-1	-2	-3	-4	-7	-8	-9
3.	Complain to a government representative about some land issue	55-1	-2	-3	-7	-8	-9	63-1	-2	-3	-4	-7	-8	-9
5.	Sign a petition about some land issue	57-1	-2	-3	-7	-8	-9	65-1	-2	-3	-4	-7	-8	-9
6.	Join in a boycott about some land issue	58-1	-2	-3	-7	-8	-9	66-1	-2	-3	-4	-7	-8	-9
7.	Being involved in an eviction	59-1	-2	-3	-7	-8	-9	67-1	-2	-3	-4	-7	-8	-9
8.	Refusing to pay rates or levies in connection with some land issue	60-1	-2	-3	-7	-8	-9	68-1	-2	-3	-4	-7	-8	-9

			ONE MENTION ONLY.		GO TO:
64.	**SHOW CARD**: There has been some talk recently about crime in South Africa. In terms of how it affects you personally, would you say that in the last year the level of crime has got worse, has not changed, or has got better?	1.	Got better	69-1	
		2.	Has not changed	-2	
		3.	Only a little worse	-3	
		4.	Got moderately worse	-4	
		5.	Got a great deal worse	-5	
		7.	No answer – (DO NOT READ OUT)	-7	
		8.	Refused – (DO NOT READ OUT)	-8	
		9.	Don't know – (DO NOT READ OUT)	-9	
65.	**OMITTED COL 56 BLANK / COL 64 BLANK**				
66a.	**ASK ALL:** Over the last year have you or your family been the victims of a crime?	1.	Yes	70-1	Q.67a
		2.	No	-2	
		7.	No answer – (DO NOT READ OUT)	-7	Q.68
		8.	Refused – (DO NOT READ OUT)	-8	
		9.	Don't know – (DO NOT READ OUT)	-9	
66b.	**OMITTED COL 5-18 BLANK**			CARD 17	
67a.	Did you or anyone report the incident to the police?	1.	Yes	19-1	Q.67b
		2.	No	-2	Q.68
		7.	No answer – (DO NOT READ OUT)	-7	
		8.	Refused – (DO NOT READ OUT)	-8	
		9.	Don't know – (DO NOT READ OUT)	-9	

67b.	IF YES IN Q.67a, ASK: Would you say that you were very satisfied, somewhat satisfied, not very satisfied, or very dissatisfied with the way the police dealt with your statement?	ONE MENTION ONLY.	
		1. Very satisfied	20-1
		2. Somewhat satisfied	-2
		3. Not very satisfied	-3
		4. Very dissatisfied	-4
		7. No answer – (DO NOT READ OUT)	-7
		8. Refused – (DO NOT READ OUT)	-8
		9. Don't know – (DO NOT READ OUT)	-9

68. SHOW CARD: How much do you agree or disagree with each statement? Would you say you agree strongly, agree, are uncertain, disagree, or disagree strongly with each of these statements? ONE MENTION ONLY PER STATEMENT.

	AGREE STRONGLY	AGREE	UNCERTAIN	DISAGREE	DISAGREE STRONGLY	NO ANSWER (DNRO)	REFUSED (DNRO)	DON'T KNOW (DNRO)
1. Crime is caused more by the failure of individual moral standards than by the failure of society and its institutions	21-1	-2	-3	-4	-5	-7	-8	-9
2. Whatever people may say, the reason behind crime in South Africa is always racial	22-1	-2	-3	-4	-5	-7	-8	-9
4. I worry a great deal about becoming a victim of crime	24-1	-2	-3	-4	-5	-7	-8	-9
5. No one is to blame for crime except the criminal; not society, not poverty, not anything but the individual himself	25-1	-2	-3	-4	-5	-7	-8	-9
6. The way the crime rate is heading today, civilized society in the country is likely to be destroyed	26-1	-2	-3	-4	-5	-7	-8	-9

69. SHOW CARD: Today, most productive land in South Africa is in the hands of white people. Most black people are quite poor and own little land. We are interested in your views about how this came to be. For each of the following factors please indicate how much you believe this inequality in South Africa today is a result of the following. ONE MENTION ONLY PER STATEMENT.

	AN EXTREMELY IMPORTANT CAUSE	AN IMPORTANT CAUSE	UNCERTAIN	A NOT VERY IMPORTANT CAUSE	NOT IMPORTANT AT ALL	NO ANSWER (DNRO)	REFUSED (DNRO)	DON'T KNOW (DNRO)
1. White people are more intelligent than black people	27-1	-2	-3	-4	-5	-7	-8	-9
2. White people still have advantages they got from the apartheid system	28-1	-2	-3	-4	-5	-7	-8	-9
3. Black people are unable to recover from the damage done by colonialism and apartheid	29-1	-2	-3	-4	-5	-7	-8	-9
4. Black people are too divided among themselves	30-1	-2	-3	-4	-5	-7	-8	-9
6. White people are more ruthless than black people – they will do anything to get what they want	32-1	-2	-3	-4	-5	-7	-8	-9

CONTINUED OVERLEAF

COL 23 BLANK
COL 31 BLANK

CARD 17

	AN EXTREMELY IMPORTANT CAUSE	AN IMPORTANT CAUSE	UNCERTAIN	A NOT VERY IMPORTANT CAUSE	NOT IMPORTANT AT ALL	NO ANSWER (DNRO)	REFUSED (DNRO)	DON'T KNOW (DNRO)
7. Black people are captives of the traditional ways	33-1	-2	-3	-4	-5	-7	-8	-9
8. Black people are less well-educated than white people	34-1	-2	-3	-4	-5	-7	-8	-9

				GO TO:
70.1	Now I'd like to ask you a few questions about the South African Constitutional Court. Would you say you are very aware, somewhat aware, not very aware or have you never heard of the South African Constitutional Court?	**ONE MENTION ONLY.**		
		1. Very aware	35-1	
		2. Somewhat aware	-2	Q.70.2
		3. Not very aware	-3	
		4. Never heard of	-4	Q.70.3
		7. No answer – **(DO NOT READ OUT)**	-7	
		8. Refused – **(DO NOT READ OUT)**	-8	
		9. Don't know – **(DO NOT READ OUT)**	-9	
70.2	**IF AWARE IN Q.70.1, ASK:** From what you have heard or read, would you say you are very satisfied, somewhat satisfied, not very satisfied or not satisfied at all with the way the South African Constitutional Court has been working?	**ONE MENTION ONLY.**		
		1. Very satisfied	36-1	
		2. Somewhat satisfied	-2	
		3. Not very satisfied	-3	
		4. Not satisfied at all	-4	Q.71.1
		7. No answer – **(DO NOT READ OUT)**	-7	
		8. Refused – **(DO NOT READ OUT)**	-8	
		9. Don't know – **(DO NOT READ OUT)**	-9	
70.3	**IF NEVER HEARD OF IN Q.70.1, ASK:** Would you say you are very satisfied, somewhat satisfied, not very satisfied or not satisfied at all with the way the South African Constitutional Court has been working?	**ONE MENTION ONLY.**		
		1. Very satisfied	37-1	
		2. Somewhat satisfied	-2	
		3. Not very satisfied	-3	
		4. Not satisfied at all	-4	
		7. No answer – **(DO NOT READ OUT)**	-7	
		8. Refused – **(DO NOT READ OUT)**	-8	
		9. Don't know – **(DO NOT READ OUT)**	-9	
71.1	**ASK ALL:** And what about Parliament? Would you say you are very aware, somewhat aware, not very aware or have you never heard of the South African Parliament?	**ONE MENTION ONLY.**		
		1. Very aware	38-1	Q.71.2
		2. Somewhat aware	-2	
		3. Not very aware	-3	
		4. Never heard of	-4	Q.71.3
		7. No answer – **(DO NOT READ OUT)**	-7	
		8. Refused – **(DO NOT READ OUT)**	-8	
		9. Don't know – **(DO NOT READ OUT)**	-9	

CARD 17

71.2	**IF AWARE IN Q.71.1, ASK:** From what you have heard or read, would you say you are very satisfied, somewhat satisfied, not very satisfied or not satisfied at all with the way the South African Parliament has been working?	**ONE MENTION ONLY.**		**GO TO:**
		1. Very satisfied	39-1	
		2. Somewhat satisfied	-2	**Q.72**
		3. Not very satisfied	-3	
		4. Not satisfied at all	-4	
		7. No answer – **(DO NOT READ OUT)**	-7	
		8. Refused – **(DO NOT READ OUT)**	-8	
		9. Don't know – **(DO NOT READ OUT)**	-9	
71.3	**IF NEVER HEARD OF IN Q.71.1, ASK:** Would you say you are very satisfied, somewhat satisfied, not very satisfied or not satisfied at all with the way the South African Parliament has been working?	**ONE MENTION ONLY.**		
		1. Very satisfied	40-1	
		2. Somewhat satisfied	-2	
		3. Not very satisfied	-3	
		4. Not satisfied at all	-4	
		7. No answer – **(DO NOT READ OUT)**	-7	
		8. Refused – **(DO NOT READ OUT)**	-8	
		9. Don't know – **(DO NOT READ OUT)**	-9	

72. **ASK ALL: SHOW CARD:** We are interested in your views about how similar various groups are to you. For each of the following, could you please tell me the extent to which you think you and the group hold similar points of view and values. Let's begin with black people in general. ONE MENTION ONLY.

	A GREAT DEAL IN COMMON	SOME THINGS IN COMMON	NOT MANY THINGS IN COMMON	LITTLE OR NOTHING IN COMMON	NO ANSWER (DNRO)	REFUSED (DNRO)	DON'T KNOW (DNRO)
1. Black people in general	41-1	-2	-3	-4	-7	-8	-9
2. White people in general	42-1	-2	-3	-4	-7	-8	-9
3. (GROUP A)	43-1	-2	-3	-4	-7	-8	-9
4. Those who advocate the expropriation of all white – owned land in South Africa, without any compensation to anyone	44-1	-2	-3	-4	-7	-8	-9
5. Those who advocate denying all land claims from the past from black people, and not providing any compensation to anyone	45-1	-2	-3	-4	-7	-8	-9

Q73.1 – Q73.2 OMITTED COL 46-49 BLANK

74. **SHOW CARD:** Please tell me how important each of the following problems are to you personally, very important, important, not very important, or not important at all. ONE MENTION ONLY PER STATEMENT.

	VERY IMPORTANT	IMPORTANT	NOT VERY IMPORTANT	NOT IMPORTANT AT ALL	NO ANSWER (DNRO)	REFUSED (DNRO)	DON'T KNOW (DNRO)
2. Drugs	50-1	-2	-3	-4	-7	-8	-9
4. Unemployment	52-1	-2	-3	-4	-7	-8	-9
5. Level of crime	53-1	-2	-3	-4	-7	-8	-9
6. Racism and discrimination	54-1	-2	-3	-4	-7	-8	-9

COL 51 BLANK

	VERY IMPORTANT	IMPORTANT	NOT VERY IMPORTANT	NOT IMPORTANT AT ALL	NO ANSWER (DNRO)	REFUSED (DNRO)	DON'T KNOW (DNRO)
7. HIV/AIDS	55-1	-2	-3	-4	-7	-8	-9
8. Corruption	56-1	-2	-3	-4	-7	-8	-9
9. Affirmative action	57-1	-2	-3	-4	-7	-8	-9
10. Illiteracy	58-1	-2	-3	-4	-7	-8	-9
11. Finding out the truth about the past	59-1	-2	-3	-4	-7	-8	-9
12. Racial reconciliation	60-1	-2	-3	-4	-7	-8	-9
13. Problems of land ownership and redistribution	61-1	-2	-3	-4	-7	-8	-9
14. Making up for the injustices of the past in South Africa	62-1	-2	-3	-4	-7	-8	-9

CARD 17

➤ INTERVIEWER INSTRUCTION: CHECK BACK TO PAGE 4 AND RECORD THE NUMBER OF THE STORY YOU ARE REQUIRED TO READ. ALSO RECORD THE VERSION.

NUMBER:

63- [ ][ ]

VERSION	Fanie + Sifiso	65-1	- ASK Q.75a – Q.81a
	Zola + Thapelo	-2	- ASK Q.75b – Q.81b

75a. And now I would like to read you a story and hear your opinions about what happened in this story.

➤ INTERVIEWER INSTRUCTION: IF STORY NUMBER: 1/3/5/7/9/11/13/15/17, ASK: SHOW CARD: First considering all aspects of the story, how fair do you think it is that Sifiso got ownership of the land? If "10" means that you believe the outcome is completely fair to Sifiso and "1" means the outcome is completely unfair to him, which number from "10 to 1" best describes how you feel?

For example, you might answer with a "4" if you think the outcome is only somewhat unfair, or a "7" if you think that it is somewhat fair that Sifiso was given ownership of the land.

The outcome is…ONE MENTION ONLY.

Completely unfair	←							→	Completely fair
66-01	-02	-03	-04	-05	-06	-07	-08	-09	10

1. Was re-read	68 [ ]	-1	97. No answer	-97 (DNRO)
2. Not re-read		-2	98. Refused	-98 (DNRO)
			99. Don't know	-99 (DNRO)

75a. INTERVIEWER INSTRUCTION: IF STORY NUMBER: 2/4/6/8/10/12/14/16/18 ASK: SHOW CARD: First considering all aspects of the story, how fair do you think it is that Fanie got ownership of the land? If "10" means that you believe the outcome is completely fair to Fanie and "1" means the outcome is completely unfair to him, which number from "10 to 1" best describes how you feel?

For example, you might answer with a "4" if you think the outcome is only somewhat unfair, or a "7" if you think that it is somewhat fair that Fanie was given ownership of the land.

The outcome is…ONE MENTION ONLY.

Completely unfair	←							→	Completely fair
69-01	-02	-03	-04	-05	-06	-07	-08	-09	10

1. Was re-read	71 [ ]	-1	97.	No answer	-97 (DNRO)
2. Not re-read		-2	98.	Refused	-98 (DNRO)
			99.	Don't know	-99 (DNRO)

76a. INTERVIEWER INSTRUCTION: IF STORY NUMBER: 1/3/5/7/9/11/13/15/17 ASK: SHOW CARD: Using the same scale, how fair is it that Fanie did not get ownership of the land? ONE MENTION ONLY.

Completely unfair	←							→	Completely fair
72-01	-02	-03	-04	-05	-06	-07	-08	-09	10

➤ INTERVIEWER: CIRCLE HERE IF THE RESPONDENT ASKS THAT THE STORY BE RE-READ

1. Was re-read	74 [ ]	-1	97.	No answer	-97 (DNRO)
2. Not re-read		-2	98.	Refused	-98 (DNRO)
			99.	Don't know	-99 (DNRO)

76a. **INTERVIEWER INSTRUCTION:** **IF STORY NUMBER:** **2/4/6/8/10/12/14/16/18 ASK:** **SHOW CARD:** Using the same scale, how fair is it that Sifiso did not get ownership of the land? ONE MENTION ONLY.

Completely unfair									Completely fair
75-01	-02	-03	-04	-05	-06	-07	-08	-09	10

➢ **INTERVIEWER:** CIRCLE HERE IF THE RESPONDENT ASKS THAT THE STORY BE RE-READ

1. Was re-read	77 ☐	-1	97.	No answer	-97	**(DNRO)**
2. Not re-read		-2	98.	Refused	-98	**(DNRO)**
			99.	Don't know	-99	**(DNRO)**

77a. **SHOW CARD:** Had the decision been entirely up to you, would you…?	**ONE MENTION ONLY.**	
	1. Give the land to Sifiso	78-1
	2. Give the land to Fanie	-2
	3. Give a portion of the land to Sifiso, a portion to Fanie (Volunteered) - **(DNRO)**	-3
	7. No answer – **(DO NOT READ OUT)**	-7
	8. Refused – **(DO NOT READ OUT)**	-8
	9. Don't know – **(DO NOT READ OUT)**	-9

➢ **INTERVIEWER:** THE STORY SHOULD NOT BE RE-READ ANYMORE, EVEN IF THE RESPONDENT REQUESTS IT. IF ASKED TO RE-READ THE STORY, SAY "I'M NOT ALLOWED TO RE-READ THE STORY FOR THE NEXT SET OF QUESTIONS."

78.1a **SHOW CARD:** Thinking back on the story, would you say that…?	**ONE MENTION ONLY.**	C18
	1. Fanie had a stronger legal right to the land than Sifiso	5-1
	2. Sifiso had a stronger legal right to the land than Fanie	-2
	3. Both had an equal legal right to the land	-3
	4. Neither had a legal right to the land - **(DO NOT READ OUT)**	-4
	7. No answer – **(DO NOT READ OUT)**	-7
	8. Refused – **(DO NOT READ OUT)**	-8
	9. Don't know – **(DO NOT READ OUT)**	-9
78.2a **SHOW CARD:** How certain are you of this?	**ONE MENTION ONLY.**	
	1. Extremely certain	6-1
	2. Fairly certain	-2
	3. Somewhat uncertain	-3
	4. Very uncertain	-4
	7. No answer – **(DO NOT READ OUT)**	-7
	8. Refused – **(DO NOT READ OUT)**	-8
	9. Don't know – **(DO NOT READ OUT)**	-9

CARD 18

79.1a **SHOW CARD**: And how much do you think that Sifiso needed the land? ONE MENTION ONLY.

Needed the land a great deal	⟵⟶								Did not need the land
7-01	-02	-03	-04	-05	-06	-07	-08	-09	10

- 97. No answer **(DNRO)**
- 98. Refused **(DNRO)**
- 99. Don't know **(DNRO)**

79.2a **SHOW CARD**: And how much did Fanie need the land?

Needed the land a great deal	⟵⟶								Did not need the land
9-01	-02	-03	-04	-05	-06	-07	-08	-09	10

- 97. No answer **(DNRO)**
- 98. Refused **(DNRO)**
- 99. Don't know **(DNRO)**

80.1a Can you remember what Sifiso's race is?	ONE MENTION ONLY.	
	1. White	11-1
	2. Black	-2
	3. Other - **(DO NOT READ OUT)**	-3
	7. No answer – **(DO NOT READ OUT)**	-7
	8. Refused – **(DO NOT READ OUT)**	-8
	9. Don't know – **(DO NOT READ OUT)**	-9
80.2a And what about Fanie's race?	ONE MENTION ONLY.	
	1. White	12-1
	2. Black	-2
	7. No answer – **(DO NOT READ OUT)**	-7
	8. Refused – **(DO NOT READ OUT)**	-8
	9. Don't know – **(DO NOT READ OUT)**	-9
81.a **SHOW CARD**: Is it important to you, one way or another, whether Fanie or Sifiso got ownership of the land?	ONE MENTION ONLY.	
	1. Very important	13-1
	2. Somewhat important	-2
	3. Not very important	-3
	4. Not at all important	-4
	7. No answer – **(DO NOT READ OUT)**	-7
	8. Refused – **(DO NOT READ OUT)**	-8
	9. Don't know – **(DO NOT READ OUT)**	-9

➢ **INTERVIEWER INSTRUCTION: GO TO QUESTION 82**

CARD 18

> **INTERVIEWER INSTRUCTION:** RECORD ANSWER TO ZOLA AND THAPELO'S STORY.

75.b   And now here are some questions concerning your opinions about what happened in this story.

INTERVIEWER INSTRUCTION: IF STORY NUMBER: 1/3/5/7/9/11/13/15/17 ASK: SHOW CARD: First considering all aspects of the story, how fair do you think it is that Thapelo got ownership of the land? If "10" means that you believe the outcome is completely fair to Thapelo and "1" means the outcome is completely unfair to him, which number from "10 to 1" best describes how you feel?

For example, you might answer with a "4" if you think the outcome is only somewhat unfair, or a "7" if you think that it is somewhat fair that Thapelo was given ownership of the land.

The outcome is…ONE MENTION ONLY.

Completely unfair	←								→	Completely fair
14-01	-02	-03	-04	-05	-06	-07	-08	-09		10

1. Was re-read   16 ☐☐   -1   97.   No answer   **(DNRO)**
2. Not re-read   -2   98.   Refused   **(DNRO)**
                                  99.   Don't know   **(DNRO)**

75.b   And now here are some questions concerning your opinions about what happened in this story.

INTERVIEWER INSTRUCTION: IF STORY NUMBER: 2/4/6/8/10/12/14/16/18 ASK: SHOW CARD: First considering all aspects of the story, how fair do you think is it that Zola got ownership of the land? If "10" means that you believe the outcome is completely fair to Zola and "1" means the outcome is completely unfair to him, which number from "10 to 1" best describes how you feel?

For example, you might answer with a "4" if you think the outcome is only somewhat unfair, or a "7" if you think that it is somewhat fair that Zola was given ownership of the land.

The outcome is…ONE MENTION ONLY.

Completely unfair	←								→	Completely fair
17-01	-02	-03	-04	-05	-06	-07	-08	-09		10

1. Was re-read   19 ☐☐   -1   97.   No answer   -97   **(DNRO)**
2. Not re-read   -2   98.   Refused   -98   **(DNRO)**
                                  99.   Don't know   -99   **(DNRO)**

76.b   **INTERVIEWER INSTRUCTION: IF STORY NUMBER: 1/3/5/7/9/11/13/15/17 ASK: SHOW CARD:** Using the same scale, how fair is it that Zola did not get ownership of the land?

The outcome is…ONE MENTION ONLY.

Completely unfair	←								→	Completely fair
20-01	-02	-03	-04	-05	-06	-07	-08	-09		10

> **INTERVIEWER:** CIRCLE HERE IF THE RESPONDENT ASKS THAT THE STORY BE RE-READ

1. Was re-read   22 ☐☐   -1   97.   No answer   -97   **(DNRO)**
2. Not re-read   -2   98.   Refused   -98   **(DNRO)**
                                  99.   Don't know   -99   **(DNRO)**

76.b	**INTERVIEWER INSTRUCTION:** **IF STORY NUMBER: 2/4/6/8/10/12/14/16/18 ASK:** **SHOW CARD:** Using the same scale, how fair is it that Thapelo did not get ownership of the land?

The outcome is...ONE MENTION ONLY.

Completely unfair	←								→	Completely fair
23-01	-02	-03	-04	-05	-06	-07	-08	-09		10

➢   **INTERVIEWER:** CIRCLE HERE IF THE RESPONDENT ASKS THAT THE STORY BE RE-READ

1. Was re-read	25		-1	97.	No answer	-97	**(DNRO)**
2. Not re-read			-2	98.	Refused	-98	**(DNRO)**
				99.	Don't know	-99	**(DNRO)**

77.b	**SHOW CARD:** Had the decision been entirely up to you, would you give the land to Thapelo or Zola?	**ONE MENTION ONLY.**	
		1. Give the land to Thapelo	26-1
		2. Give the land to Zola	-2
		3. Give a portion of the land to Thapelo, a portion to Zola (Volunteered)	-3
		7. No answer – **(DO NOT READ OUT)**	-7
		8. Refused – **(DO NOT READ OUT)**	-8
		9. Don't know – **(DO NOT READ OUT)**	-9

➢   **INTERVIEWER: THE STORY SHOULD NOT BE RE-READ ANYMORE, EVEN IF THE RESPONDENT REQUESTS IT. IF ASKED TO RE-READ THE STORY, SAY "I'M NOT ALLOWED TO RE-READ THE STORY FOR THE NEXT SET OF QUESTIONS."**

78.1b	**SHOW CARD:** Thinking back on the story, would you say that...?	**ONE MENTION ONLY.**	
		1. Zola had a stronger legal right to the property than Thapelo	27-1
		2. Thapelo had a stronger legal right to the property than Zola	-2
		3. Both had about the same legal right to the property	-3
		4. Neither had a legal right to the property - **(DO NOT READ OUT)**	-4
		7. No answer – **(DO NOT READ OUT)**	-7
		8. Refused – **(DO NOT READ OUT)**	-8
		9. Don't know – **(DO NOT READ OUT)**	-9
78.2b	**SHOW CARD:** How certain are you of this?	**ONE MENTION ONLY.**	
		1. Extremely certain	28-1
		2. Fairly certain	-2
		3. Somewhat uncertain	-3
		4. Very uncertain	-4
		7. No answer – **(DO NOT READ OUT)**	-7
		8. Refused – **(DO NOT READ OUT)**	-8
		9. Don't know – **(DO NOT READ OUT)**	-9

79.1b **SHOW CARD**: And how badly do you think that Thapelo needed the land? ONE MENTION ONLY.

Very badly needed the land	←								→	Did not need the land
29-01	-02	-03	-04	-05	-06	-07	-08	-09		10

97.   No answer **(DNRO)**
98.   Refused **(DNRO)**
99.   Don't know **(DNRO)**

79.2b **SHOW CARD**: And how badly did Zola need the land?

Very badly needed the land	←								→	Did not need the land
31-01	-02	-03	-04	-05	-06	-07	-08	-09		10

97.   No answer **(DNRO)**
98.   Refused **(DNRO)**
99.   Don't know **(DNRO)**

80.1b Can you remember what Thapelo's race is?	**ONE MENTION ONLY.**	
	1. White	33-1
	2. Black	-2
	7. No answer – **(DO NOT READ OUT)**	-7
	8. Refused – **(DO NOT READ OUT)**	-8
	9. Don't know – **(DO NOT READ OUT)**	-9
80.2b And what about Zola's race?	**ONE MENTION ONLY.**	
	1. White	34-1
	2. Black	-2
	7. No answer – **(DO NOT READ OUT)**	-7
	8. Refused – **(DO NOT READ OUT)**	-8
	9. Don't know – **(DO NOT READ OUT)**	-9
81.b **SHOW CARD**: Would it really matter very much to you, one way or another, whether Zola or Thapelo got ownership of the land?	**ONE MENTION ONLY.**	
	1. Would matter a great deal to me	35-1
	2. Would matter some to me	-2
	3. Would not matter much to me	-3
	4. Wouldn't matter to me at all	-4
	7. No answer – **(DO NOT READ OUT)**	-7
	8. Refused – **(DO NOT READ OUT)**	-8
	9. Don't know – **(DO NOT READ OUT)**	-9

82.	**ASK ALL. SHOW CARD: And now on a different subject.** How hopeful are you about **your** future?	**ONE MENTION ONLY.**	
		1. Extremely hopeful	36-1
		2. Somewhat hopeful	-2
		3. Not very hopeful	-3
		4. Not hopeful at all	-4
		7. No answer – **(DO NOT READ OUT)**	-7
		8. Refused – **(DO NOT READ OUT)**	-8
		9. Don't know – **(DO NOT READ OUT)**	-9
83.	**SHOW CARD:** Have you happened to have heard any talk or news about compensation for apartheid that is, the lawsuits between apartheid victims and big business?	**ONE MENTION ONLY.**	
		1. Heard a great deal about it	37-1
		2. Heard some	-2
		3. Haven't heard very much	-3
		4. Haven't heard anything at all	-4
		7. No answer – **(DO NOT READ OUT)**	-7
		8. Refused – **(DO NOT READ OUT)**	-8
		9. Don't know – **(DO NOT READ OUT)**	-9
84.	**SHOW CARD:** Do you have any idea about roughly how many black people in South Africa were actually harmed, by apartheid? Would you say…?	**READ OUT. ONE MENTION ONLY.**	
		1. Nearly all black people were harmed	38-1
		2. Most black people were harmed	-2
		3. Only some black people were harmed	-3
		4. Few, if any, black people were harmed	-4
		7. No answer – **(DO NOT READ OUT)**	-7
		8. Refused – **(DO NOT READ OUT)**	-8
		9. Don't know – **(DO NOT READ OUT)**	-9
85.	**SHOW CARD:** To what extent do you think that large companies in South Africa are to blame for the harms done to black people under apartheid? Would you say large companies in South Africa…?	**READ OUT. ONE MENTION ONLY.**	
		1. Are very much to blame for the harm	39-1
		2. Are somewhat to blame for the harm	-2
		3. Should not be blamed very much	-3
		4. Should not be blamed at all	-4
		5. Was no harm (volunteered) – **(DO NOT READ OUT)**	-5
		7. No answer – **(DO NOT READ OUT)**	-7
		8. Refused – **(DO NOT READ OUT)**	-8
		9. Don't know – **(DO NOT READ OUT)**	-9

86.	**SHOW CARD**: And what about large companies outside South Africa? Would you say they…?	**READ OUT. ONE MENTION ONLY.**	
		1. Are very much to blame for the harm	40-1
		2. Are somewhat to blame for the harm	-2
		3. Should not be blamed very much	-3
		4. Should not be blamed at all	-4
		5. Was no harm (Volunteered) – **(DO NOT READ OUT)**	-5
		7. No answer – **(DO NOT READ OUT)**	-7
		8. Refused – **(DO NOT READ OUT)**	-8
		9. Don't know – **(DO NOT READ OUT)**	-9
87.	Some people in South Africa are going to court against large companies both inside and outside the country seeking compensation for harms or injuries they experienced under apartheid. Would you say that you strongly support, support, oppose, or strongly oppose making companies pay compensation for the harms they caused people during the apartheid period?	**READ OUT. ONE MENTION ONLY.**	
		1. Strongly support	41-1
		2. Support	-2
		3. Oppose	-3
		4. Strongly oppose	-4
		7. No answer – **(DO NOT READ OUT)**	-7
		8. Refused – **(DO NOT READ OUT)**	-8
		9. Don't know – **(DO NOT READ OUT)**	-9
88.	The South African government opposes the compensation lawsuits, saying that forcing these companies to pay for harms they caused under apartheid would be bad for the country today. Do you agree strongly, agree, are uncertain, disagree, or disagree strongly with the government's position?	**READ OUT. ONE MENTION ONLY.**	
		1. Agree strongly	42-1
		2. Agree	-2
		3. Uncertain	-3
		4. Disagree	-4
		5. Disagree strongly	-5
		7. No answer – **(DO NOT READ OUT)**	-7
		8. Refused – **(DO NOT READ OUT)**	-8
		9. Don't know – **(DO NOT READ OUT)**	-9
89.	**OMITTED**		

90. **SHOW CARD:** Do you agree strongly, agree, are uncertain, disagree, or disagree strongly with the following statements? ONE MENTION ONLY PER STATEMENT.

INTERVIEWER: READ OUT INTRODUCTION BELOW ONLY FOR STATEMENTS 1 - 3.

INTRODUCTION: The land problem in Zimbabwe is relevant to South Africa's problem since…

	AGREE STRONGLY	AGREE	UNCERTAIN	DISAGREE	DISAGREE STRONGLY	NO ANSWER (DNRO)	REFUSED (DNRO)	DON'T KNOW (DNRO)
1. It shows how the land issue should NOT be handled	43-1	-2	-3	-4	-5	-7	-8	-9
2. It shows just how dangerous it is not to deal with the land expectations of the people	44-1	-2	-3	-4	-5	-7	-8	-9
3. It shows how the land issue should be handled in South Africa	45-1	-2	-3	-4	-5	-7	-8	-9
4. Zimbabwe's experiences are completely irrelevant to South Africa	46-1	-2	-3	-4	-5	-7	-8	-9

DEMOGRAPHICS

➤ **INTERVIEWER READ OUT: AND NOW JUST A FEW MORE QUESTIONS ABOUT YOURSELF.**

91.	In what year were you born?	**WRITE IN YEAR:** 47-	
		97. No answer	-9997
		98. Refused	-9998
		99. Don't know	-9999
92.	**SHOW CARD:** What is your highest school standard you have passed? **ONE MENTION ONLY**	1. Standard 1/ Grade 3	51-01
		2. Standard 2/ Grade 4	-02
		3. Standard 3/ Grade 5	-03
		4. Standard 4/ Grade 6	-04
		5. Standard 5/ Grade 7	-05
		6. Standard 6/ Grade 8	-06
		7. Standard 7/ Grade 9	-07
		8. Standard 8/ Grade 10	-08
		9. Standard 9/ Grade 11	-09
		10. Standard 10/ Grade 12	-10
		97. No answer– **(DO NOT READ OUT)**	-97
		98. Refused– **(DO NOT READ OUT)**	-98
		99. Don't know– **(DO NOT READ OUT)**	-99

Q.93 OMITTED

94.	**SHOW CARD:** What is the highest level of education you personally have achieved? **ONE MENTION ONLY**	1.	No schooling	53-01
		2.	Some primary school	-02
		3.	Primary school completed	-03
		4.	Some high school	-04
		5.	Matric	-05
		6.	Artisan's certificate obtained	-06
			POST-MATRIC (DEGREES/DIPLOMAS/CERTIFICATES)	
		7.	Technikon diploma/degree completed	-07
		8.	University degree completed	-08
		9.	Professional	-09
		10.	Technical	-10
		11.	Secretarial	-11
		97.	No answer– **(DO NOT READ OUT)**	-97
		98.	Refused– **(DO NOT READ OUT)**	-98
		99.	Don't know– **(DO NOT READ OUT)**	-99

95.	**SHOW CARD:** What language do you speak **mostly** at home? **ONE MENTION ONLY**	1.	SiSwati	55-01
		2.	Shangaan	-02
		3.	Ndebele	-03
		4.	Indian language	-04
		5.	Afrikaans	-05
		6	English	-06
		7.	Portuguese	-07
		8.	Xhosa	-08
		9.	Zulu	-09
		10.	Venda	-10
		11.	South Sotho/ Sesotho	-11
		12.	Setswana/ Tswana	-12
		13.	North Sotho/ Sepedi	-13
		14.	Other European (SPECIFY):	-14
		15.	Other Black (SPECIFY):	-15
		16.	Other (SPECIFY):	-16
		17.	Multi-lingual (Volunteer) – **(DO NOT READ OUT)**	-17
		97.	No answer – **(DO NOT READ OUT)**	-97
		98.	Refused – **(DO NOT READ OUT)**	-98
		99.	Don't know – **(DO NOT READ OUT)**	-99

CARD 18

96.	**SHOW CARD**: How often do you now attend or go to a place of worship? **ONE MENTION ONLY**	1.	More than once a week	57-1
		2.	Once a week	-2
		3.	2 to 3 times a month	-3
		4.	Once a month	-4
		5.	Often, but less than once a month	-5
		6.	2 – 3 times a year	-6
		7.	Hardly ever/seldom	-7
		97.	No answer – **(DO NOT READ OUT)**	-8
		98.	Refused – **(DO NOT READ OUT)**	-9
		99.	Don't know – **(DO NOT READ OUT)**	-0

97.	Which specific religious institution (church, synagogue congregation, etc.) do you attend? ➤ e.g. Wynberg, Catholic Church	**WRITE IN:**	59-

98.	**SHOW CARD**: When you yourself, hold a strong opinion, do you ever find yourself persuading your friends, relatives or fellow workers to share your views?	1.	Often	63-1
		2.	From time to time	-2
		3.	Rarely	-3
		4.	Never	-4
		7.	No answer – **(DO NOT READ OUT)**	-7
		8.	Refused – **(DO NOT READ OUT)**	-8
		9.	Don't know – **(DO NOT READ OUT)**	-9

99.1 **SHOW CARD**: How would you evaluate the following statements about the South African Constitutional Court? Would you say that you agree strongly, agree, are uncertain, disagree, and disagree strongly with each of the following statements? ONE MENTION ONLY PER STATEMENT.

		AGREE STRONGLY	AGREE	UNCERTAIN	DISAGREE	DISAGREE STRONGLY	NO ANSWER (DNRO)	REFUSED (DNRO)	DON'T KNOW (DNRO)
1.	If the South African Constitutional Court started making a lot of decisions that most people disagree with, it might be better to do away with the court altogether	64-1	-2	-3	-4	-5	-7	-8	-9
3.	The South African Constitutional Court can usually be trusted to make decisions that are right for the country as a whole	65-1	-2	-3	-4	-5	-7	-8	-9
4.	The South African Constitutional Court treats all people who bring their cases to it black, white, coloured, and Asian the same	66-1	-2	-3	-4	-5	-7	-8	-9

99.2	**OMITTED COL 67-69 BLANK**

100.	**OMITTED**

CARD 18

101.	**SHOW CARD**: What is your current employment status?	ONE MENTION ONLY.		
		1.	Unemployed (not looking for work)	70-01
		2.	Unemployed (looking for work)	-02
		3.	Housewife (not looking for work)	-03
		4.	Housewife (looking for work)	-04
		5.	Student/scholar	-05
		6.	Pensioner	-06
		7.	Army/armed forces	-07
		8.	Work in informal sector (looking for permanent work)	-08
		9.	Work in informal sector (not looking for permanent work)	-09
		10.	Self-employed (part-time)	-10
		11.	Self-employed (full-time)	-11
		12.	Employed (part-time)	-12
		13.	Employed (seasonally)	-13
		14	Employed (full-time)	-14
		15.	Disabled not looking for permanent work	-15
		97.	No answer – **(DO NOT READ OUT)**	-97
		98.	Refused – **(DO NOT READ OUT)**	-98
		99.	Don't know – **(DO NOT READ OUT)**	-99
102.	**SHOW CARD**: How much does the thought worry you that, during the next 12 months, you or some member of your family might become unemployed?	ONE MENTION ONLY.		
		1.	Not at all worried	72-1
		2.	Not very worried	-2
		3.	A little worried	-3
		4.	Very worried	-4
		5.	No one is employed/all unemployed - **(DO NOT READ OUT)**	-5
		7.	No answer – **(DO NOT READ OUT)**	-7
		8.	Refused – **(DO NOT READ OUT)**	-8
		9.	Don't know – **(DO NOT READ OUT)**	-9
103.	Have you or a member of your family become unemployed in the last 12 months?	1.	Yes	73-1
		2.	No	-2
		7.	No answer – **(DO NOT READ OUT)**	-7
		8.	Refused – **(DO NOT READ OUT)**	-8
		9.	Don't know – **(DO NOT READ OUT)**	-9

CARD 18/19

| 104. | SHOW CARD: How would you evaluate the following statements about the South African Parliament? Would you say that you agree strongly, agree, are uncertain, disagree, or disagree strongly with each of the following statements? ONE MENTION ONLY PER STATEMENT. |

		AGREE STRONGLY	AGREE	UNCERTAIN	DISAGREE	DISAGREE STRONGLY	NO ANSWER (DNRO)	REFUSED (DNRO)	DON'T KNOW (DNRO)
1.	If the South African Parliament started making a lot of decisions that most people disagree with, it might be better to do away with parliament altogether.	74-1	-2	-3	-4	-5	-7	-8	-9
2.	The South African Parliament can usually be trusted to make decisions that are right for the country as a whole	75-1	-2	-3	-4	-5	-7	-8	-9
3.	The South African Parliament treats all people who come before it, be black, white, coloured, and Asian the same	76-1	-2	-3	-4	-5	-7	-8	-9

105.	SHOW CARD: How likely is it that you will be living in South Africa 10 years from now?	1.	Extremely likely	77-1
		2.	Quite likely	-2
		3.	Not very likely	-3
		4.	Highly unlikely	-4
		7.	No answer – (DO NOT READ OUT)	-7
		8.	Refused – (DO NOT READ OUT)	-8
		9.	Don't know – (DO NOT READ OUT)	-9

			C19	DO NOT OWN THIS	OWN THIS	NO ASWER (DNRO)	REFUSED (DNRO)	DON'T KNOW (DNRO
106a.	Do you or anyone else in your household own a...?	1.	Radio	5-1	-2	-7	-8	-9
		2.	Television	6-1	-2	-7	-8	-9
		3.	Computer	7-1	-2	-7	-8	-9
		4.	Refrigerator	8-1	-2	-7	-8	-9
		5.	Telephone (landline) in dwelling	9-1	-2	-7	-8	-9
		6.	Cell phone	10-1	-2	-7	-8	-9
		7.	Microwave oven	11-1	-2	-7	-8	-9
		8.	Bank account	12-1	-2	-7	-8	-9
		9.	Pension fund	13-1	-2	-7	-8	-9
		10.	Car	14-1	-2	-7	-8	-9
106b.	OMITTED COL 15-17 BLANK							

107.	ASK ALL: SHOW CARD: Finally, we are interested in your experiences under the old system of apartheid. In general, how would you judge your life under apartheid compared with now? Would you say it was...?		READ OUT.	
		1.	A lot worse	18-1
		2.	A little worse	-2
		3.	About the same	-3
		4.	A little better	-4
		5.	A lot better	-5
		6.	Not here during apartheid – (DO NOT READ OUT)	-6
		7.	No answer – (DO NOT READ OUT)	-7
		8.	Refused – (DO NOT READ OUT)	-8
		9.	Don't know – (DO NOT READ OUT)	-9

CARD 19

108.	Were you ever personally harmed or injured by apartheid?			
		1.	Yes	19-1
		2.	No	-2
		3.	Didn't live here during apartheid – (DO NOT READ OUT)	Q. 111 -3
		4.	Apartheid was before my time – (DO NOT READ OUT)	-4
		7.	No answer – (DO NOT READ OUT)	-7
		8.	Refused – (DO NOT READ OUT)	-8
		9.	Don't know – (DO NOT READ OUT)	-9

109. Here is a list of things that happened to people under apartheid. Please tell me which, if any, of these experiences you have had. READ OUT. ONE MENTION ONLY PER STATEMENT.

		YES	NO	NO ANSWER (DNRO)	REFUSED (DNRO)	DON'T KNOW (DNRO)
1.	Required to move my residence	20-1	-2	-7	-8	-9
2.	Lost my job because of apartheid	21-1	-2	-7	-8	-9
3.	Was assaulted by the police	22-1	-2	-7	-8	-9
4.	Was imprisoned by the authorities	23-1	-2	-7	-8	-9
5.	Was psychologically harmed	24-1	-2	-7	-8	-9
6.	Was denied access to education of my choice	25-1	-2	-7	-8	-9
7.	Was unable to associate with people of different race and colour	26-1	-2	-7	-8	-9
8.	Had to use a pass to move about	27-1	-2	-7	-8	-9
9.	Profited from the system	28-1	-2	-7	-8	-9

Q.110 OMITTED
COL 29-32 ON CARD 19 BLANK

111.	What kind of housing are you living in at the moment?			
		1.	Office	33-01
		2.	House in suburb	-02
		3.	House in township	-03
		4.	Townhouse/cluster	-04
		5.	Flat	-05
		6.	Hotel/residential hotel	-06
		7.	Hut	-07
		8.	Room in backyard	-08
		9.	Shack in backyard	-09
		10.	Squatter camp	-10
		11.	House on employer's property	-11
		12.	Compound	-12
		13.	Domestic accommodation room	-13
		14.	Farm worker's house	-14
		15.	Shack in rural area	-15
		16.	House in rural area	-16
		17.	House in village	-17
		18.	House on farm, farmhouse	-18
		19.	Other (specify)	-19
		98	Refused - (DNRO)	-98

CARD 19

111.1 How long have you been living here in this community of ... (MENTION NAME OF THE LOCAL SUBURB)?	1.	RECORD NUMBER OF YEARS	
		....	35-
	2.	IF LESS THAN ONE YEAR: RECORD NUMBER OF MONTHS	
		....	38-
		OFFICE	40-
	997	No answer - (DNRO)	-997
	998	Refused - (DNRO)	-998
	999	Don't know - (DNRO)	-999
111.2 Is there a traditional leader in this area?	1.	Yes	45-1
	2.	No	-2
	7.	No answer - (DNRO)	-7
	8.	Refused - (DNRO)	-8
	9.	Don't know - (DNRO)	-9
b. IF YES: What is his/her name?		WRITE IN:	
		....	46-
	7.	No answer - (DNRO)	-9997
	8.	Refused - (DNRO)	-9998
	9.	Don't know - (DNRO)	-9999
c. Do you consider him/her to be your leader?	1.	Yes	50-1
	2.	No	-2
	7.	No answer - (DNRO)	-7
	8.	Refused - (DNRO)	-8
	9.	Don't know - (DNRO)	-9

111.3 We would like to know if you are a member of any of the following organisations: MMP.	MULTIMENTIONS POSSIBLE. READ OUT	Mentions	No answer DNRO	Refused DNRO	Don't know DNRO
INTERVIEWER INSTRUCTION: If a person IS a member, circle the relevant code. If they are not a member of any of the listed organisations, leave question blank.	1. Religious or church organisation	51-01	-97	-98	-99
	2. Labour unions	53-02	-97	-98	-99
	3. Political parties or groups	55-03	-97	-98	-99
	4. Local community action groups on issues such as land	57-04	-97	-98	-99
	5. Youth groups or organisations	59-05	-97	-98	-99
	6. Women's groups or organisations	61-06	-97	-98	-99
	7. Business groups or organisations	63-07	-97	-98	-99
	8. Farm groups or organisations	65-08	-97	-98	-99
	9. Rate payers associations	67-09	-97	-98	-99

> ➤ **INTERVIEWER READ OUT:** Thank you for participating in this research survey. We may want to contact your household again in a few years to learn more about how life changes for South African families. Could you please give us information about **TWO** people who **DO NOT LIVE IN THE HOUSEHOLD** and would know where you or other household members are, or how to reach you, in the future?

112.	FULL NAME:		C20
	RELATIONSHIP TO YOU:		C21
	CURRENT ADDRESS:		C22
			C23
			C24
			C25
	CURRENT PHONE NUMBER:		C26
B.	FULL NAME:		C27
	RELATIONSHIP TO YOU:		C28
	CURRENT ADDRESS:		C29
			C30
			C31
			C32
			C33
	CURRENT PHONE NUMBER:		

CARD 34-40 BLANK

CARD 41

113.	IF NO IN Q.112, ASK: IF NOT, PLEASE PROVIDE THE CONTACT DETAILS OF SOMEONE WHO MIGHT HELP US IN CONTACTING YOU AGAIN. What is your relationship with the contact person? ➤ **INTERVIEWER: RECORD ALTERNATIVE ADDRESS:** .... Tel no:	1. Parent	5-01
		2. Child	-02
		3. Sibling	-03
		4. Other family member	-04
		5. Friend	-05
		6. Colleague	-06
		7. Employer	-07
		8. Other	-08
		97. No answer	-97
		98. Refused	-98
		99. Don't know	-99
114.	Do you know someone close to you, a relative or a close friend, who has died of AIDS?	1. Yes	7-1
		2. No	-2
		7. No answer – **(DO NOT READ OUT)**	-7
		8. Refused – **(DO NOT READ OUT)**	-8
		9. Don't know – **(DO NOT READ OUT)**	-9
115.	Are there people close to you who have AIDS or who are HIV positive?	1. Yes	8-1
		2. No	-2
		7. No answer – **(DO NOT READ OUT)**	-7
		8. Refused – **(DO NOT READ OUT)**	-8
		9. Don't know – **(DO NOT READ OUT)**	-9

THANK YOU FOR PARTICIPATING IN OUR SURVEY. IN THE NEXT FEW DAYS MY SUPERVISOR MIGHT CONTACT YOU TO EVALUATE THE QUALITY OF MY WORK AND ANSWER ANY QUESTIONS YOU MIGHT HAVE ABOUT THE INTERVIEW.

CARD 41

> **INTERVIEWER REMARKS:** (TO BE COMPLETED AFTER THE SURVEY IS FINISHED).	**TIME INTERVIEW ENDED: 24-HOUR CLOCK** 9-	

> **INTERVIEWER INSTRUCTION:** (RECORD TOTAL DURATION OF ACTUAL INTERVIEW IN MINUTES	45 - 47 **MINUTES**	

1.	In general, what was the respondent's attitude towards the interview?	1.	Friendly	13-1
		2.	Cooperative but not particularly interested	-2
		3.	Impatient and restless	-3
		4.	Hostile	-4
2.	Did the respondent understand the questions?	1.	Well	14-1
		2.	Not very well	-2
		3.	Poorly	-3
3.	Was the respondent able to read the showcards?	1.	Without any apparent difficulty	15-1
		2.	With some difficulty	-2
		3.	With a great deal of difficulty	-3
		4.	Could not read the showcards	-4
4.	Compared to other respondents, how well did the respondent understand the story?	1.	Well	16-1
		2.	Not very well	-2
		3.	Poorly	-3
5.	Was the respondent…?	1.	About as clever as most respondents	17-1
		2.	Not as clever as most respondents	-2
		3.	Somewhat more clever than most respondents	-3
		4.	A great deal more clever than most respondents	-4
		5.	Can't compare	-5
6.	Compared to other respondents, was the respondent…?	1.	About as honest and open as most respondents	18-1
		2.	Not as honest and open as most respondents	-2
		3.	Somewhat more honest and open than most respondents	-3
		4.	A great deal more honest and open than most respondents	-4
7.	Was the spouse of the respondent present?	1.	Yes	19-1
		2.	No	-2
8.	Were any children of the respondent present?	1.	Yes	20-1
		2.	No	-2
9.	Were other adults present?	1.	Yes	21-1
		2.	No	-2
10.	How would you evaluate the living quarters of the respondent?	1.	Clearly much better off then most people	22-1
		2.	About as well off as most people	-2
		3.	Clearly less well off than most people	-3
		4.	Interview did not take place in living quarters of respondent	-4

CARD 41

11.	In what type of dwelling was the interview conducted?	1.	Office	23-01
		2.	House in suburb	-02
		3.	House in township	-03
		4.	Townhouse/cluster	-04
		5.	Flat	-05
		6.	Hotel/residential hotel	-06
		7.	Hut	-07
		8.	Room in backyard	-08
		9.	Shack in backyard	-09
		10.	Squatter camp	-10
		11.	House on employers property	-11
		12.	Compound	-12
		13.	Domestic accommodation room	-13
		14.	Farm workers house	-14
		15.	Shack in rural area	-15
		16.	House in rural area	-16
		17.	House in village	-17
		18.	House on farm, farmhouse	-18
		19.	Other (SPECIFY):	-19
			....	
12.	What would you say is the socio-economic status of the respondent?	1.	Upper, upper middle class	25-1
		2.	Middle, non-manual workers	-2
		3.	Manual workers – skilled, semi-skilled	-3
		4.	Manual workers – unskilled, unemployed	-4
13.	How well could the respondent read?	1.	Was able to read without difficulty	26-1
		2.	Was able to read, but with some difficulty	-2
		3.	Was able to read, but with great difficulty	-3
		4.	Was not able to read	-4
		5.	Could not judge	-5
14.	In what language was most of the interview conducted?	1.	Afrikaans	27-1
		2.	English	28-1
	ONE MENTION ONLY	3.	North Sotho	29-1
		4.	South Sotho	30-1
		5.	Tswana	31-1
		6.	Tsonga	32-1
		7.	Venda	33-1
		8.	Xhosa	34-1
		9.	Zulu	35-1

CARD 41

15.	Was it necessary to use a mixture of languages to conduct the interview?	1.	Languages were often mixed	36-1
		2.	Languages were occasionally mixed	-2
		3.	Languages were not mixed	-3
15.1	How would you rate the respondent's language skills?	1.	Was quite adept at expressing his or her thoughts	37-1
		2.	Spoke reasonably well and was able to express his or her thoughts	-2
		3.	Had some difficulty expressing his or her thoughts	-3
		4.	Had a great deal of difficulty expressing his or her thoughts	-4

15.2 In your opinion, compared to the range of skin colours seen throughout South Africa, please rate the colour of the respondent's skin.

Very light			Light			Dark			Very dark		
38-01	-02		-03	-04	-05	-06	-07	-08	-09	-10	

16.	**INTERVIEWER'S GENDER:**	1.	Male	40-1
		2.	Female	-2
17.	**INTERVIEWER'S RACE:**	1.	Black	41-1
		2.	Coloured	-2
		3.	White	-3
		4.	Indian	-4

Please record the GROUP selected at the various questions below:

'RACE GROUP' Q.21

'GROUP A' Q29.1/Q.29.3

'LAND GROUP' .... Q32 and Q50.1 – 50.9

References

Aliber, Michael, and Reuben Mokoena. 2005. "The Land Question in Contemporary South Africa." In *State of the Nation: South Africa 2003–2004*, eds. John Daniel, Adam Habib, and Roger Southall. Cape Town: HSRC Press. Pp. 330–346.

Aliber, Michael, Maxine Reitzes, and Marlene Roefs. 2006. "Assessing the Alignment of South Africa's Land Reform Policy to People's Aspirations and Expectations: A Policy-Oriented Report Based on a Survey in Three Provinces." *Human Sciences Research Council.*

Alvarez, R. Michael, and John Brehm. 2002. *Hard Choices, Easy Answers.* Princeton: Princeton University Press.

Aronson, Elliot, Phoebe C. Ellsworth, J. Merrill Carlsmith, and Marti Hope Gonzales. 1990. *Methods of Research in Social Psychology*, 2nd ed. New York: McGraw-Hill.

Asabere, Paul K. 1994. "Public Policy and the Emergent African Land Tenure System: The Case of Ghana." *Journal of Black Studies* 24 (March): 281–289.

Banner, Stuart. 2000. "Conquest by Contract: Wealth Transfer and Land Market Structure in Colonial New Zealand." *Law & Society Review* 34 (1): 47–96.

Barry, Brian. 2005. *Why Social Justice Matters.* Malden, Mass. Polity Press.

Benjamin, Chantelle. 2006. "Commission Sets Deadline for Land Claims: Land Will Be Expropriated If Negotiations Dragged on More Than Three Years." *Business Day Monday,* July 23, 2007. http://www.businessday. co.za/Articles.aspx?ID=1887779 (accessed July 24, 2007).

Bennett, T. W. 1995. *Human Rights and African Customary Law under the South African Constitution.* Cape Town: Juta & Co.

Bierbrauer, Gunter. 1994. "Toward an Understanding of Legal Culture: Variations in Individualism and Collectivism between Kurds, Lebanese, and Germans." *Law & Society Review* 28 (2): 243–264.

Blankenburg, Erhard. 1994. "The Infrastructure for Avoiding Civil Litigation: Comparing Cultures of Legal Behavior in the Netherlands and West Germany." *Law & Society Review* 28 (4): 789–808.

Bobo, Lawrence D., and Mia Tuan. 2006. *Prejudice in Politics: Group Position, Public Opinion, and the Wisconsin Treat Rights Dispute.* Cambridge, Mass. Harvard University Press.

Bratton, Michael, Robert Mattes, and E. Gyimah-Boadi. 2005. *Public Opinion, Democracy, and Market Reform in Africa.* New York: Cambridge University Press.

Brewer, Marilynn B., and Samuel L. Gaertner. 2004. "Toward Reduction of Prejudice: Intergroup Contact and Social Categorization." In *Self and Social Identity,* eds. Marilynn B. Brewer and Miles Hewstone. Malden, Mass: Blackwell Publishing. Pp. 298–318.

Brislin, Richard W. 1970. "Back-Translation for Cross-Cultural Research." *Journal of Cross-Cultural Psychology* 1 (September): 185–216.

Caldeira, Gregory A., and James L. Gibson. 1995. "The Legitimacy of the Court of Justice in the European Union: Models of Institutional Support." *American Political Science Review* 89 (2, June): 356–376.

Chambers, David L. 2000. "Civilizing the Natives: Marriage in Post-Apartheid South Africa." *Daedelus* 129 (Fall): 101–124.

Chong, Dennis, and Anna-Maria Marshall. 1999. "When Morality and Economics Collide (or Not) in a Texas Community." *Political Behavior* 21 (June): 91–121.

Citrin, Jack, and Donald Philip Green. 1990. "The Self-Interest Motive in American Public Opinion." *Research in Micropolitics* 3: 1–27.

Cohen, Jacob, Patricia Cohen, Stephen G. West, and Leona S. Aiken. 2003. *Applied Multiple Regression/Correlation Analysis for the Behavioral Sciences,* 3rd ed. Mahwah, N.J.: Lawrence Erlbaum Associates.

Cousins, Ben. 2000. "Uncertainty and Institutional Design: Proposals for Tenure Reform in South Africa." Presented at the biennial conference of the International Association for the Study of Common Property, Bloomington, Indiana.

Cousins, Ben. 2007. "Agrarian Reform and the 'Two Economies': Transforming South Africa's Countryside." In *The Land Question in South Africa: The Challenge of Transformation and Redistribution,* eds. Lungisile Ntsebeza and Ruth Hall. Cape Town: HSRC Press. Pp. 220–245.

Darby, B. W., and Barry R. Schlenker. 1989. "Children's Reactions to Transgressions: Effects of the Actor's Apology, Reputation and Remorse." *British Journal of Social Psychology* 28 (December): 353–364.

Davis, Darren W. 2006. *Negative Liberty: Public Opinion and the Terrorist Attacks on America.* New York: Russell Sage Foundation.

Davis, Darren W., and Brian D. Silver. 2004. "Civil Liberties vs. Security: Public Opinion in the Context of the Terrorist Attacks on America." *American Journal of Political Science* 48 (January): 28–46.

Dawson, Michael C. 1994. *Behind the Mule: Race and Class in African American Politics.* Princeton: Princeton University Press.

de Villiers, Bertus. 2003. *Land Reform: Issues and Challenges. A Comparative Overview of Experiences in Zimbabwe, Namibia, South Africa and Australia.* Johannesburg: Konrad Adenauer Foundation.

Druckman, James N. 2004. "Political Preference Formation: Competition, Deliberation, and the (Ir)relevance of Framing Effects." *American Political Science Review* 98 (November): 671–686.

Du Bois, François. 2008. "Reparation and the Forms of Justice." In *Justice and Reconciliation in Post-Apartheid South Africa*, eds. François du Bois and Antje du Bois-Pedain. New York: Cambridge University Press. Pp. 116–143.

Duch, Raymond M., and Harvey D. Palmer. 2001. "It's How You Play the Game: Self-Interest, Social Justice, and Mass Attitudes toward Transition to a Market Economy." Presented at the 2001 Annual Meeting of the Midwest Political Science Association, Chicago.

Duch, Raymond M., and Harvey D. Palmer. 2004. "It's Not Whether You Win or Lose, but How You Play the Game: Self-Interest, Social Justice, and Mass Attitudes toward Market Transition." *American Political Science Review* 98 (3, August): 437–452.

Duckitt, John, Jane Callaghan, and Claire Wagner. 2005. "Group Identification and Outgroup Attitudes in Four South African Ethnic Groups: A Multidimensional Approach." *Personality and Social Psychology Bulletin* 31 (May): 633–646.

du Toit, Pierre. 2006. "The Rule of Law, Public Opinion and the Politics of Land Restitution in South Africa." Paper delivered at the conference on Land, Memory, Reconstruction and Justice: Perspectives on Land Restitution in South Africa, Houw Hoek (South Africa), September 13–15, 2006.

Eisenberg, Andrea. 1993. "Different Constitutional Formulations of Compensation Clauses." *South African Journal on Human Rights* 9: 412–421.

Ferree, Karen E. 2006. "Explaining South Africa's Racial Census." *Journal of Politics* 68 (November): 803–815.

Field, Sean, ed. 2001. *Lost Communities, Living Memories: Remembering Forced Removals in Cape Town.* Cape Town: David Philip.

Fife, Ian. 2004. "A Costly Constitution: Judges Tell Our Law Makers to Keep Their Promises to Owners and Squatters." *Financial Mail*, 11 June 2004.

Finkel, Norman J. 1995. *Commonsense Justice: Jurors' Notions of the Law.* Cambridge: Harvard University Press.

Finkel, Norman J. 2001. *Not Fair! The Typology of Commonsense Unfairness.* Washington, D.C.: American Psychological Association.

Friedman, Steven. 2004. "Why We Vote: The Issue of Identity." *Electionsynopsis* 1 (2): 2–4.

Funk, Carolyn L. 2000. "The Dual Influence of Self-Interest and Societal Interest in Public Opinion." *Political Research Quarterly* 53 (March): 37–62.

Gibson, James L. 1997. "Mass Opposition to the Soviet Putsch of August 1991: Collective Action, Rational Choice, and Democratic Values in the Former Soviet Union." *American Political Science Review* 91 (September): 671–684.

Gibson, James L. 1998. "A Sober Second Thought: An Experiment in Persuading Russians to Tolerate." *American Journal of Political Science* 42 (July): 819–850.

Gibson, James L. 2000. "Being Democratic in a Deeply Divided Society: Racial, Ethnic, Linguistic Conflict over Democratic Values in the New South Africa." Presented at the 58th Annual Meeting of the Midwest Political Science Association, Chicago.

Gibson, James L. 2001. "The Land Question in South Africa – Clouds on the Horizon." *The Institute for Justice and Reconciliation.* http://www.ijr.org.za/art_pgs/art23.html.

Gibson, James L. 2002. "Truth, Justice, and Reconciliation: Judging the Fairness of Amnesty in South Africa." *American Journal of Political Science* 46 (July): 540–556.

Gibson, James L. 2003a. "The Legacy of Apartheid: Racial Differences in the Legitimacy of Democratic Institutions and Processes in the New South Africa." *Comparative Political Studies* 36 (September): 772–800.

Gibson, James L. 2003b. "Russian Attitudes towards the Rule of Law: An Analysis of Survey Data." In *Law and Informal Practices: The Post-Communist Experience,* eds. Denis J. Galligan and Marina Kurkchiyan. Oxford: Oxford University Press. Pp. 77–91.

Gibson, James L. 2004a. *Overcoming Apartheid: Can Truth Reconcile a Divided Nation?* New York: Russell Sage Foundation.

Gibson, James L. 2004b. "Linking Identities and Intolerance: Conditional Relationships." Presented at the 2004 Annual Meeting of the American Political Science Association, Chicago.

Gibson, James L. 2006. "Do Strong Group Identities Fuel Intolerance? Evidence from the South African Case." *Political Psychology* 27 (October): 665–705.

Gibson, James L. 2007. "Changes in American Veneration for the Rule of Law." *DePaul Law Review* 56 (Winter): 593–614.

Gibson, James L. 2008a. "The Evolving Legitimacy of the South African Constitution Court." In *Justice and Reconciliation in Post-Apartheid South Africa.* Edited by François du Bois and Antje du Bois-Pedain. New York: Cambridge University Press. Pp. 223–266.

Gibson, James L. 2008b. "Group Identities and Theories of Justice: An Experimental Investigation into the Justice and Injustice of Land Squatting in South Africa." *Journal of Politics* 70 (3, July): 700–716.

Gibson, James L., and Gregory A. Caldeira. 1996. "The Legal Cultures of Europe." *Law & Society Review* 30 (1): 55–85.

Gibson, James L., and Marc Howard. 2007. "Russian Anti-Semitism and the Scapegoating of Jews." *British Journal of Political Science* 37 (2, April): 193–223.

Gibson, James L., Raymond M. Duch, and Kent L. Tedin. 1992. "Democratic Values and the Transformation of the Soviet Union." *Journal of Politics* 54 (May): 329–371.

Gibson, James L., and Amanda Gouws. 1997. "Support for the Rule of Law in the Emerging South African Democracy." *International Social Science Journal* 152 (June): 173–191.

Gibson, James L., and Amanda Gouws. 1999. "Truth and Reconciliation in South Africa: Attributions of Blame and the Struggle over Apartheid." *American Political Science Review* 93 (September): 501–517.

Gibson, James L., and Amanda Gouws. 2000. "Social Identities and Political Intolerance: Linkages Within the South African Mass Public." *American Journal of Political Science* 44 (April): 278–292.

Gibson, James L., and Amanda Gouws. 2001. "Making Tolerance Judgments: The Effects of Context, Local and National." *Journal of Politics* 63 (November): 1067–1090.

Gibson, James L., and Amanda Gouws. 2003. *Overcoming Intolerance in South Africa: Experiments in Democratic Persuasion.* New York: Cambridge University Press.

González, Roberto, and Rupert Brown. 2003. "Generalization of Positive Attitude as a Function of Subgroup and Superordinate Group Identifications in Intergroup Contact." *European Journal of Social Psychology* 33 (2): 195–214.

Gosling, Melanie. 2004. "Land Returned but We Still Have Nothing." *Cape Times*, August 18: 5.

Gran, Thorvald. 2005. "Land Politics and Trust Relations in Government: Findings from Western South Africa." In *Trust in Public Institutions in South Africa*, eds. Steinar Askvik and Nelleke Bak. Burlington, Vt.: Ashgate. Pp. 103–119.

Graubard, Stephen R. 2001. "Preface to the Issue 'Why South Africa Matters.'" *Daedalus* 130 (Winter): V–VIII.

Graybill, Lyn S. 1998. "South Africa's Truth and Reconciliation Commission: Ethical and Theological Perspectives." *Ethics and International Affairs* 12 (March): 43–62.

Groenewald, Yolandi. 2005. "Late Land Claimants Want Another Chance." *Mail & Guardian*, July 8–14: 12.

Hall, Ruth. 2007. "Transforming Rural South Africa? Taking Stock of Land Reform." In *The Land Question in South Africa: The Challenge of Transformation and Redistribution*, eds. Lungisile Ntsebeza and Ruth Hall. Cape Town: HSRC Press. Pp. 87–106.

Hall, Ruth, and Lungisile Ntsebeza. 2007. "Introduction." In *The Land Question in South Africa: The Challenge of Transformation and Redistribution*, eds. Lungisile Ntsebeza and Ruth Hall. Cape Town: HSRC Press. Pp. 1–24.

Hamilton, V. Lee, and Joseph Sanders. 1992. *Everyday Justice: Responsibility and the Individual in Japan and the United States.* New Haven: Yale University Press.

Hayner, Priscilla B. 2001. *Unspeakable Truths: Confronting State Terror and Atrocity.* New York: Routledge.

Hegtvedt, Karen A., and Karen S. Cook. 2001. "Distributive Justice: Recent Theoretical Developments and Applications." In *Handbook of Justice*

Research in Law, eds. Joseph Sanders and V. Lee Hamilton. New York: Kluwer Academic/Plenum. Pp. 93–132.

Henrich, Joseph, Robert Boyd, Samuel Bowles, Colin Camerer, Ernst Fehr, Herbert Gintis, and Richard McElreath. 2001. "In Search of Homo Economicus: Behavioral Experiments in 15 Small-Scale Societies." *American Economic Review* 91 (May): 73–78.

Hochschild, Jennifer L. 1981. *What's Fair? American Beliefs about Distributive Justice*. Cambridge: Harvard University Press.

Hofstätter, Stephan. 2004. "Whites Stake Land Claim." *This Day*, August 5, Issue 212, p. 1.

Horowitz, Donald L. 1985. *Ethnic Groups in Conflict*. Berkeley: University of California Press.

Huchzermeyer, Marie. 2004. *Unlawful Occupation: Informal Settlements and Urban Policy in South Africa and Brazil*. Trenton, N.J.: Africa World Press.

Huddy, Leonie. 2001. "From Social to Political Identity: A Critical Examination of Social Identity Theory." *Political Psychology* 22 (March): 127–156.

Huo, Yuen J. 2003. "Procedural Justice and Social Regulation across Group Boundaries: Does Subgroup Identity Undermine Relationship-Based Governance?" *Personality and Social Psychology Bulletin* 29 (March): 336–348.

Huo, Yuen J., Heather J. Smith, Tom R. Tyler, and E. Allan Lind. 1996. "Superordinate Identification, Subgroup Identification, and Justice Concerns: Is Separatism the Problem; Is Assimilation the Answer?" *Psychological Science* 7 (January): 40–45.

Huo, Yuen J., and Tom R. Tyler. 2000. *How Different Ethnic Groups React to Legal Authority*. San Francisco: Public Policy Institute of California.

Jacoby, William G. 2005. "Values and American Public Opinion: Difficult Choices or Hierarchical Structure?" Presented at the 2005 Annual Meeting of the Midwest Political Science Association, Chicago.

James, Wilmot, and Jeffrey Lever. 2000. "South Africa – The Second Republic: Race, Inequality and Democracy in South Africa." In *Three Nations at the Crossroad [Beyond Racism: Embracing an Interdependent Future]*. Atlanta, Ga.: The Southern Education Foundation. Pp. 42–59.

Johnson, R.W., and Lawrence Schlemmer, eds. 1996. *Launching Democracy in South Africa: The First Open Election, April 1994*. New Haven: Yale University Press.

Jung, Courtney. 2000. *Then I Was Black: South African Political Identities in Transition*. New Haven: Yale University Press.

Kinder, Donald R. 1986. "The Continuing American Dilemma: White Resistance to Racial Change 40 Years after Myrdal." *Journal of Social Issues* 42 (2): 151–171.

Kinder, Donald R., and D. Roderick Kiewiet. 1979. "Economic Discontent and Political Behavior: The Role of Personal Grievances and Collective

Economic Judgments in Congressional Voting." *American Journal of Political Science* 23 (3, August): 495–527.

Kinder, Donald R., and Thomas R. Palfrey, eds. 1993. *Experimental Foundations of Political Science*. Ann Arbor: University of Michigan Press.

Klandermans, Bert, Marlene Roefs, and Johan L. Olivier. 2001. *The State of the People: Citizens, Civil Society and Governance in South Africa, 1994–2000*. Pretoria: Human Sciences Research Council.

Kluegel, James R., David S. Mason, and Bernd Wegener, eds. 1995. *Social Justice and Political Change: Public Opinion in Capitalist and Post-Communist States*. New York: Aldine de Gruyter.

Lahiff, Edward. 2000. "*Communal Tenure in South Africa: A Comparative Study*." Johannesburg: National Land Committee.

Leung, Kwok, and Michael W. Morris. 2001. "Justice through the Lens of Culture and Ethnicity." In *Handbook of Justice Research in Law*, eds. Joseph Sanders and V. Lee Hamilton. New York: Kluwer Academic/Plenum. Pp. 343–378.

Lind, E. Allan, and Tom R. Tyler. 1988. *The Social Psychology of Procedural Justice*. New York: Plenum Press.

Macfarlane, David. 2003. "True Lies or False Truths?" *Mail & Guardian*, June 6–12: 3.

Mattes, Robert. 1995. *The Election Book: Judgement and Choice in South Africa's 1994 Election*. Cape Town: Idasa.

Mattes, Robert, and Jessica Piombo. 2001. "Opposition Parties and the Voters in South Africa's General Election of 1999." *Democratization* 8 (Fall): 101–128.

Mattes, Robert, Helen Taylor, and Cherrel Africa. 1999. "Public Opinion & Voter Preferences: 1994–1999." In *Election '99 South Africa: From Mandela to Mbeki*, ed. Andrew Reynolds. New York: St. Martin's Press. Pp. 37–63.

Mbeki, Thabo. 1998. *Statement at the Opening of Debate on "Reconciliation And Nation Building," National Assembly of South Africa*, Cape Town, May 29. http://www.anc.org.za/ancdocs/history/mbeki/1998/sp980529.html (accessed January 30, 2008).

Michelbach, Philip A., John T. Scott, Richard E. Matland, and Brian H. Bornstein. 2003. "Doing Rawls Justice: An Experimental Study of Income Distribution Norms." *American Journal of Political Science* 47 (July): 523–539.

Miller, Dale T. 2001. "Disrespect and the Experience of Injustice." *Annual Review of Psychology* 52: 527–553.

Miller, David. 1991. "Review Article: Recent Theories of Social Justice." *British Journal of Political Science* 21 (July): 371–391.

Miller, David. 1999. *Principles of Social Justice*. Cambridge: Harvard University Press.

Miller, D. L. Carey, with Anne Pope. 2000. *Land Title in South Africa*. Kenwyn, South Africa: Juta & Co.

Mitchell, Thomas W. 2001. "The Land Crisis in Zimbabwe: Getting Beyond the Myopic Focus upon Black and White." *Indiana International and Comparative Law Review* 11: 587–603.

Murphy, John. 1996. "The Restitution of Land after Apartheid: The Constitutional and Legislative Framework." In *Confronting Past Injustices: Approaches to Amnesty, Punishment, Reparation and Restitution in South Africa and Germany*, eds. M. R. Rwelamira and G. Werle. Durban: Butterworths. Pp. 113–132.

Murray, Christina, and Catherine O'Regan, eds. 1990. *No Place to Rest: Forced Removals and the Law in South Africa*. Cape Town: Oxford University Press.

Mutz, Diana C., and Jeffery J. Mondak. 1997. "Dimensions of Sociotropic Behavior: Group-Based Judgments of Fairness and Well-Being." *American Journal of Political Science* 41 (January): 284–308.

Neuwirth, Robert. 2005. *Shadow Cities: A Billion Squatters, A New Urban World*. New York: Routledge.

Nicholson, Stephen P., Adrian Pantoja, and Gary M. Segura. 2006. "Political Knowledge and Issue Voting among the Latino Electorate." *Political Research Quarterly* 59 (June): 259–271.

North, Douglass C. 2005. *Understanding the Process of Economic Change*. Princeton, N.J.: Princeton University Press.

Ntsebeza, Lungisile. 2005. *Democracy Compromised: Chiefs and the Politics of Land in South Africa*. Cape Town: HSRC Press.

Ntsebeza, Lungisile. 2007. "Land Redistribution in South Africa: The Property Clause Revisited." In *The Land Question in South Africa: The Challenge of Transformation and Redistribution*, eds. Lungisile Ntsebeza and Ruth Hall. Cape Town: HSRC Press. Pp. 107–131.

Ntsebeza, Lungisile, and Ruth Hall. 2007. *The Land Question in South Africa: The Challenge of Transformation and Redistribution*. Cape Town: HSRC Press.

Ohbuchi, Ken-ichi, Masuyo Kameda, and Nariyuki Agarie. 1989. "Apology as Aggression Control: Its Role in Mediating Appraisal of and Response to Harm." *Journal of Personality and Social Psychology* 56 (2): 219–227.

O'Regan, Catherine. 1989. "No More Forced Removals – An Historical Analysis of the Prevention of Illegal Squatting Act." *South African Journal on Human Rights* 3: 361–394.

Pillay, Udesh, Benjamin Roberts, and Stephen Rule, eds. 2006. *South African Social Attitudes: Changing Times, Diverse Voices*. Cape Town: HSRC Press.

Piombo, Jessica, and Lia Nijzink. 2006. *Electoral Politics in South Africa: Assessing the First Democratic Decade*. Cape Town: HSRC Press.

Platzky, Laurine, and Cherryl Walker. 1985. *The Surplus People: Forced Removals in South Africa*. Johannesburg: Ravan Press.

Posel, Deborah. 2001. "What's in a Name? Racial Categorisations under Apartheid and Their Afterlife." *Transformation* 47 (2001): 50–74.

http://www.transformation.und.ac.za/issue%2047/47%20posel1.pdf (accessed June 3, 2003).

Powell, Anél. 2006a. "We Will Petrol-Bomb Your Homes, Say Delft Residents." *Cape Times*, July 27: 1, 3.

Powell, Anél. 2006b. "Removal Trucks Stoned in Delft, Two Held." *Cape Times*, July 28: 3.

Robbennolt, Jennifer K., John M. Darley, and Robert J. MacCoun. 2003. "Symbolism and Incommensurability in Civil Sanctioning: Decision Makers as Goal Managers." *Brooklyn Law Review* **68** (4): 1121–1158.

Roberts, Benjamin. 2006. "The Happy Transition? Attitudes to Poverty and Inequality after a Decade of Democracy." In *South African Social Attitudes: Changing Times, Diverse Voices*, eds. Udesh Pillay, Benjamin Roberts, and Stephen Rule. Cape Town: HSRC Press. Pp. 101–130.

Robinson, Paul H., and John M. Darley. 1995. *Justice, Liability, and Blame: Community Views and the Criminal Law*. Boulder, Colo.: Westview Press.

Robinson, Paul H., and John M. Darley. 1998. "Objectivist versus Subjectivist Views of Criminality: A Study of the Role of Social Science in Criminal Law Theory." *Oxford Journal of Legal Studies* **18** (Autumn): 409–447.

Roth, Alvin E., Vesna Prasnikar, Masahiro Okuno-Fujiwara, and Shmuel Zamir. 1991. "Bargaining and Market Behavior in Jerusalem, Ljubljana, Pittsburgh, and Tokyo: An Experimental Study." *American Economic Review* **81** (December): 1068–1095.

Roux, Theunis. 2004. "Pro-Poor Court, Anti-Poor Outcomes: Explaining the Performance of the South African Land Claims Court." *South African Journal on Human Rights* **20**: 511–543.

Roux, Theunis. 2006. "*Land Restitution and Reconciliation in South Africa.*" Presented at the Conference on Transitional Justice in South Africa, Cambridge University.

Sanders, Joseph, and V. Lee Hamilton. 2001. "Justice and Legal Institutions." In *Handbook of Justice Research in Law*, eds. Joseph Sanders and V. Lee Hamilton. New York: Kluwer Academic/Plenum. Pp. 3–27.

Scher, Steven J., and John M. Darley. 1997. "How Effective Are the Things People Say to Apologize? Effects of the Realization of Apology Speech Act." *Journal of Psycholinguistic Research* **26** (January): 127–140.

Schneider, Saundra K., and William G. Jacoby. 2007. "Reconsidering the Linkage between Public Assistance and Public Opinion in the American Welfare State." *British Journal of Political Science* **37** (July): 555–566.

Scott, John T., Richard E. Matland, Philip A. Michelbach, and Brian H. Bornstein. 2001. "Just Deserts: An Experimental Study of Distributive Justice Norms." *American Journal of Political Science* **45** (October): 749–767.

Sears, David O. 1995. "Symbolic Politics: A Socio-Psychological Theory." In *Explorations in Political Psychology*, eds. Shanto Iyengar and William J. McGuire. Durham, N.C.: Duke University Press. Pp. 113–149.

Sears, David O., and Jack Citrin. 1985. *Tax Revolt: Something for Nothing in California.* Cambridge: Harvard University Press.

Seekings, Jeremy, and Nicoli Nattrass. 2002. "Class, Distribution and Redistribution in Post-Apartheid South Africa." *Transformation* 50: 1–30.

Seekings, Jeremy, and Nicoli Nattrass. 2005. *Class, Race, and Inequality in South Africa.* New Haven: Yale University Press.

Sides, John, and Jack Citrin. 2007. "European Opinion about Immigration: The Role of Identities, Interests and Information." *British Journal of Political Science* 37 (July): 477–504.

Skitka, Linda J. 2003. "Of Different Minds: An Accessible Identity Model of Justice Reasoning." *Personality and Social Psychology Review* 7(4): 286–297.

Skitka, Linda J., Jennifer Winquist, and Susan Huchinson. 2003. "Are Outcome Fairness and Outcome Favorability Distinguishable Psychological Constructs? A Meta-Analytic Review." *Social Justice Research* 16 (December): 309–341.

Smith, Heather J. 2002. "Thinking about Deservingness." *Social Justice Research* 15 (December): 409–422.

Sniderman, Paul M., Joseph F. Fletcher, Peter H. Russell, and Philip E. Tetlock. 1996. *The Clash of Rights: Liberty, Equality, and Legitimacy in Pluralist Democracy.* New Haven: Yale University Press.

"Surplus People Project." 1983. *Forced Removals in South Africa.* Cape Town: Surplus People Project.

Tajfel, Henri. 1981. *Human Groups and Social Categories.* New York: Cambridge University Press.

Tamanaha, Brian Z. 2004. *On the Rule of Law: History, Politics, Theory.* New York: Cambridge University Press.

Tarman, Christopher, and David O. Sears. 2005. "The Conceptualization and Measurement of Symbolic Racism." *The Journal of Politics* 67 (August): 731–761.

Thompson, Leonard, and Andrew Prior. 1982. *South African Politics.* Cape Town: David Philip.

Turner, Stephen, and Hilde Ibsen. 2000. *Land and Agrarian Reform in South Africa: A Status Report.* Cape Town: Programme for Land and Agrarian Studies, School of Government, University of the Western Cape, and Centre for International Environment and Development Studies, Agricultural University of Norway.

Tutu, Desmond Mpilo. 1999. *No Future Without Forgiveness.* New York: Doubleday.

Tyler, Tom R., and Steven L. Blader. 2000. *Cooperation in Groups: Procedural Justice, Social Identity, and Behavioral Engagement.* Philadelphia: Psychology Press.

Tyler, Tom R., and E. Allan Lind. 1992. "A Relational Model of Authority in Groups." *Advances in Experimental Social Psychology* 25: 115–191.

Tyler, Tom R., and E. Allan Lind. 2001. "Procedural Justice." In *Handbook of Justice Research in Law*, eds. Joseph Sanders and V. Lee Hamilton. New York: Kluwer Academic/Plenum. Pp. 65–92.

Tyler, Tom R., Robert J. Boeckmann, Heather J. Smith, and Yuen J. Huo. 1997. *Social Justice in a Diverse Society*. Boulder, Colo.: Westview Press.

van Wilsem, Johan. 2004. "Criminal Victimization in Cross-National Perspective: An Analysis of Rates of Theft, Violence and Vandalism across 27 Countries." *European Journal of Criminology* 1 (1): 89–109.

Vidmar, Neil. 2001. "Retribution and Revenge." In *Handbook of Justice Research in Law*, eds. Joseph Sanders and V. Lee Hamilton. New York: Kluwer Academic/Plenum. Pp. 31–63.

Villa-Vicencio, Charles. 2000. "Getting on with Life: A Move Towards Reconciliation." In *Looking Back, Reaching Forward: Reflections on the Truth and Reconciliation Commission of South Africa*, eds. Charles Villa-Vicencio and Wilhelm Verwoerd. Cape Town: University of Cape Town Press. Pp. 199–209.

Villa-Vicencio, Charles, and S'fiso Ngesi. 2003. "South Africa: Beyond the 'Miracle.'" In *Through Fire with Water: The Roots of Division and the Potential for Reconciliation in Africa*, eds. Erik Doxtader and Charles Villa-Vicencio. Claremont, South Africa: David Philip. Pp. 266–302.

Visser, Daniel, and Theunis Roux. 1996. "Giving Back the Country: South Africa's Restitution of Land Rights Act, 1994 in Context." In *Confronting Past Injustices: Approaches to Amnesty, Punishment, Reparation and Restitution in South Africa and Germany*, eds. M. R. Rwelamira and G. Werle. Durban: Butterworths. Pp. 89–111.

Walker, Cherryl. 2000. "Relocating Restitution." *Transformation* 44: 1–16.

Walker, Cherryl. 2002. *Agrarian Change, Gender and Land Reform: A South African Case Study*. Geneva, Switzerland: United Nations Research Institute for Social Development. Social Policy and Development Programme Paper Number 10, April.

Walker, Cherryl. 2005a. "The Limits of Land Reform: Rethinking 'the Land Question.'" *Journal of Southern African Studies* 31 (December): 805–824.

Walker, Cherryl. 2005b. "Misplaced Agrarianization? Reflections on Ten Years of Land Restitution." *Social Research* 72 (Fall): 647–670.

Walker, Cherryl. 2007. "Redistributive Land Reform: For What and for Whom?" In *The Land Question in South Africa: The Challenge of Transformation and Redistribution*, eds. Lungisile Ntsebeza and Ruth Hall. Cape Town: HSRC Press. Pp. 132–151.

Weiner, Bernard, Sandra Graham, Orli Peter, and Mary Zmuidinas. 1991. "Public Confession and Forgiveness." *Journal of Personality* 59 (June): 281–312.

Wolpert, Robin W., and James G. Gimbel. 1998. "Self-Interest, Symbolic Politics, and Public Attitudes toward Gun Control." *Political Behavior* 20 (September): 241–262.

Index

Books in the Series *(continued from page iii)*